MY NINE LIVES

MY NINE LIVES

Sixty Years in Israeli and Biblical Archaeology

William G. Dever

SBL PRESS

Atlanta

Copyright © 2020 by William G. Dever

All rights reserved. No part of this work may be reproduced or transmitted in any form or by any means, electronic or mechanical, including photocopying and recording, or by means of any information storage or retrieval system, except as may be expressly permitted by the 1976 Copyright Act or in writing from the publisher. Requests for permission should be addressed in writing to the Rights and Permissions Office, SBL Press, 825 Houston Mill Road, Atlanta, GA 30329 USA.

Library of Congress Control Number: 2020950570

For my children
Sean, Jordana, Hannah, and Zeb

CONTENTS

List of Figures..ix
Foreword..xi

1. Beginnings: My First Life 1
2. Off to a Tropical Paradise: My Second Life............................. 9
3. Finding Myself: My Third Life...21
4. On to a Protestant Seminary: My Fourth Life......................33
5. Finishing School: My Fifth Life 45
6. The Jerusalem Years: My Sixth Life......................................71
7. The Desert Blooms, and So Do I: My Seventh Life..........141
8. In Limbo: My Eighth Life..173
9. Cyprus: My Ninth Life 179
10. Does Biblical Archaeology Have a Future?.......................189

Epilogue 209
Further Reading..211
Works Cited..219
General Index...227

FIGURES

1.	My grandmother, Sudie Murphy Dever	1
2.	My grandfather, Lee Dever	2
3.	My father and his sister in their parents' shack	2
4.	My father and Henry Gwinn	3
5.	My mother's family	4
6.	My father and mother, shortly after their wedding	5
7.	My family in Minerva, Ohio	7
8.	My father in Jamaica at the mission compound in Ewarton	18
9.	The school quartet, Milligan College, 1952	26
10.	The Oak Grove Christian Church, on Powder Branch	28
11.	Our wedding, July 1, 1953	30
12.	The Harmony Christian Church, Leisure, Indiana	34
13.	My first trip to Israel, summer of 1957: H. L. Ginsberg, Abraham Katsh, Martin Buber, Ze'ev Vilnay	37
14.	Graduation at Christian Theological Seminary, 1959	46
15.	At Shechem, my first dig, 1957	51
16.	Bethany Congregational Christian Church, Quincy	54
17.	Our house at 41 Homer Road, Quincy	55
18.	Hebrew Union College, Nelson Glueck School of Biblical Archaeology, Jerusalem	57
19.	The first season at Gezer, fall 1964	61
20.	Gezer advisors Nelson Glueck and G. Ernest Wright, with me and Associate Director H. Darrell Lance	66
21.	Graduation, Harvard, 1966, with my parents	68
22.	The dig camp at Gezer, established in 1966	73
23.	Me instructing the Gezer volunteers on balk-trimming	74
24.	Nelson Glueck, end of the Six-Day War, 1967, with Père de Vaux at the École Biblique et Archéologique in Jerusalem	85
25.	Inscription 3 from Tomb II at Khirbet el-Qôm	93
26.	The staff at Jebel Qa'aqir in 1971, in Cemetery B	94

27. The Arab village of Samiyeh, where we lived — 95
28. Sean's christening at St. Andrew's Presbyterian Church, Jerusalem, May 1969 — 100
29. Albright's visit to the high place at Gezer, April 1969 — 101
30. Mrs. Albright, on one of her visits after her husband's death — 103
31. Sy Gitin in the garden of the Albright Institute — 110
32. Nelson Glueck, cover of *Time* magazine — 113
33. Moshe Dayan and I, circa 1970 — 115
34. Yigael Yadin at Gezer, flanked by me and Magen Broshi on the left and Darrell Lance and Nelson Glueck on the right — 117
35. Pamela at Gezer, spring 1969 — 121
36. Staff at Gezer, 1971 — 121
37. The director's house at the W. F. Albright Institute — 123
38. Père Roland de Vaux at Gezer — 124
39. The living room of the Albright Institute director's house — 131
40. Reception in the garden of the Albright Institute — 132
41. G. Ernest Wright at Harvard Divinity School — 133
42. Dame Kathleen Kenyon's visit to Gezer in 1967 — 135
43. Rudy Cohen and I — 144
44. The camp at Be'er Resisim in 1980; site in background — 145
45. Casa de la Paloma Blanca — 146
46. Frequent visits to the excavations in Israel, here with David Ussishkin and Israel Finkelstein at Megiddo — 148
47. Yigal Shiloh and I at the Ciy of David excavations, 1982 — 151
48. With graduate students University of Arizona, here Michael Hasel — 154
49. Sean at sixteen, a few weeks before diagnosis — 156
50. Pamela and I at our wedding in Concord, with Jordana Lee Gaber (now Saletan) and Hannah Susan Gaber — 159
51. With Zeb and Sean shortly before the end — 169
52. Lecture tours while in New York, 2002–2008 — 175
53. The 1842 millhouse in Montoursville, Pennsylvania — 181
54. Our old farmhouse in Alampra, Cyprus, circa 2008 — 183
55. Pamela in the field at Idalion — 186
56. Hannah Gaber, Zeb Dever, Julian Hall, Sasha Hall, Jordana Saletan, Pamela, and me — 188
57. Reading pottery with Ruth Amiran — 194

FOREWORD

I have put off writing this book—my memoirs—for many years, for several reasons. For one thing, the idea seemed self-serving (it is, of course). Then I thought I'd wait until nearer the end of the journey (that could be soon, the way things are going). Finally, to tell some of the best stories I had to wait until a few people died (that is happening).

Many colleagues and friends, however, have convinced me to write this book not so much to recount my own adventures as to tell the larger story of the momentous changes in "biblical" or "Syro-Palestinian" (now "Levantine") archaeology that I have been privileged to be a part of these last sixty years. Retirement and then a period of confinement after surgery persuaded me that it was time to reflect and to tell the story now.

Some of the following is quite personal, sometimes painfully so. But I have tried to be as honest as possible, despite occasionally portraying myself (and others, too) in a negative light. My hope is that readers, especially young people, will find courage in seeing how one can overcome difficulties in both family life and career.

Part of my rationale is that archaeology is not a science but an art—a very subjective human art in which creative imagination plays a pivotal role. That is why I have told so many candid stories, not only about myself, but more significantly about a remarkable generation of giants in archaeology in Israel whom I was privileged to know personally. A similar personal memoir of an archaeological career has recently been published by Michael Coe, a distinguished New World archaeologist, entitled *Final Report: An Archaeologist Excavates His Past* (Thames & Hudson, 2006). I only hope that mine is not *quite* the final report. Since the framework of this narrative about changes in my branch of archaeology is my own story, I have not hesitated to recount many of my own achievements, but always, I hope, in the larger context of what was happening at the time in archaeology in the Middle East and America. (In any case, fake modesty would not fool anyone who knows me.) Some people will feel left out, while others may wish that they had not been mentioned at all. Many will have a different perspective on events I discuss. But this is, unabashedly, *my* story. It will appear in 2020, near the sixty-fifth anniversary of my first trip to Israel and my first exposure to the seductions of archaeology. Thus the title, and also the focus, is on Israel, not the only locale of importance, but the place where nearly all of my experiences took place. The focus is also on the Old Testament, or better Hebrew Bible, since historically biblical archaeology has been largely concerned with the Bronze and Iron Ages, not the classical era of Judaism and early Christianity or with archaeology in Jordan (on the latter, see the bibliography). These are important studies but must be left for others to tell.

Much of my boldness comes from the fact that I happen to have been right in the middle of nearly all of the changes in archaeology that I describe, sometimes even instrumental in them. Much of this good fortune was simply a matter of being in the right place at the right time and possessed of enough self-confidence to plunge in. Of course, I worked very hard through good times and bad. But I was also one very lucky fellow. I know personally nearly every person (and site) mentioned in this story. That means I am indebted to many people.

First and foremost would be my parents, Lonnie Earl and Claudine Watts Dever. From them I learned, more by example than by word, the importance of what I call "moral earnestness." I also got from them an overarching sense of duty and responsibility, self-reliance, and persistence in the face of adversity.

I owe more than I could ever repay to my teachers, especially Ernest Wright, without whose inspiration and guidance I would likely have been an obscure Congregational minister somewhere in New England. I am also indebted to Rabbi Nelson Glueck, of blessed memory, who took a chance in 1965 in hiring me at Hebrew Union College in Jerusalem, where I got my professional start. Richard Scheuer, also now of blessed memory, was a patron for forty-five years. To the latter two, I dedicate this volume.

I have learned more from my graduate students than I have taught them, and when so many other things seemed futile, they made the investment seem worthwhile. They will be my best legacy.

I want to add my profound thanks to the staff of SBL Press—Bob Buller, Nicole Tilford, Heather McMurray, and Lindsay Lingo—for their skill and patience in transforming a rough manuscript and a miscellany of photographs into a finished book. I am delighted to be publishing a second book with them.

Innumerable colleagues and friends, both in Israel and in America, have made my odyssey an even more rewarding journey.

Both of my families loom large in this story, as they should: Norma and Sean in the earlier years; Pamela, Jordana, Hannah, and Zeb in the later years. I am grateful for their support and forbearance. In the end, they matter more than anything else.

I really have had nine lives, some of them so different that they seem contradictory. But each was a response, whether subconscious or deliberate, to a set of different circumstances. That it seems to have turned out reasonably well is a source of constant amazement and satisfaction to me.

The last chapter is not (I hope) a postmortem but a postscript on the likely future of biblical archaeology after my time. The subsequent annotated bibliography will guide serious readers to some of the scholarly literature that will flesh out the story. (For instance, all the dozens of sites here will be encountered in full detail in Stern 1993–2008.) When publications of my own are referred to only by year, they can be found easily in the complete list of my publications in Gitin, Wright, and Dessel 2006 (see also the bibliography below). There is no adequate history of biblical or Israeli archaeology, however, and this account certainly makes no pretense to be one.

Alampra, Cyprus
January 2019

1
BEGINNINGS: MY FIRST LIFE

I am a fifth-generation Irish-English-Welsh American, and I have all the well-known foibles of the Irish temperament. My forebears on my father's side came over from County Donegal and County Mayo in northern Ireland during the potato famine in the l840s. The name Dever is the Anglicized form of Gaelic "Ó Duibhidir" (related to the name Dwyer). They were Protestants, dirt poor, and nearly illiterate. The whole clan settled in Kentucky for some reason, many of them becoming day laborers in Louisville, where I was born in November of 1933. My ancestors on my mother's side were largely of English and Welsh derivation (her maiden name was Watts), similarly poor immigrants. But I never knew my maternal grandparents, since they died when my mother was a very small girl.

My paternal grandparents were of sturdy but coarse Irish stock. My grandmother's maiden name was Sudie Murphy (fig. 1), born in LaRue County, Kentucky, in 1881. She never went beyond the third grade and could barely read and write. My father, who wrote to her every week, was the only person who could decipher her handwriting. But Sudie could talk—and how! She was a tiny woman, not five feet tall, but she had a voice like a foghorn and a sailor's slang to match. I remember her chasing Grandfather Lee (fig. 2) out of their ramshackle house right on the railroad tracks in Louisville, brandishing a broom at him and shouting loudly enough to be heard a block away.

Fig. 1. My grandmother, Sudie Murphy Dever.

Fig. 2. My grandfather, Lee Dever.

Fig. 3. My father and his sister in their parents' shack in Harlan County, Kentucky.

He had been a terrible drunkard some years earlier, and she never quite forgave him. And he never did much except work on the railroad. In fact, they had gotten a divorce while my father was in college. Eventually Lee reformed, however, and my father persuaded them to get remarried. They agreed, and he, by now a minister, performed the marriage ceremony himself. I've always imagined it: "Do you, Father, take this woman, my mother, to be your lawful wife?"

Parents

My father, Lonnie Earl Dever, was born in Louisville in 1909 (fig. 3). He had two brothers and a sister. One brother spent his whole life in the Navy, roaming around the world; the other was something of a dandy, a wanna-be jockey and, later, horse trainer at Churchill Downs in Louisville. His sister married a ne'er-do-well and settled into dreary domesticity. I never really knew any of my cousins and apparently didn't miss much.

Education was not the priority in my family that it was for some immigrant groups. My father was the first person ever in his family to finish high school and go on to college. His parents were estranged at the time and desperately poor. As a teenager, he got up at 3 a.m. to drive a horse-drawn ice wagon before school time, delivering blocks of ice to local homes and businesses. Not only did he complete his high school degree, however, but he went on to obtain three college degrees, one a graduate degree in theology from Lexington Theological Seminary. I vaguely remember his graduation from the latter school in 1936, when I was three.

Fig. 4. My father and Henry Gwinn.

My father would probably not have amounted to anything, however, had it not been for a remarkable man named Henry Gwinn (fig. 4). He was a local Fundamentalist minister and a prison chaplain, who somehow befriended my father when he had been a teenager. It was he who encouraged Father to stay in school and make something of himself, unlike anyone in the family thus far. My middle name is Gwinn because my father so admired his mentor. Gwinn gave my father an Elgin double-cased gold pocket watch (dated 1912), which he passed on to me and which my wife had restored as my seventieth birthday present. What an *enormous* difference one individual with a dream can make. (The watch has now passed to my son Zeb.)

Father was also a people person, a man with a huge heart, which made him as good a pastor as he was a preacher. Father was also an incurable optimist, always assuming that others were as upbeat as he was. He was ebullient, generous in spirit, and a bit naive in some of his good-intentioned schemes, as we kids were later to see. But from my father's example I learned moral courage—the most important gift he could have given me. I also inherited from him a big voice, which in time I learned to use to good advantage in another pulpit, one that he could hardly have imagined.

My mother, Claudine Watts Dever (fig. 5), an orphan, had been raised largely in a boarding school run by the Christian Normal Institute in Grayson, Kentucky. In those days a normal educational institution was a remedial school of sorts, meant to train young women in the only trade

Fig. 5. My mother's family; she is the girl on the right.

they should learn, teaching. The Grayson institute itself was an unaccredited four-year Bible college, and there Mother naturally enrolled in due course. And there she met Father when he chose to attend college at the institute. They were married during their early college years, in 1932, when she was twenty-one and he was twenty-three (fig. 6). Upon graduation, Father went off to Lexington for a three-year Bachelor of Divinity degree (now a Master of Divinity), then returned to Grayson to become minister of the local Christian church there.

My sister Myma Sue, four years younger, was born in Grayson, and we lived there until I was six and ready for grade school. My earliest memories are of these years, living in a small isolated religious community, in which the church and the authority of the church dominated every aspect of our lives. One simply did not question any of this. Moral rectitude was the order of the day.

My parents were totally devoted to each other, not only out of religious conviction, but also because with their deprived childhoods they found solace in the security of marriage. I am certain that they were completely faithful. My father would occasionally glance at other women when we were going somewhere, but one frown from my mother ended that. They were not very vocal about their love and certainly not very demonstrative physically around us children. My mother was simply too emotionally

Fig. 6. My father and mother, shortly after their wedding.

repressed for any of that. But my sister and I could see from their everyday behavior that our parents were inseparable, and a large part of what kept them together was the absolute assurance that this was right in the sight of God and the church.

After their deaths (both in their early sixties), my sister found a note that Father had left for Mother. He wrote "I've always loved you. I will see you on the other side." Sometimes I wish that I believed such things or had the assurance of divine sanction. But I don't—and perhaps I never did. Yet I owe much to my parents' beliefs and especially to their abiding sense of vocation. Mine has not been a career but a vocation—for better or worse, a calling.

School Days

When I was six, we moved to the small town of Sebring, Ohio. The church there was larger but no more sophisticated. While I was in the first grade, my mother became ill with tuberculosis and was in a sanitarium for about six months. My sister, now two, was farmed out to a local caring family, and my father juggled church work and housekeeping to look after me. We could visit the sanitarium, but only to look in through a window. I'm sure that these long months in total isolation further deepened my mother's depression, but they also seem to have taught her greater self-reliance. I now understand, too, what it means to be a loner. But I do not regret it, much less regard it as a weakness.

I remember little of the first and second grades in Sebring. There were no frills such as school buses, so we all walked to school, about a mile for me, through bleak Ohio winters. All I recall about classes is that I learned quickly but was a social misfit, always feeling like a goodygoody. I had absolutely no athletic ability and hated what little playground activity there was. I do recall playing after school with a few neighborhood kids, but my mother was very protective, openly judgmental about any family outside our circle. Our lives revolved almost totally around church activities—Sunday morning and evening services, Wednesday night prayer meetings, some social activities.

Even summer family vacations were spent in a couple of weeks at a sort of camp meeting. There dozens of families from the churches of our denomination would gather for intensive Bible study, inspirational preaching services, and sessions with missionaries on home leave to encourage our evangelistic efforts. But we kids had some time off to play. I remember boating, fishing, and swimming at Winona Lake in Indiana. Now some of my books have been published there by Eisenbrauns. Maybe something took after all.

My father, despite his soft-heartedness where needy people were concerned, was a typical fire-breathing Fundamentalist in the pulpit. He would flourish an open Bible in one outstretched hand, while the other jabbed his points home. He used to tell the story of one of his college classmate preachers who held weekend revival meetings in Harlan County Kentucky, noted for its moonshine and roughneck lads. He would ride in on horseback, dismount, stride into the tent, and stand up in a makeshift pulpit. He would then reach down into one boot, pull out a Bible, and declare, "I mean to preach the Gospel." Then he would reach into the other boot to produce a pistol. "And I mean to have order!"

When I was eight, we moved to Erwin in the mountains of eastern Tennessee, which would become in many ways a sort of home base. My parents moved back to nearby Johnson City when my father retired many years later, and they are both buried there. My sister, my only sibling, is also buried there. I also went to school at Milligan College near there, got married there, and began my career there.

In Erwin I went to the third and fourth grades. Again, I remember only that school was easy for me, although to be sure the standards in a tiny railroad town in east Tennessee were hardly challenging. Again our family life revolved around the local church my father served.

When the predictable denouement came after two years, we were off to Ohio again, this time to Minerva, a small town near Akron (fig. 7). There I went to the fifth and sixth grades. Again, I have very few specific memories of school itself. If there was ever any homework, it didn't make an impression on me. I do recall winter sports such as ice skating. In fact, we often ice skated along the frozen river to school. In the congregation in Minerva there were a few more sophisticated people. Among them were a physician and his wife who traveled, encouraged their children's taste in reading and in art, and gave them music lessons. My mother then began to send us kids to piano and violin lessons. I even recall attending a Fritz Kreisler concert in Akron when I was about ten or eleven. But otherwise my experience growing up in Minerva was that of many other Middle Americans of that era: parochial and isolated from larger world events. I remember the day World War II ended in 1945 but little else of those tumultuous years.

Fig. 7. My family in Minerva, Ohio, when I was about eleven years old, my sister eight.

Trying to Grow Up

Porter Junior High in Barberton had the typical racial and ethnic mix of many northern and Midwestern big cities. This was really the first time that I had encountered what anthropologists would call the "Others," and I was mostly terrified. They were not only different from the small-town church people I had known, but they were aggressively different. Timid as always, I was miserable. The gym and the locker room were the worst, because the other boys were more developed, and their vulgar talk—especially about girls—horrified me. Nevertheless, I decided to try to fit in. So, not being at all athletic, I joined the football team as a sort of gofer. I helped to sort out and repair the football gear before and after practice on the field. I went to all the games, even away games, and stood on the sidelines to fetch water for the big boys.

Occasionally I got to run out on the field with water during time out. I even earned a letter. As I look back on all this, it seems rather pathetic; I wanted so desperately to belong. But on the whole, it was a beneficial experience in some ways. Never again would I stand on the sidelines. I would be a player—a major player. As it turned out, in adult life I would become the CEO of nearly every organization I ever served.

2
OFF TO A TROPICAL PARADISE: MY SECOND LIFE

My father was always a missionary of sorts (so my friends tell me that I come by it naturally). In the spring of 1947, I was fourteen and in junior high in Barberton, Ohio, where my father was the minister at a Christian church. Somehow he had a vision of the poor black folk in Jamaica who needed his ministry more than the local congregation, many of whom may well have agreed.

On the Road

So it was that my father began to pursue the possibilities of joining a mission station on the island of Jamaica, sponsored by a volunteer association of a number of Christian churches in the South and Midwest. None of them were affiliated, out of principle, with any central denominational body. This included the Disciples of Christ, from which our independent movement had seceded in the fundamentalist-modernist controversy of the early twentieth century, which had split many a Protestant denomination. So for my father to raise money for this venture, he had to begin traveling widely among these independent Christian churches to drum up their support. It was to be an uphill struggle, requiring enormous confidence—or, as my mother would have put it, foolhardiness.

Father sold the nearly new 1946 Chevrolet that he had waited eighteen postwar months for and bought a Jeep Wagoneer station wagon. We got rid of or stored nearly all the household things, packed our clothes in the Jeep, and drove to Miami, where we loaded the car on a small boat bound for the port of Kingston. We boarded an old Douglas two engine DC-3 and flew off, stopping briefly in Havana on the way to Jamaica. My sister and

I were enthralled at the promise of a new and exotic life off somewhere in the jungle. My father was nonplussed, secure in the knowledge that he was fulfilling his vocation. My mother was skeptical—the only one, it turned out, who was realistic.

Jamaica, Long before the Tourists

We arrived late at night in Kingston. To this day I remember the smells of the dark, humid tropical night, the scent of jasmine heavy in the air, the smells of acrid ground coffee beans and rotten sugar cane left over from processing rum that will always define Kingston for me. The head of the mission station out in the bush, near Spanish Town, met us. His name was Luke Elliot, and he was to missionary work what Harrison Ford was to archaeology. Elliot was about 6 feet 11 inches, gaunt and sharp-featured but striking in appearance. He was dressed, as always, in a freshly pressed white linen suit, with a wide brimmed Panama hat. He had an imperious manner about him, especially, I noticed, when dealing with the natives who handled our gear. Their black faces in the pitch black gardens outside the airport and Elliot's snow-white garb struck me as a paradox. It was the first of many that would define our brief adventure in Jamaica.

We all drove off into the night in Elliot's car, full of excitement and trepidation. The mission station, near the village of Ewarton, was on a large, hilly plot of land, densely covered with all sorts of lush tropical vegetation: coconut palms, citrus trees, breadfruit trees, banana plants, flowering trees, and shrubs. There was Elliot's rambling, self-contained manor house on the highest rise, two smaller houses flanking a large water reservoir below that, a large workshop between these houses, a seminary building with classrooms and several dormitory rooms down the slope, and the little mission church building well down by the roadway. As we drove up the hill that first night, there were, of course, no lights. The mission station had neither electricity, running water, toilet facilities, nor any of the other niceties of civilized life. All around us the dark jungle, the "bush," closed in on us mysteriously and oppressively. It was a bit creepy, but what an adventure!

Elliot had made rudimentary preparations for us in the house that we had been assigned. That first night, however, I slept on the floor on a coconut-husk mattress, awakened by lizards clambering over me. Eventually we got a cat to deal with them, but they often fought back ferociously, even latching onto the cat's tongue and biting him as he thrashed them about.

There were other amusements. We simply could not manage to keep the ants out of the sugar no matter how we tried. So we accepted the situation. At meals my sister and I would put the sugar into the cold tea or lemonade, wait till the ants floated to the top, then scoop them up and pile them beside our plate. It was a contest to see who had the biggest pile. My mother never delighted in this practice as much as we did. Only reluctantly would she go into the kitchen, a semidetached alcove with primitive facilities, no running water, and an old wood-burning cook stove. There were bugs everywhere, rodents at night, pots and pans whose cleanliness was dubious, but my sister and I would often hang out in the kitchen with the servants, because it was cozy, and they were great fun with their patois dialects and their simple jokes about the smallest affairs of everyday life.

Things Are Not What They Appear to Be

Our first Jamaican housekeeper and cook was an attractive girl named Ada, whom Elliot had brought in from another village before our arrival. He explained that he had installed her in a one-room hut just behind his house on the hill, since that would be convenient. So it was—for him, as we later found out.

Our simple house had floors made of handsawn and planed mahogany boards, some 2 feet wide. Maintaining them entailed periodically dying them with a dark purplish vegetable dye, then waxing them and buffing them to a high polish. The polishing was done by the housekeeper, who got down on her knees with a half-coconut husk in each hand, the rough fibers serving as an efficient brush. One day when Ada was polishing floors, she disappeared. We eventually found her under a bed, fast asleep on the floor. The mystery was solved when we realized that she simply was not getting enough sleep at night in her little hut behind Elliot's house. Ada soon left us.

How we found Ada's replacement I don't recall. She was an ebullient local girl about eighteen named Sylvia. But we called her "Girlie." Girlie, despite her lack of a proper background, was proud—especially of the fact that, unlike most of the other teenage girls in the bush, she had no illegitimate babies, not even one. That did seem an achievement. Girlie kept our house neat and clean, and she also did most of the cooking. She would have served at table as well, but my mother could never quite adjust to having servants.

Our "houseboy" was an orphan, an impish fourteen-year old from the bush whom we only knew, naturally, as "Boysie." Boysie cleaned the brush, swept the patio, delighted in washing the Jeep, chopped firewood, and ran all kinds of errands. He and Girlie were like two playful kittens, constantly amusing my sister and me—but always keeping a respectful distance. They would speak somewhat proper English to us, then lapse into patois and also into giggles. But we soon learned patois and shared their jokes.

At breakfast, which I often took a bit late and alone, Girlie would come in from the kitchen, doff her sandals, and say cheerfully, "Manin, Massa Bill! How keeping?" Then she would bring breakfast, such as it was. One day she was taking a tub bath in the outdoor bathhouse/outhouse, and she ran out of rinse water. She heard me passing by outside and shouted to ask if I would fetch her some more water. I declined, since my sense of propriety (as a precocious fourteen-year old) differed somewhat from Girlie's.

We also had a laundry woman who came two or three days a week, "Sister B," whom everyone called "Sta B." We had imported a gasoline-powered wringer washing machine. When we cranked it up, it sent out loud clanging noises and a great cloud of smoke. Sta B gave it a wide berth. But she did all the ironing, using old-fashioned sad irons heated alternately on a charcoalfired brazier. We had a fancy white, gas-fired iron, with a pump to pressurize the fuel and provide steam, but that was too much for Sta B. One day as I was visiting her in the palmfrond lean-to that was our laundry, she listened to one of my many explanations. Then she declared, "Massa Bill, you have a fine mind. You must save it!" I did.

At first I had no bedroom, but in time my father and I, with the help of the seminary students, added one onto the house. Like the house itself, the room was of native wattle-and-daub construction. Wooden poles served as two-by-fours; the space in between was filled with interwoven split bamboo lathes; and the interior and exterior surfaces were coated with rough hand-smeared plaster. The cement floor was left bare. Here as elsewhere in the house, there were no glass windows, only openings equipped with screens and roll-up canvas blinds. The tropical climate was always warm, even at night, and only during the heavy monsoon season did we even need the canvas blinds. Of course, our house was never locked. At night the breeze, often flower-scented, was delightful.

Our furniture was all handmade in the mission shop. We had no real living room, only a sort of screen porch in which there was a heavy-frame daybed and some similar lounge chairs. The dining room was pleasant, with a high paneled ceiling, whitewashed walls, and the usual dark-burnished mahogany floor. We had a kerosene-operated refrigerator in the dining room, which always amused me. You had to tend the little flame in the bottom compartment to make cold, but it worked.

We had no local electricity, and it turned out to be too expensive to run the big Army surplus generator we had brought. We also had no running water, only what we caught from roof run-off and stored in a large open outdoor reservoir. The water was a bit green and slimy, but we boiled what we drank. In the bathroom we had an old-fashioned basin and pitcher. For a shower, we had rigged up a barrel on the roof, which Boysie kept filled by hauling buckets up a ladder. The sun warmed the water enough to take the chill off, at least during the daytime. We periodically emptied the barrel and tarred it to keep it rust-free. But one time Mother took a shower before the tar was quite dry, and she came out almost tarred herself. Burning off the accumulation in the outdoor two-holers with kerosene to keep the roaches down could have similar disastrous effects if Boysie forgot to wipe off the oily residue on the seats.

Since we had no electricity, we ate the evening meal around a kerosene Aladdin table lamp whose tall chimney and fragile mesh mantle gave off a soft, flickering light. Sometimes we would linger to read around the table. But we had no newspapers or magazines whatsoever, and only a few books that we could get by mail from the public library in Kingston. A rare treat on Saturday night was waffles. We would crank up the little generator in the woodworking shop, string a long extension cord to our house, and cook waffles on the old chrome waffle iron we had brought from the States.

Father was quite proud of the battery-powered Zenith Trans-Atlantic short-wave radio that he had had the foresight to bring along. But for the most part we couldn't tune in a clear station on any one of the impressive wave bands and got only squeals and whistles. We were almost totally isolated out in the bush, but I soon came to relish the solitude. Gradually the dangerous world that my parents warned me about receded.

School and Shop

My days were pretty much the same. Mornings were spent in the mission workshop, where we made all the mission furniture, as well as windows, doors, pulpits, and communion tables for the forty or so mission churches scattered around the island. Often we would prefabricate a whole church building, truck the stuff to the site, and spend several days assembling it all with the help of the local church members. Then there would be a joyous dedication service, with abandoned singing and testimonials. A few people would play tambourines, penny-whistles, or any instrument they could find, and the singing and dancing might go on all night.

The workshop was a large, rambling shed, the dirt floor ankle deep in sawdust, the side flaps opened high during the day to let the breeze through. Elliot, a consummate craftsman (among his other skills), had contrived several ingenious handmade woodworking tools. All were driven either by a gasoline engine or, in some cases, by an electric motor powered by a small generator. We had a large table saw, a band saw, a drill press, even a lathe. The eight resident seminary students were expected to spend mornings working in the shop, and I always joined them. Sometimes Elliot would look in on us, but mostly we were left to our own resources. The students were always in high spirits, often breaking into hymns and folksongs as they worked. Like our house servants, they were delightful company but always maintained a slightly deferential attitude. When the church furniture was done, they were allowed to make a few things for themselves—mostly small wooden suitcases that they used for their required weekend trips to serve the churches around the island.

The wood we used was sometimes exotic tropical hardwood: mahogany, cedar, a type of jungle walnut, rosewood, ironwood (lignum vitae), even ebony. The trees were felled in the jungle and hauled to the shop. There they were rolled up onto a raised platform above a deep pit, and two men—one above and one below—pulled a long, thin saw up and down the length of the log, slowly detaching one board after another. The boards were air-dried for many months, then hand-planed to rough thicknesses.

To this day, I love to plane wood, relishing the sound and the smell and the feel of the shavings.

I made my own cedar-wood bed and chest for my newly added bedroom. I also learned to use the lathe and made some simple jewelry boxes, one of which I still have. I remember with great pleasure those sweaty mornings in the woodworking shop, often preoccupied with my own thoughts. I learned not only the skills that enabled me to do advanced cabinet-making throughout my life but also the joys of solitude that have been equally satisfying all these years.

Afternoons were spent doing my correspondence high-school assignments, again working alone at the small homemade desk in my bedroom. I would do the readings, then write the required essays and mail them to the American School in Chicago, which served diplomatic, military, and other American personnel all over the world. The periodic exams would be mailed to me in sealed envelopes, which I completed and returned to receive my grades. I rarely consulted my parents, and it was in these private lessons that I learned the self-reliance that would serve me so well in later life. Even today, with several hundred publications, I have written only two joint articles. That solipsism might be regarded by some as a weakness, but I consider it one of my strengths.

The Rhythms of Life on the Missionary Station

Meals were simple and a bit monotonous. We had whatever fruits and vegetables were in season: lots of oranges, grapefruits, and coconuts from the extensive mission grounds. A local churchman, Mr. English, brought us a whole bunch of ripe bananas each week on his small donkey. The price for 100–150 bananas? The equivalent of one dollar. There was also breadfruit, a large tree-borne growth with a spongy center that when sliced and fried tasted something like French toast. Cassava root, dug from our garden, substituted for potatoes; when sufficiently drowned in gravy, it could almost fool one. We had meat, but we were never quite sure what it was. We raised our own chickens and rabbits.

One night a week we would drive into the tiny village of Ewarton, a few miles away, to buy meat at the local butchery. My mother hated this weekly excursion, but I recall how fascinating it seemed. The large, open shed was unlit except by lantern light, the freshly killed carcasses of sheep, goats, pigs, and cows hanging from the rafters, the warm, musky-smelling blood dripping onto the dirt floor. You simply pointed to the approximate part of the carcass that you wanted, and the seller would whack off a piece, weigh it, and deliver it to you wrapped in a newspaper. The meat was cheap, but much of it was tough no matter how it was prepared.

My sister Myma, now ten, had acquired a billy goat, thinking that it might make a good pet. The goat, however, thought otherwise. It was so unruly that we finally decided to get rid of it. But how? The servants decided that the recalcitrant goat would make a delicious dinner. They tied it to a tree and tried to slit its throat. But the cut was so shallow that the goat got away and ran all over the place, bleating madly and spewing blood everywhere until it finally succumbed. The servants then strung it up in a tree by its hind legs, gutted it, and dismembered the carcass. After carrying the body parts to our kitchen, they decided to have some fun with the entrails before converting the intestines into tripe—a great delicacy. They pulled the slippery intestines like jumping ropes. My sister and I watched all this with a sense of satisfaction: that mean goat had gotten what it deserved. But that night at the table, we were all so disgusted that we could not eat any of that goat. My sister also had a pet donkey, equally stubborn, but we did not eat him either.

On Sunday mornings and evenings, all three missionary families dressed up in our finest and walked down to services in the little frame church building down by the road. The white folks all sat together in the front row or two, quietly prim and proper, while the black congregation warmed up to the occasion. The men were dressed in their Sunday best, as far as a poor income allowed, some of them cast-offs from our missionary barrels. The women and older girls were all in long white dresses topped by big headwraps. The sermon was usually to be delivered by one of the missionaries, so the black leaders, elders or deacons, conducted all the preliminaries, mostly music. And what music it was!

There were no songbooks, except for an occasional one the song leader might have. In that case, he would "line out" the hymn, that is, recite the next line while the congregation held onto the last note of the previous line. Then off they would go again. The alternation of moving lines and sostenuto notes was mesmerizing. Many of the hymns were from the Anglican hymnal or even the old Scottish Psalter, thanks to lingering

British influence in the former colony. But if the melodies were traditional, the syncopated rhythms of our congregants transformed them into an almost jazz-like medium. All the hymns were sung in harmony, often improvised: the low voices of the men droning like a continua, the women sopranos singing a high descant—and always the instinctive, driving rhythm, usually accompanied by syncopated clapping.

Many of the most popular church songs were originally folk songs, set now to sacred themes. One I recall was:

> I am on the battlefield for my Lord.
>   I will fight 'til I die;
> I will never run away.
>   I am on the battlefield for my Lord.

These lyrics would be repeated again and again, the intensity rising, then gradually falling away, until at last voices began to drop out and finally everything drifted into silence. Then one heard murmurs throughout the church. "Massa, me son." "O sister, sing it!" "Hallelujah!" "Amen." Then from the back somewhere would come an anonymous voice beginning a new song, soon joined by other voices until there was a great swell of singing. So it would go on for an hour or more before the service would begin.

For my sister and me, these were some of our most memorable experiences. Soon we knew all the songs and joined in, our parents a bit scandalized by our fraternizing with the natives. Once we organized an all-night sing and invited people from all around the bush for free food and drink, a big bonfire, and a promise to record their songs. We did try, on the Webcor wire recorder we had brought from the States, but the recently invented device invariably spun the thin wire out of control and off the spool, so in the end we could not salvage anything. I've always regretted that loss. One memorable event was the death of Brother Byfield, Girlie's father and a revered elder in the local congregation. He died suddenly at a local clinic where he was being treated. Father and I went in the Jeep Wagoneer to fetch the body, and we brought it back to the mission, iced down in view of the heat. That night the men and women gathered at the mission. The men worked with me and the other missionary men to make a wooden coffin, while the women washed and dressed the body. There was food for everyone as we worked into the night. The next day Brother

Byfield was lowered into a simple grave dug in the churchyard, Girlie herself giving one of the tributes.

Saving the "Heathen"

My father and I made many weekend trips to the mission churches scattered around the island, and I remember how at fifteen I treasured these times together. Sometimes we would drive as far as we could on the back roads (I got to drive now and then), then meet the church elders and deacons and go the rest of the way on the mules they had brought for us. We would stay for a couple of nights with the congregants in their simple huts, sharing what little food they had. We drank, however, out of thermoses we had brought, because we knew that the water was always contaminated. When we could, we also brought food to contribute. But pride usually dictated that the local folk would feed their honored quests as well as they were able.

Fig. 8. My father in Jamaica at the mission compound in Ewarton, 1947.

One time when the whole family went on a trip to a remote church, we realized that the local boys and girls had never seen any white children. That night, as we sat on the platform in the crude bamboo-and-thatch church building, lit only by a few lanterns, they would reach in between the slats to stroke my sister's long hair, which hung down to her waist.

Another time I recall sitting in a similar church in a monsoon rain so heavy that it was leaking through the roof. One concerned congregant approached my mother and said, "Sista D., are you wetting?" Often, to welcome us, they would say "Come in and make yo'self homely."

At church services in the more backward rural areas, the local Obeah adherents—witch doctors who practiced voodoo—would come to our services. This was partly out of curiosity, but it was mostly to subvert our attempts to convert the locals to a "pagan" religion such as Christianity. At first they would mass quietly in the back of the church, mostly white-robed women, but gradually they would begin their own rival songs, then move more aggressively up front. By now my father would be in the pulpit trying to be heard. But it was a losing battle: we were outnumbered. I would watch this show from the platform behind my father, trying to hide my amusement. Some of the women would throw themselves on the floor, writhing in a trance and muttering words inspired by some strange spirit. We couldn't compete with these crowd-pleasing spectacles. I knew then that the "heathen" would prevail, and they did.

Trouble in Paradise

One thing my father noticed (and soon so did I) was that in almost every church we visited there was an attractive young black woman who seemed more forward than other folks, as though she were more at home with the white missionaries. My father soon began to suspect that these women, several of them only teenagers, were "Elliot's girls," and when questioned most of them acknowledged it with pride. They saw nothing immoral in this, and they were pleased with their special status as the white man's mistress. My father was so angered by the discovery of these liaisons that he vowed to drive Elliot from the island—and he did, by reporting him to our constituents back in the States.

I recall overhearing my father discussing all this with my mother late at night behind closed doors. One of Elliot's favorite girl's, I heard, was his own secretary, a stunning young black woman whom even I had noticed was always at his side And, of course, he had installed our first house girl,

Ada, in the little house behind his to serve his remaining needs. My father even approached Mrs. Elliot with his accusations, but she dismissed him haughtily, saying that she could no longer accommodate him. Then we discovered that she was having an affair with a local mulatto doctor—so much for saving the "heathen"! Which ones *were* they?

Of course, as a blossoming lad of fifteen, I was more fascinated than horrified by all these titillating revelations. But for my mother, this was the last straw: we were wasting our time, and we needed to go back home. So we did.

I have never been back to Jamaica in the nearly seventy years since. I would rather remember it the way it was: fearful and wonderful. This was long before the advent of mass tourism, of course. When we used to take the servants over to the north coast for an outing, we would be the only people at places like Ocho Rios, having the river and magnificent waterfalls all to ourselves. To go back now would be to court disillusionment. As it was then, Jamaica was idyllic, a brief but formative interlude in my young life. Later, I was to seek paradise elsewhere. I had my sixteenth birthday on the little boat we took back to Miami. It was a stormy passage.

3
FINDING MYSELF: MY THIRD LIFE

After about two years abroad in Jamaica, I landed back home in Erwin, Tennessee, where I had gone to the third and fourth grades. Although I had never attended high school, I had done correspondence work in Jamaica and had completed fifteen hours of credits. I skipped geometry, and I have skipped all math ever since, with no apologies. Back then I supposed that I could get into college with only fifteen credits, so I simply forfeited a high school diploma.

Missionary Work Again

Our family settled into a tiny walk-up rented apartment, and my father found a job as director of the Appalachian Mountain Evangelizing Association. This was a voluntary association of local Christian churches, the Churches of Christ, the same fundamentalist sect that had sponsored our work in Jamaica. We were missionaries again.

My father's work consisted of traveling throughout the mountains of eastern Tennessee and southeastern Kentucky, where we had our roots, encouraging local churches in various evangelistic efforts, occasionally holding a week or two of revival meetings. This characteristically southern form of religious life entailed nightly worship services, sermons by the visiting preacher, and other activities intended to revitalize the congregation and thus to stimulate its missionary efforts. (Today we might call them outreach activities.)

Now and then in rural areas my father would hold these meetings in a large tent, as he had done in Kentucky when he was a young college and seminary student. I still remember a few of these revival meetings.

My father had a big, sharply resonant voice, and he used it to full effect. When he thundered about the fires of hell, you could smell the hair of your body singeing.

Having nothing special to do that fall of 1948 in Tennessee, I audited several courses at the local high school. One was a required science course; another was a woodworking class in which I used the wood from the boxes we shipped from Jamaica to make a desk. Finally, there was band, where I tried unsuccessfully to master a tuba that was a big as I was.

I have forgotten everything about the science course, I never learned to play the tuba well enough to march with the band (and I didn't like most group activities, then or now), and the desk has since disappeared. However, one memorable thing did happen. A few teachers, simply hearing me say a few words with the voice that was by now a deep bass, suggested that I should be the master of ceremonies for the spring commencement. I borrowed an ill-fitting tux, looked up a few jokes in a standard joke book, and did my best. I was out of touch with popular American culture, with high school students in particular, and completely out of my element. I suspect that I made a fool of myself, but I learned something: never speak on a subject unless you control it, and never speak unless you are fully prepared. I also learned that speaking *style* is important. I was only sixteen, but I was on the road to overcoming my innate shyness.

Growth Pains

In the summer of 1949 we moved a few miles away to Johnson City, where my parents finally put down more permanent roots. My father had managed to buy a partially finished house and had done the construction work needed to make it livable. At sixteen, I was too young to go to college, even if I had gotten in, so I applied for a job in a local establishment, the Parks-Belk Department Store. Much to my surprise, I was hired. There must have been no child-labor laws back then. This was the largest local department store in the area, and its low advertised prices catered to the working classes in and around Johnson City, especially the local low-income farmers.

At first I was sent to the men's work-clothes department, where I sold blue jeans, overalls, and Dickie-brand khakis. This was easy, since working men knew exactly what they wanted and always bought the same clothes.

If you had their size in stock, that was it. I didn't really have to sell anything, so I was quite happy. I had Wednesday afternoons off, so I usually went to the movie theater down the street. One night a week I had to stay late to lock up after the cleaning crew, and I would wander over to the men's department and try on their best clothes, imagining how I would look dressed in something besides the cast-off clothes from the missionary barrel that I still wore. In time I saved enough money from my $35 weekly salary to buy a Varsity Town suit from a nearby haberdashery, a few Arrow shirts, and some neckties. I was so skinny (about 125 pounds) that the tailor had to measure for alterations. When he was adjusting the pants and asked, "On which side do you dress, Sir?" I didn't know what he was talking about. But relative to my salary back then, this was the best suit I have ever had. Again, I realized that style *does* matter.

I bought my first car that fall, a 1934 Plymouth for which I paid $200. It was the one year that Plymouth made a big car: a four-door sedan with a rear luggage rack, a fold-out front windshield, two outboard spare tires set into the front fenders, a louvered hood, enormous headlights, and twin chrome trumpet horns. It even had roll-down interior curtains and flower vases. That big black Plymouth looked just like the gangster cars in the movies and did not seem to suit my rather retiring personality. I named the car "Dreamboat," had a rebuilt engine installed, and reupholstered and painted it myself. Dreamboat saw me through part of college and into marriage. I have often wondered why I hit upon the name Dreamboat. My dreams back then were scarcely formed, certainly not articulated.

I was, of course, a regular churchgoer and volunteered to teach a Sunday school class for junior high boys. I also sang in the church choir. Teaching and choral work would remain lifelong passions. I became interested in a girl in the church youth groups whose parents worked, like me, in a department store. We went out every Saturday night in my old car, mostly to the movies, sometimes (when I could afford it) to dinner at a local eatery. I had absolutely no idea about how to treat a young woman, and I must have seemed like a real nerd. But we dated for several months, a lot of the time geared to church activities. At that time I began to be invited to speak for various youth group meetings, both in Johnson City and in nearby towns. Part of my appeal was that I appeared to be somehow exotic: a returned missionary. Almost no one in these local congregations had ever been anywhere abroad, unless possibly in the military. I even went to

Milligan College to speak, and my future wife told me that she sat on the floor to hear me speak and wondered what it would be like to know "such a dedicated young man."

At Parks-Belk I was soon transferred to the ladies' and children's shoe department, which was headed by a martinet who drove me mercilessly. The salespeople here worked largely on commissions, but I was so shy that I didn't compete aggressively for customers the minute they walked in the way the other salespeople did. I preferred to hang back in the stockroom, reshelving the rows of shoeboxes, since that was a chore no one else liked to do.

I was terrified of the department head and tried to avoid him, but he would hound me, driving me out onto the floor to sell shoes. I was so distressed that I wanted to quit. Some days I was so unnerved that I nearly did. But eventually I began to see pressure as a challenge. Soon I became more angry than depressed, determined now to prove myself—and I did. I became a confident salesman; what is more, I learned how to interact better with people. I have many memories of poor folk whom I helped into the best shoes they could afford for their children.

I remained a shoe salesman full-time for nearly a year and even continued part-time into my freshman year in college. Although the workplace was a harsh introduction to real life and my boss was a slave-driver, I look back on this year when I was sixteen–seventeen as one of the most significant turning points in my life. I had faced down a challenger who seemed to be my superior, and in the process I had discovered the self-confidence that would mark the rest of my life and career.

A College Man

Now seventeen, I decided that it was time to go to college—if I could get in. However, my horizons were so limited then that I never even thought to apply anywhere except at a local school, Milligan College. The college had begun in the 1860s as the Buffalo Male and Female Institute, an ominous-sounding name, but it reflected mostly the location, under the shadow of Buffalo Mountain, part of the Appalachian chain. Now Milligan College, it was affiliated with my denomination, the Churches of Christ, a separatist fundamentalist offshoot of the Disciples of Christ denomination. Milligan billed itself as a Christian liberal arts college, and its motto was "Christian education, the hope of the world." In fact, it was mostly a Bible college. Its faculty, students, and mandate were strictly denominational. The college, with only about 250 students, was unaccredited until a year after I graduated. Few of the faculty had mainstream university doctorates, if a graduate degree at all. However, many were dedicated teachers, at least within the confines of their limited worldview.

I always thought that Milligan's motto was a dead giveaway: *Christian* clearly meant only our kind of Christian; *education* meant mostly indoctrination; *hope* obviously amounted to Christian triumphalism; and Milligan's *world* was so parochial that it had little to do with the real world that I would eventually discover. Even the stated goal—liberal arts—was a misnomer: there was no art to speak of and absolutely nothing that was liberal. The emphasis and one strong major was religion, although there were departments of premed, prelaw, accounting, physical education, history, and education (where teaching certificates were earned).

But initially I couldn't even get into *that* college. Upon applying I was told by the registrar (I can still see her face) that I was not college material. At any rate, I didn't have a high school diploma. Eventually I was accepted, on probation, for one semester, after being warned that I would not be able to do the work. Four years later, without working very hard at it, I graduated cum laude with a major in religion.

The only courses that I recall as being of any value were two years of New Testament Greek and a class in music appreciation taught by a disabled local woman who had no graduate degree but exposed me for the first time in my life to classical music, which remains one of my great loves. I joined the college choir as a low bass and soon was a member of the college junior quartet (fig. 9). It was the beginning of a lifetime's involvement with choral work, but my musical tastes were far from being formed.

Girls—At Least, One Girl

As I said, I joined the college choir. After a bit my eyes landed on one particular girl in the choir. Being very shy, I did not approach her at first but told someone that I would like to go out with her. That person told

Fig. 9. The school quartet, Milligan College, 1952. I'm second from the left.

the girl, and by the time I got up courage to approach her and say that I knew someone who wanted a date, she laughed and said, "I know it, too, and it's you!"

As part of the social scene, a hayride through the rural hinterland around Milligan was planned. It was a dark, brisk October night, and I sat alone on the hay at first, socially inept as usual and wishing that I were somewhere else. The girl I had noticed in the choir, an outgoing sophomore named Norma Spangler, teased me into joining the hayride. I recall that we held hands. Soon we were going together, despite that fact that she had a lingering boyfriend in the background, an older man. By November, when I turned eighteen, we became one of the prominent pairs of the little college community.

I had never seriously dated any other girl, and I guess I assumed that this was it. We had a common small-town background, although she was a Baptist and thus, my parents declared, hell-bound (at this point I no longer worried about that). We saw each other constantly: in class, in choir, and at all kinds of college functions. Dates were simple because I was paying for my own college expenses while living at home and had very little money. We went to movies, to burger stands, and sometimes to drive-in movies (where we did the usual necking).

Despite growing frustration, we never seriously considered "doing it." One didn't, unless married. Before too long, I think, we simply assumed that we would get married in due course. I have no hesitation in saying that, despite the end of that marriage many years later, Norma and I were as much in love as we were capable of being and certainly so by the standards of the day. But looking back, we were extraordinarily naïve—at least I was.

The Boy Preacher

In October of my freshman year, while I was still seventeen, the pastorate of a country church near Milligan was vacated by the professor who had held it. For reasons I will never know (except possibly the fact that my father was a well-known local preacher), I was asked to fill in, that is, to preach on Sunday mornings and evenings, as well as leading Wednesday prayer meetings. After several weeks, when no one more suitable applied for the pulpit, I was asked by the church elders and deacons to become their pastor. So in December I became the full-time minister of the Oak Grove Christian Church on Powder Branch (fig. 10). The name Powder Branch came from a Civil War gun-powder mill on the creek that ran through the valley, and there really was a grove of large, old oak trees, in the midst of which on the hilltop stood the neat white frame church building with a tall steeple. Surrounding it were the tombstones of several generations of members, mostly descendants of the Scots-Irish immigrants who had originally settled so much of the Appalachian mountains. There were about 150 members, and church attendance ran a hundred or so most Sundays. My salary was the same as it had been at the department store: $35 a week. I continued to work on Saturdays at the store because my parents were unable to help me, and I was on my own.

So I was now a full-time student at a college that didn't want me, a full-time pastor of a church that did, and a part-time shoe salesman. I was barely eighteen. If a pastorate at the tender age seems anomalous, it was. Mainline Protestant denominations required a three-year graduate degree (the MDiv) for ordination, but my little sect (for so it was) thought that ordination—the laying on of hands, as in the New Testament church—was not about education, which was optional, but about vocation, being called.

Fig. 10. The Oak Grove Christian Church, on Powder Branch, east Tennessee.

I was called, and I answered. My father and some ministerial friends organized an ad hoc ordination service for me. I didn't know until much later that all this was highly unusual—even in my benighted little community.

Having to prepare and deliver sermons twice a week did not trouble me at all. I quickly discovered that I had oratorical talents as well as a pulpit voice. Since I was studying New Testament Greek, I would do a careful exegesis of the biblical text that each sermon was based on. No social gospel for me! Looking back, I wonder what those simple but pious farm folk thought; it was all Greek to them. But they indulged the boy preacher, since he was something of a novelty.

Pastoral obligations posed a greater challenge, since despite my growing pulpit prowess, I was still a rather shy, awkward teenager. I duly visited congregants in the hospital or convalescing at home, but I inquired about diseases or symptoms gingerly, especially when confronting women, who were still a mystery to me, and the less said the better.

I would also go calling, as a pastor was expected to do, visiting congregants in their homes. I would set off in my old Plymouth when I had an afternoon free of classes, making the rounds in the back country near the college. I would drop in unannounced, wherever I ran across the house of a parishioner, stopping to "set a spell," as the local dialect had it. I'd ask, "Granny McKeehan [a real name], how are you?" She'd reply, "Oh, feeling right peert, able to sit up and take nourishment."

Speaking of nourishment, how we did eat! Often Norma and I would be invited for Sunday dinner at one of the farm families' homes. There would be heaping plates of homemade southern fried chicken, piles of mashed potatoes and buckets of brown gravy, deviled eggs, all kinds of fresh vegetables in season, and at least half a dozen pies and cakes. Several times a year in warm weather the Oak Grove Christian Church would host an event called an "All-Day Preaching and Dinner on the Ground." Several sister congregations would gather; there would be morning, afternoon, and evening sermons by several preachers. Combined choirs would sing gospel hymns, sometimes from old-fashioned shaped-note songbooks for those who couldn't read music (most folks).

The real attraction, however, may have been the food: an alfresco feast the likes of which I have never seen since. Each church family would try to outdo the others, both in the quality and the quantity of food. The feast was laid out on long folding tables on the church lawn, and after piling our plates we gathered in small groups and ate picnic-style off tablecloths spread on the ground. I was young and pencil-thin then, so I indulged myself shamelessly and guilt-free.

Starting Married Life

Norma and I seemed almost the parson and his wife that first, and even the second, year at Oak Grove Christian Church. But although soon engaged, we did not get married until June 1, 1953, at the end of her junior and my sophomore year (fig. 11). Since we had almost no money, we got college friends to decorate the little church sanctuary by draping everything in white bedsheets with hand-picked flowers all around. Norma had a beautiful bride's dress given to her by her sophisticated cousin who lived in New York City. Bridesmaids were dressed in various pastel long gowns. I had a new, double-breasted gray suit. Norma's parents, two brothers, and a few friends drove over from her hometown, Jonesville, Virginia. My father performed the wedding ceremony. Unfortunately, we had mistakenly gotten the wedding license in the neighboring county, where we were going to live, so that ceremony was not valid. We decided to keep that quiet, so after the church wedding was over we went back to my father's house in Johnson City and had a private, legal ceremony. We drove off in

Dreamboat, festooned with ribbons and tied-on tin cans, for a five-day honeymoon in Ashville, North Carolina, and Gatlinburg, Tennessee, gateway to the Smoky Mountains. We were nineteen, virgins, as required, and somewhat anxious, not about each other but about life as adults.

Fig. 11. Our wedding, July 1, 1953.

Both sets of our parents were not only supportive of our marriage, but they virtually organized it (better to legitimize the inevitable). Norma's parents promised to continue paying her modest tuition, and mine offered the use of their basement apartment if we would fix it up. My parents had already lent me the money for the engagement ring ($150), and now they helped us to open a charge account for some furniture. I bought a used electric stove and refrigerator and repainted them. We acquired a real sofa, chair, and rug. I had my own homemade bedroom set, brought from Jamaica. I made a solid walnut desk from wood I found at a local sawmill. (I sit at that same desk as I write these lines, sixty-five years later.) So it was that we set up housekeeping on our own. I was worried about how we would live on little more than $35 a week. I went to the church board and suggested that, if I quit my Saturday work at the department store, I would have more time for church work. In that case, could they give me a raise to $50—especially since I would return $5 a week as a tithe (mandated, in our tradition)? They agreed, so I now had a net salary of $45 a week—a fortune.

We had no checking account, so we bought groceries with cash, stretching it as far as we could. Our only recreation was an occasional movie—if we could go through our pockets and find $2. We worked on class preparation most weekday evenings, excepting Sundays and Wednesdays at the church. If I had an afternoon with no classes, I would go calling, as described above. Since congregants were well aware of the modest preacher's salary that they could pay, they would help out by giving me food on my rounds. At one house, I'd get a brown bag (a "poke" in the local dialect) of fresh ripe tomatoes; at another, a dozen "roastin ears" right out of the field; elsewhere a box of big brown country eggs; sometimes a pecan pie (my favorite to this day); or even a live chicken.

My junior and senior years followed pretty much along expected lines. Although busy, I continued to do well in classes—except for one or two where I was beginning to flex the antiauthoritarian muscles that would get me into considerable trouble later. One was a class on the book of Acts, taught by an idiosyncratic New Testament professor who thought that his rather rare earned doctorate (a ThD from Southern Baptist Theological Seminary) gave him some sort of apostolic authority. He demanded that all students take down his class lectures almost word for word, then turn in the notes for his approval. I delayed, then simply refused (he wasn't that interesting). He warned me that my grades would suffer. I took my chances, made a 97 on the final exam, and got a C for the course. I was quite proud of that grade because principle was involved. The professor harangued me, declaring that I had "no academic future." Some years later, when I had completed my Harvard doctorate and sported a growing bibliography, the professor was jailed on fraud charges. Since he had time on his hands, I thought I might send him some of my publications to read. However, remembering the proverbial injunction to imitate God, who "tempers the wind to the shorn lamb," I decided against my initial impulse.

Maybe the World Isn't So Dangerous

My horizons began to expand a bit through travel. The college quartet was now traveling to promote the school, and we made trips to the Midwest and even to Florida. I sang with the quartet and did the promotional speaking in churches along the way on these trips.

Milligan College never noticed my later success, not even when I became an internationally recognized scholar. They negotiated with an Israeli colleague my age to send students to his dig, but they never invited me back to lecture, and I soon lost track completely. Then in 1999—forty-five years after graduation—Milligan invited me to come to Tennessee to accept some sort of award for service. By then I had converted to Judaism, a fact of which the college officials were unaware. When they learned, they tried desperately to uninvite me. I went, partly, I admit, to teach these bigots a lesson! The banquet and awards ceremony constitute one of the strangest nights of my life. Every other recipient was lauded for his Christian family and his service to the Lord. When my turn came, a few publications were mentioned, and I received a handshake and plaque. When I got back to Tucson, I threw it in the trash.

My senior year I attended a week of lectures at Southern Baptist Theological Seminary in Louisville, where I was born. Some of the lectures were given by the distinguished conservative British Old Testament scholar H. H. Rowley. I was already taken by the breadth of the Old Testament narratives, and I began to focus on that Bible rather than the New Testament (which Frank Cross, later my teacher at Harvard, always called "that late Hellenistic postscript to the Bible"). I thought of applying to Southern Seminary, but something held me back.

Dean Walker suggested his old school of Butler School of Religion, where a friend of his (and conservative fellow-traveler) taught Biblical Hebrew. Toyozo Watanabi Nakarai was a Japanese Buddhist turned Christian and a great Zionist. He was quite proud of his Hebrew name "Tovia" ("Yahweh is good"). A trained linguist, he had written a Hebrew grammar that apparently no other biblicist could understand. Moreover, he spoke Modern Hebrew as badly as I came later to speak it myself. But it was Professor Nakarai who turned me on to Israel and, by chance, to archaeology.

4
ON TO A PROTESTANT SEMINARY: MY FOURTH LIFE

As graduation at Milligan approached, I applied only to the School of Religion at Butler University. My father and others helped me to make contact with a country church near Elwood, Indiana, about an hour's drive north of Indianapolis. I was invited to the Harmony Christian Church at Leisure, for what we called back then a "trial sermon." The whole four-year affair became a trial during which there was neither harmony nor leisure. Names do matter, and I should have guessed. The last names of my three immediate predecessors, each of whom had been fired in turn, were Smelser, Pugh, and Stanke, and the nearest town was named Aroma (central Indiana was hog country). But I preached my sermon, and I was hired.

Indiana Gothic

Norma and I packed our few belongings in a rented truck, got a beautiful black cocker spaniel dog, and drove to Leisure. There we installed ourselves in the parsonage, an old but spacious frame house across the street from the turn-of-the-century brick church building (fig. 12). Leisure was literally a crossroad on Indiana Route 37. The only buildings were the church, the parsonage, four or five other houses, a gas station, a feed store, a blacksmith shop, and a small cafe. The population was twenty-six, including the two of us. The church, however, drew on the farmlands that stretched for miles in every direction, and it had some three hundred members. My salary was up to $65 a week; with Norma's income from a teaching position in nearby Elwood, we thought we were rich. We were, in many ways.

Fig. 12. The Harmony Christian Church, Leisure, Indiana.

The First Chinks in the Armor

At Butler School of Religion I began a three-year course toward a ministerial degree, the BD, or Bachelor of Divinity degree (now an MDiv). I drove a hundred miles a day, four days a week, through freezing Indiana winters, leaving well before sunrise each day. In the process I wore out four cars. In those days Butler, now Christian Theological Seminary, was the leading seminary of the Disciples of Christ denomination, liberal in its theological orientation and deeply involved in the World Council of Churches and the then-trendy ecumenical movement. I knew instinctively (if my parents had not already told me) that all this was the work of the devil. I resisted mightily the critical approach to the Old Testament in the classroom; after all, *critical* meant negative, didn't it? With several fellow Milliganites, I also cut the required daily chapel services (covering as best I could) to play pool over lunch hour. I was now very worldly—but only selectively. Intellectually I was still a fundamentalist, yet determined somehow to persevere in my ambition to get a graduate degree and prepare myself for a teaching career. I just didn't intend to teach this stuff.

I took additional courses in New Testament and New Testament (Koine) Greek, but I was gravitating more and more to the Old Testament. Even the dreaded Documentary Hypothesis (source criticism) did not dissuade me. I took two years of Septuagint Greek, the arcane dialect into which the Hebrew Bible was translated about 150 BCE, and I began Hebrew with Professor Nakarai. I still remember our first words to translate, from the opening lines of the book of Ruth:

wa-yehi ra'av ba-'arets
And there was a famine in the land.

This famine had led an Israelite family to move to Moab, of course. I was fascinated by the cadences of the Hebrew text, but it was years before I began to wonder if the land of Moab was real. We read from the Hebrew text in order to learn the language inductively, but we also had to master grammar. It was arduous, but I knew already that this was one of the basic tools of the trade that I was determined to learn.

Nakarai also offered an occasional course in biblical archaeology, so when it was available I took it. It was not memorable. Nakarai had no hands-on field experience, there were no slides or any other visual aids, and the course focused on a few sensational discoveries such as the Dead Sea Scrolls. That was not going to turn me on to archaeology. However, Nakarai unwittingly did that in another way.

My First Trip to Israel

Nakarai had been president of the National Association of Biblical Instructors, an organization that fostered, in particular, the teaching of Hebrew. A close associate in that organization was Professor Abraham Katsh of New York University. Katsh directed a travel study program in Israel called "Workshop in the Lands of the Bible" that catered to non-Jews. The idea was simply to attract Christian pastors and teachers to Israel and then send them home with favorable impressions that they might incorporate into their work. Many years later, in 2006, when I was lecturing at Christie's in New York City, an elderly lady came up to me and said, "I wonder if you ever knew my late husband, Abraham Katsh." Astonished, I replied, "Madame, your husband sent me on my first trip to Israel, fifty years ago. Without him, I wouldn't be in this field today."

One day toward the end of my second year in seminary, Nakarai approached me, told me about the workshop, and said that, if I wanted to participate during the coming summer, he could get me a partial scholarship. But there would still be a fee of $700, more than one-fifth of my annual salary. I hesitated but then figured that, if I borrowed the money, I could probably pay it back with speaking fees when I returned. The scheme worked. In rural Indiana, part of the Bible Belt, a Christian minister talking about his experiences in Israel was a big hit. Over the next two years, collecting $10–12 lecture fees one at a time, I repaid the loan—and the trip in the summer of 1957 repaid me many times over.

In New York I met Katsh with others in the little group. It may sound incredible, but in all my twenty-three years he was the first Jew I had ever encountered. There simply were no Jews in the small towns in the South and Midwest where I grew up. But at least I had no negative impressions. My fundamentalist father believed sincerely that, unless Jews converted, they could not be saved, but I had never heard expressions such as "Christ-killers."

Katsh was a charming, worldly gentleman with an infectious love of Israel, and I took to him immediately. Our group of a dozen or so included a couple of pastors, a Southern Baptist Seminary professor, a school teacher or two, and a dour New England matron who was determined to teach me good manners. I was the only student and years younger than anyone else, but I'm afraid that she taught me little.

We spent three weeks in Jerusalem in daily study sessions, broken up by walking tours of the city. Several Israeli scholars came to the hotel for lectures, some of them young but promising. Our Hebrew teacher was the noted scholar Chaim Rabin. A course on the Dead Sea scrolls was taught by Jacob Licht. The history of ancient Israel was covered by a lively young scholar of Viennese extraction, still working on his doctorate. His name was Avraham Malamat, and later he became one of Israel's most prominent biblical historians. Today he is deceased, but Malamat was among the small circle of old friends I still saw when I went back to Jerusalem each summer. Recently I found my notebook from Malamat's 1957 course. We both had amounted to something after all. On off-hours walking tours of the city, I often went alone, something I have always loved to do in cities abroad. I explored the Orthodox Quarter in Mea Shearim, alternately fascinated and appalled by the religious fanaticism that I saw. So these were the Pharisees my father always talked about! Other days I would try to find dead-end streets that led up to the no man's land that divided Jerusalem after the armistice that ended the 1948 war. I tried to get up high enough to sneak a photograph. I thought to myself, "I'll never get to see the Old City."

Katsh arranged some memorable visits for us. One day he said that we would be going to Martin Buber's house for lunch. I had already encountered Buber's marvelous book *I and Thou*, but I couldn't believe that we were actually going to meet him. Another day we were on the bus to our destination, and Katsh was conversing with an excitable little man who stuttered. I wasn't particularly impressed, but it was H. L. Ginsberg, whose elegant translations of the Ugaritic epic poems have related them to the poetry of Psalms in the Hebrew Bible. Still another day we went to the president's house, where Golda Meir spoke to us. For a kid from nowhere, these were experiences I could never even have imagined, and they opened a new world for me. Within less than ten years I was to move freely in such circles in Jerusalem myself.

Fig. 13. My first trip to Israel, summer of 1957. Left to right: H. L. Ginsberg, Abraham Katsh, Martin Buber, Ze'ev Vilnay.

So This Is What Archaeologists Do!

The field trips were the highlights of that summer in 1957. Our guide was none other than the legendary author Ze'ev Vilnay, a great Russian bear of a man who exuded enthusiasm for every square inch of the land. We spent three weeks with Vilnay, devouring his classic *Israel Guide*. At each stop he would bound out of the bus, stretch out his arms like Joshua in the Valley of Aijalon, and exclaim, "Now we are in this historic place!" I soon learned that every place in Israel is historic. Actually, we did go to the Aijalon Valley and even clambered up the overgrown mound of Gezer, where I have now spent more than fifty-five years of my life. But I knew nothing about Gezer then, and I scarcely have any memories of that first day.

The most memorable visit for me was at the great mound of Hazor in Lower Galilee, where Yigael Yadin was in his third season of excavations. Yadin, then retired as chief of staff of the Israel Defense Forces, had recently completed his PhD dissertation on ancient warfare. Always a superb organizer and promoter, he saw the Hazor dig not only as the excavation of a major Canaanite-Israelite site but as a training ground for the next generation of Israeli archaeologists. Several of his young proteges were there, all of whom would in time become my closest friends and colleagues—many, like me, now retired. They included Amnon Ben-Tor, Yigal Shiloh, Ephraim Stern, David Ussishkin, and others. The senior staff members, including Ruth Amiran, Trude and Moshe Dothan, Miriam Tadmor, and Yohanan Aharoni, were those who so warmly welcomed me when I returned to Israel in 1964. However, I didn't actually meet any of these Israeli archaeologists on our visit to Hazor that day. I just observed them at work down in the trenches, marveling at why any sane person would want to make a profession of that. It looked like hot and dirty work, and I couldn't see that they were finding anything. That was my introduction to archaeology. While it doesn't sound promising, there is no doubt in my mind that a tiny seed was planted that day, and it would take fruit. Toyozo Watanabi Nakarai had inadvertently steered me toward my real vocation.

Ze'ev Vilnay, our venerable guide on the 1957 tour, was someone I got to know better when I returned to Israel to take up my first position there. Many years later, in 1973, when I was director of the Albright Institute,

Vilnay sometimes came to the school for social occasions. One Saturday evening when I had invited the resident fellows over to the director's house for drinks after dinner, Vilnay and his wife showed up at the door. I was a bit taken back, especially when he exclaimed "How nice of you to invite us!" We hadn't invited him, but since we were all sitting around, well dressed and having a drink, I welcomed him as our honored guest. He captivated the fellows with wonderful stories, and they were delighted to have met the famous Vilnay. I have always wondered where he was *supposed* to be that night.

Archaeology in the 1950s: The First Generation

The Hazor Excavations of 1955–1958, which I visited in 1957, were the first large-scale Israeli field project after the 1948 War of Liberation, directed by Israel's former chief of staff, Yigael Yadin. He has just completed his doctoral dissertation in 1955, published as *The Art of Warfare in Biblical Lands* (surprise, surprise). Hazor was the training ground for the coming generation of younger Israeli archaeologists, among them Amnon Ben-Tor, Ephraim Stern, Yigal Shiloh, David Ussishkin, and others, only in their twenties then (below).

While Yadin was director (no doubt about that, for he was already an imperious figure), the real heart and soul of Hazor was Immanuel Dunayevsky, another veteran of the Palestine days. He was not primarily an archaeologist but rather a well-trained architect whose orientation toward building levels, rather than empirically observed strata, dominated Israeli field methods for many years. In 1973, in a volume of essays in Dunayevsky's honor, I ventured to attack this method as antiquated, inferior to Kathleen Kenyon's balk-debris-layer method that we had adapted at Gezer.

There were, however, a number of other Israeli archaeologists of the older generation at Hazor, such as Nahman Avigad, Yohanan Aharoni, Ruth Amiran, Pesach Bar-Adon, Dan Barag, Claire Epstein, Moshe and Trude Dothan, Miriam Tadmor, and others (even non-Israeli archaeologists such the legendary French archaeologist, Jean Perrot). Others of that first generation were the prehistorians Jacob Kaplan and Moshe Stekelis, the Second Temple expert Michael Avi-Yonah, the venerable Avraham

Biran, Eliezer Sukenik, and, of course, the grand old man of Israeli archaeology and biblical studies: Benjamin Mazar.

Mazar was later to become the rector of the Hebrew University, now confined to a new campus in West Jerusalem, the Israelis having lost the Mount Scopus campus in the 1948 war. The Archaeology Department there was founded by Yadin's father, Eliezer Sukenik, in 1925. In addition to rebuilding the Hebrew University and its archaeological and field training programs, the Israelis had to revamp the now-defunct British Mandate Department of Archaeology and renew its publications, as well as replace the national library and collections of the Rockefeller Museum in the Old City (opened in 1938).

Shmuel Yeivin, a veteran of the Jewish *yishuv* (settlement) in Mandatory Palestine, was appointed director of antiquities in July 1948 and served in that capacity until 1959. The dramatic story of these early days in Israeli archaeology has now been told in Raz Kletter's *Just Past? The Making of Israeli Archaeology* (2006).

One of the first acts of the new department was to replace the old *Quarterly of the Department of Antiquities in Palestine* (1938–1948) with a new publication, *The Israel Exploration Journal* (1950–). It was sponsored by the Israel Exploration Society and designed to replace the old Palestine Exploration Society and its journal, *The Palestine Exploration Quarterly* (still published in Great Britain).

There were a few other early Israeli excavations, such as those of Mazar at Tell Qasile (1948–1951) and Beth Shearim (1953–1954), of Kaplan in the Tel Aviv/Jaffa area (1955–), of Aharoni in Surveys in Galilee (1955–), and of Moshe Prausnitz in the Phoenician cemetery of Achziv (1958–).

All of the Israeli excavations—especially Hazor, as the principal training ground—were heavily influenced by the extraordinary American orientalist and founder of biblical archaeology, William Foxwell Albright (1891–1971). He had pioneered excavations in Palestine in the 1930s and long directed the American Schools of Oriental Research in Jerusalem (1920–1929, 1933–1936). Albright had trained virtually all of the American archaeologists of the period from the late 1920s to his retirement in 1958. Since all my teachers at Harvard had been students of Albright, I am in effect a third-generation Albrightian (although something of a renegade, as we shall see). In the 1950s, Albright was not only the doyen of American biblical archaeology but also the dominant influence on the first generation of Israeli archaeologists. That was particularly evident in the basic orientation of Mazar, Yadin, and Aharoni—the founding fathers of Israeli-style biblical archaeology.

In my brief visit to Israel in the summer of 1957, I met only Yadin and a few of his proteges at Hazor. But by the mid-late 1960s, when I was resident in Israel, I had come to know all the first-generation archaeologists mentioned above (except for Sukenik, who died in 1953). One reason I have dared to write this book is that I am unique among American archaeologists in having been privileged to know this pioneering generation personally.

There were also excavations in the West Bank in the 1950s, then part of the Hashemite kingdom of Jordan, although the heartland of ancient Israel. There were, of course, no Israeli excavations until after the Six-Day War in 1967. Americans were excavating at Shechem under Wright and others from 1957 on and at Tell el-Jib (biblical Gibeon) under James B. Pritchard (1956–1962). The French excavations at Tell el-Farʿah (biblical Tirzah; 1946–) were directed by the venerable Père Roland de Vaux of the École Biblique in Jerusalem. Finally, Kathleen Kenyon's epoch-making excavations at Jericho were carried out from 1955 to 1958. All of these foreign archaeologists, too, I came to know personally by the 1960s, especially those in Jerusalem after the Six-Day War. (Some of their stories will follow in due course.) But meanwhile, I was to seek my fortune in Israel proper, because in those days one had to choose: work in either Israel or the Arab world. I chose Israel, not for any ideological reasons (then or now), but simply because the opportunities for me arose there—even though I had begun in 1962 at Shechem, in Jordan, under the tutelage of Ernest Wright, who had only visited Israel once in 1958, incognito.

Back Home

Apart from the brief glimpse of the wider world that I got in my six weeks in Israel in 1957, the everyday world in which I lived in Leisure, Indiana, was still parochial—even more so than in my undergraduate days in Tennessee. We had no FM radio station within reach, no television whatsoever, only one local newspaper. I don't remember subscribing even to any popular magazines such as *Time* or *Newsweek*. I was immune from the draft, so

I didn't serve in Korea. If asked whether I was a Republican or a Democrat, I would have been perplexed; I didn't even vote in local elections.

During four years living in Leisure, I never went to a concert, an opera, or a lecture on public affairs. The one-hundred-mile drive to Indianapolis and back was just too difficult. We did have a record player, and after hearing an extraordinarily moving work on the radio one evening I bought the record. I didn't know what the piece was until the announcer identified it at the end. It was Mozart's *Requiem*, a piece that I now know well and have sung in concert, as well as singing the Verdi *Requiem* in Carnegie Hall.

I didn't miss the wider world because I had rarely experienced anything of it. From my early childhood, I recall my parents constantly warning me about the dangers of being worldly. That was their explanation of why any particular thing was sinful. Smoking, drinking, going to the movies, playing cards, dancing, reading secular literature, putting on airs—and especially sex outside of marriage: all these things were wrong because they were worldly. (Now we know that some of these things really *are* wrong because they are silly, destructive, and even might kill you.) I denied myself such things because I was focused on the next world, the world of eternity with God. I grew up with the fundamental concept of being saved—precisely from the real world.

Only much later did I discover the forbidden delights of that world, as well as some of its risks. But in my seminary years I remained a staunch other-worldly fundamentalist, scarcely aware of anything beyond the tiny splinter sect in which I had grown up. During these years in Indiana, my father moved much closer to us, to Illinois, where he became a professor of apologetics (whatever that was) at Lincoln Bible College, and he supported my rebelliousness as a student at a liberal seminary. Ironically, a few years later I was appointed an adjunct professor (in absentia) at Christian Theological Seminary, while I was director of the Albright Institute in Jerusalem. Nevertheless, the early experiences there were so negative that ever since then my Freudian slip gives me away—a Protestant cemetery.

Approaching our mid-twenties and the completion of seminary, Norma and I thought that it was time to have children. But nothing happened. After some time we both underwent a battery of medical tests and were informed that it was very unlikely that we would ever be able to conceive. We abandoned birth control and in time simply put out of mind the notion of being parents. Since we were still unsettled, adopting didn't seem like an option. But if the biological clock was ticking, I wasn't counting. Little by little I was beginning to focus on a career, although I was only dimly aware of where that might lead me. For better or worse, career would become vocation, the driving force in my life.

I wouldn't have made a very good parent back then; as it turned out, Norma and I became parents only after sixteen years of marriage, when we were both better prepared. Still, I confess that I never managed to balance career and parenthood as I should have, at least in my earlier years.

5
FINISHING SCHOOL: MY FIFTH LIFE

During my last year at Christian Theological Seminary in 1959, I moved beyond my Bachelor of Divinity degree (now an MDiv), designed for ordination as a pastor, to the completion of an MA in Semitics, an academic degree that usually led to a PhD (fig. 14). Given my still-conservative and somewhat apologetic leanings, it is not surprising that I chose as my thesis topic "The Revival of Old Testament Theology." In the 1950s, Protestant (and even Roman Catholic) theology had begun to turn away from the classical liberalism of an earlier era, spurred on by a movement called neo-orthodoxy. Although not fundamentalist, as European scholars charged, this was a movement that sought to restore the authority of Scripture.

George Ernest Wright was a distinguished Old Testament scholar and a leading light of neo-orthodoxy. In 1958 he had moved from McCormick Theological Seminary in Chicago to become Parkman Professor of Divinity in the Harvard Divinity School. In researching my thesis topic the following year, I was delighted to discover Wright's works, especially his little book *God Who Acts: Biblical Theology as Recital.* Here Wright declared: "In Biblical faith everything depends upon whether the central events actually occurred" (1952, 127). So the Bible was not a myth but historical. I was overjoyed—rescued at last from the wasteland of a liberal seminary.

After my defense before my skeptical professors, I was somehow awarded my MA summa cum laude (fig. 14). But the revival of biblical theology was to be short-lived. Not anticipating that, I was so taken with Wright's positivism that I was all set to study with him. I confidently applied only to Harvard. In April of 1959, I was shocked to get a letter rejecting my application. No explanation, but apparently I was not Harvard material. What to do?

My father had duly warned me about "Eastern finishing schools": they would (and did) finish my faith. But I was determined to go. So I resigned my pastorate in Indiana, and Norma resigned her tenured position in the Elwood Public Schools. We sent all our earthly possessions to Boston in a Mayflower van and into storage. Then we drove across the country in our little canary yellow Fiat 1600 roadster, sights set on the brave new world. We had no jobs, no prospects, little money in our pockets, and not a single friend or connection in all of New England. All we had was a naïve notion that this was supposed to be, that something would turn up. It did.

Fig. 14. Graduation at Christian Theological Seminary, 1959.

A Congregational Clergyman Now

I had the address of the Boston offices of the United Church of Christ, representing the Congregational Churches of New England that were affiliated with my own denomination, the Disciples of Christ. The United Church of Christ was a much more liberal denomination than my own, but I thought I might manage anyway as a pastor, given a chance. The office sent me down to Fall River to try out with a sermon before the congregation, but I decided that it was too far to commute (if I ever did get in at Harvard). I also negotiated with a congregation in Medford, Massachusetts. I could have had that position, but the old wooden colonial church building was in need of extensive repairs, and the congregation had dwindled to a few hardy souls. Then, providentially (?), I made contact with the Bethany Congregational Church in Quincy, a historic town on the South Shore.

A former undergraduate professor of mine had been associate minister there some years before while he was doing his graduate work at Harvard, and I had a letter of introduction from him. The senior minister, the Rev. John Banks, invited Norma and me for dinner at the home of one of the parishioners. Their house was right on Quincy Point, looking across Boston Harbor. We went swimming, and while we were standing waist high in the water we talked about a possible position for me. Within a few days Banks hired me, sight unseen, as it were. For the next five years I would serve as his minister of education—one of the most satisfying experiences of my life. I was still a believer but about to get an introduction to liberal Christianity.

Norma soon got a secretarial position at the Walter Baker Chocolate Factory in Milton Lower Falls, then the next year a position as a high school teacher in Weymouth. She taught there for four years, before leaving yet another tenured position, this time to go to Israel with me in 1964. With the help of bankers and realtors who were members of the congregation, we soon bought a small Dutch Colonial house a few blocks from Wollaston Beach, overlooking a salt marsh where we heard the gulls crying. I remember what the house cost: $19,000, four times my salary and a fortune to us. We were ecstatic: two kids from the sticks in Boston, with good jobs, our first house of our own, and newly found friends! So I wasn't in Harvard, but I would be.

Getting into School via the Back Door—Again

I soon drove over to Cambridge to keep an appointment I had made with G. Ernest Wright, whom, of course, I had never met. I was apprehensive, sure that I was way out of my element. But Wright, a man of patrician good looks but with a down-to-earth manner, was quite cordial. He explained to me that, while my BD with honors in Greek and Hebrew and my MA summa cum laude were adequate, I had no French or German. Furthermore, he and Frank Cross had surmised that I came from a fundamentalist background, and they thought that I might not fit in at Harvard. But he said that if I leaned French and German with tutors and came back for oral exams in the spring, they would reconsider my application. I did, and they did. So after a year as a full-time pastor, I became a full-time pastor and a full-time doctoral student at Harvard. I was terrified. Now they would find out that I really wasn't Harvard material.

Church and School

The first year at the Bethany church was a challenge. I was in charge of a large church school with a varied educational program, which I soon expanded to include adult education. I had my own office and secretary. Teaching teachers, I knew now that was what I wanted to do, more than pastoral counseling, for instance. But I was also able to indulge my other passion, preaching. Once or so a month, the other associate minister and I were given the pulpit. At first my sermons were pretty conventional, but gradually I began to feel the pull of the social gospel. One of my sermons on fair housing for minorities even made the Congressional Record. The church was one of the largest on the South Shore, with a beautiful stone Gothic building, a magnificent pipe organ, and a very upscale congregation. Banks, then turning forty, was a wonderful mentor who was tolerant of my parochial background. Because he did not wear a clerical collar, I didn't have to.

He even agreed that I didn't have to officiate at infant baptisms, anathema in my theology. Gradually I began to feel at home in the New England Congregational tradition and in the environs of Boston. I was twenty-five, already a minister for eight years and married for six. A new world was opening up for me, and I was ready.

There were eight students in my incoming class at Harvard. All had previous graduate degrees, and the clerics among them (the majority) came from much more liberal, mainstream Christian communities. The two Roman Catholic priests were multilingual, knew Rome intimately, and seemed to have a book of blank checks signed by the pope, so they could buy the books I could not afford. Several of the incoming students had won teaching assistantships, but we were on our own financially, with Norma's salary and mine. Fortunately, tuition was greatly reduced after a student passed the two-year MA-level qualifying exams and was granted doctoral residency status. My MA was accepted and qualified me for advanced standing, although I felt as though I was still the poor kid on the block.

My minor professor was Frank Moore Cross Jr., a thirty-six-year old *Wunderkind*, protege of Albright and world-renowned authority on the Dead Sea Scrolls. The first day of class in Ugaritic (a Canaanite dialect akin to Biblical Hebrew), he called on some of the students to read and translate several lines from one of the mythological poems. My heart sank. I had had two years of Greek and two of Hebrew, but this was a new language! That first year there were days when I half-hoped I would have a fender bender while driving the Southeast Expressway to Cambridge and would thus escape being called on in class.

The first two years I frequently was terrified that I would never be able to pass the written general examinations that led to the dissertation stage. I took the required courses in Old Testament introduction, history and religion of Israel, exegesis, epigraphy (inscriptions in ancient Northwest Semitic languages), Mesopotamian history, and Akkadian (Assyrian and Babylonian). I also worked on the advanced Hebrew we had to complete on our own, aided by sitting in on Tom Lambdin's courses in grammar. Several of us tried to get together over lunch to read several chapters in the Hebrew Bible—by sight, of course, since we would be responsible for the whole Hebrew Bible in the general examinations.

I also took the only courses Ernest Wright, my major professor, offered in archaeology, a one-semester introduction and a beginning seminar. When it was offered my second year, I also took Wright's course on Old Testament theology. This was what I had been waiting for, but I must confess that it was a great disappointment. Wright had defined Old Testament theology as a basically historical discipline, as in *God Who Acts* and *Magnalia Dei, the Mighty Acts of God* (the title of his Festschrift volume ten years later). It had not yet occurred to me to question whether the saving event had actually *happened* in history, but it did strike me that in this recital of the past there was nothing new, nothing dynamic. By now I was also beginning to be suspicious about the essentially dogmatic nature of all theological systems: historical, systematic, dogmatic, and now even biblical theology began to look like a dead end to me.

Near the end of the second year, I was struggling to maintain an A average while commuting and holding down a full-time pastorate. I had survived even the notorious 200 Seminar, in which you submitted a paper in advance, and students and faculty alike then ganged up to shred you to pieces. More than one grown man (there were no women then) had been reduced to tears in that seminar. Still, I began to experience a crisis in confidence. Did I have what it takes to sustain an academic career? Beyond that, what if my faith could not be grounded in actual historical events?

I certainly had the capacity for hard work, and I loved the Bible and the biblical world, but I didn't think that I would ever be an intellectual. So I went shamefacedly to tell Ernest that I was dropping out of the program. I would be only a pastor. He listened for a bit, then rocked back in his chair, swept his hand through that great mane of white hair (a gesture I would come to know well in future years), smiled, and said: "Well, Frank says you'll never be much of a Hebraist. I never was myself. But why don't you try archaeology? I'll find you some money, and you can come with me to Shechem next summer as an area supervisor. Maybe you'll be better suited to that." That brief moment marked the most critical turning point of my life. Ernest saw in a hesitant young man something I couldn't see in myself, and that something was the beginning of the self-confidence that has been the secret of whatever success I have enjoyed.

Archaeology Trumps Everything

Ernest got me a Robert H. Pfeiffer Traveling Fellowship for the summer of 1962. With several other Harvard students who had already declared an archaeological major (Jack Holladay, Darrell Lance, and Joe Seger, later my core staff members at Gezer), I raised enough money to buy a preordered VW microbus in Cologne. Flying to Germany, we picked up the van and set off for a whirlwind eight-day drive across Germany, Austria, Yugoslavia, Bulgaria, Greece, Turkey, and Syria, on our way to Jordan. We slept out in the open in sleeping bags, lived off canned Bully Beef and local beer (which I had just discovered), and pooled our money to buy gas. The total expenses for the six of us came to about $40 apiece for this two-thousand-mile journey.

The last night, quite late, we drove down the Jordan Valley and up from Jericho to Jerusalem. About midnight we pulled in through the gates of the American School of Oriental Research (later the Albright Institute). Finding no one still up, we pitched our sleeping bags on the balcony of the annual professor's apartment. The next day we all got bills from the school's director, Paul Lapp, for one day's full board—plus afternoon tea. I was so put off by that that I vowed never to spend another night at the American School, and I never did—until I became the director in 1971. But the smell of the night dew on the dusty pines in the garden has stayed with me to this day. Little did I know that the American School would dominate my personal and professional life for these sixty years.

The 1962 season at Shechem lasted six weeks. We lived in a tent camp set up in the schoolyard of the village of Balatah near Nablus. Ernest, already partly incapacitated by a heart condition, lived in the Qubr-Yousef, a small Muslim shrine thought by locals to be the tomb of Joseph. The staff was made up of about thirty Americans and one British chap, all men but two women (wives), the rest seminary students like me or seminary professors. The sponsors were Ernest's old school, the McCormick Theological Seminary in Chicago, and Drew Theological Seminary in New Jersey. Harvard lent little besides its good name (which was also the case later at Gezer).

The dig hired about seventy-five Arab men and boys from the village, including an impressive man named Mustapha Tawfeek as foreman and several technical men, specialists who had been trained by Kenyon at Jericho. The workday was from 5 am to 1 pm, then after lunch and a nap a couple of hours back in the field doing cleanup, drawing, and photography. There were no scheduled evening lectures or weekend field trips, indeed, no formal attempt at educating us neophytes in field method. However, Ernest clearly saw Shechem as a pioneer in modern methods, as

Fig. 15. At Shechem, my first dig, 1957.

well as a field school. In retrospect, what we learned at Shechem was often what not to do.

I was given a 5 meter square and a few Arab workers. I didn't know a word of Arabic, nor did the workers speak any English. Most had dug at Shechem before, so they proceeded, full of high spirits and good cheer (as far as I could make out from their laughter). But what was I supposed to record? I had been put into Field V, the area of a monumental fortress temple of the second millennium BCE, supervised by Professor Robert Bull, a Drew University professor of church history. (I wasn't sure about the connection—or much of anything else.) Bull seemed to take charge, but he was often away from the field. I supervised the digging of a deep trench in the forecourt of the temple, and I soon learned intuitively what to look for.

One could see the more or less regular layering of the successive fills, so I tried to separate these layers and the pottery they produced, since that was apparently what was meant by *stratigraphy*. I had been told to give every discrete soil layer a locus number and to record it. But what was a locus? A place, I guessed. And so it went. When the trench was done and I moved elsewhere, the dig architect—the legendary (and somewhat idiosyncratic) draftsman G. R. H. (Mick) Wright—came in to draw the section. I never saw the drawing, so I wondered if what he drew matched what I had dug and thought I saw.

Because of his heart condition, Ernest was able to make only a brief morning tour of the widely scattered excavation areas. In my two years in the field at Shechem, he was never in any of my squares, but I enjoyed his friendly greeting as he appeared high above me on the edge of the trench each day. He spent much of his time in the schoolhouse, reading pottery. It was the date assigned to the pottery from each dirt layer that gave us a timeline. Ernest was at the time one of the foremost experts in the world in the arcane discipline of Palestinian ceramic chronology. But in the afternoon, the only time I had to rest a bit, I rarely went to the schoolhouse to look over his shoulder and learn the rudiments.

I simply did not yet appreciate the necessity of mastering ceramic typology, which the great pioneer Sir Flinders Petrie had called "the essential alphabet of Palestinian archaeology." Little did I know that in only four years I would be in charge of pottery reading in my own excavations at Gezer. I have always regretted this lost opportunity, but there was no formal training program at Shechem, and we students learned hands-on as best we could. Ernest's senior staff—people such as Bob Bull, Joe Callaway, Ted Campbell, Siegfried Horn, Paul Lapp, Larry Toombs, and Jim Ross—were competent and experienced, but there was too little coordination, not even a uniform recording system.

Shechem was typical of American biblical archaeology in the 1960s: (1) a site chosen for its biblical significance, (2) sponsoring institutions that were primarily religious, and (3) a staff made up of clergy. Being still a clergyman myself, I felt pretty much at home at Shechem. But that was the beginning of a long, and sometimes painful journey that I was to make that took my younger colleagues and me toward archaeology as a secular discipline, highly specialized and professionalized. Ernest saw it coming, but he was never reconciled to these developments.

We did meet some famous visiting Palestinian archaeologists that summer, such as James Pritchard, then excavating at Gibeon, and Roland de Vaux, digging at Tell el-Farʿah (biblical Tirzah). We students also profited from weekend trips on our own. Since I had only been to Israeli Jerusalem in 1957, I delighted in staying in cheap hostels in the Old City, exploring every back street. One weekend we toured Petra, another weekend other biblical sites such as Samaria. There was also the Rockefeller Museum with its collections of fabulous things we had known only by name.

All this was an important part of our ad hoc education in archaeology, and I think it was then that I fell in love with the Old City. However, today, although hardly comparing myself with Jesus, I stand on the Mount of Olives and weep over Jerusalem. Living in Jerusalem for a long time is like an unfortunate love affair in which one can live neither with nor without one's love.

Getting the Preliminaries Out of the Way

At the end of the summer at Shechem, Ernest took me aside and told me that he had plans for me. He said that he would like to start a new excavation, a spin-off of Shechem, possibly in Israel, with the Harvard group as staff. He hinted that I might be the leader. I don't really know what Ernest saw in me that early, but his confidence gave me confidence. Later, while I was doing my dissertation, he gave me a copy of his book *Shechem: The Biography of a Biblical City*, inscribed "For Bill, with expectations of great things." Now I have the same expectations of my own doctoral students. But it all began at Shechem.

Back in Boston I continued my coursework at Harvard, but now I knew that archaeology would be my major—and that I would finish my degree. My devotion to church work continued unabated; I had not yet realized that soon I would have to choose. To be sure, Ernest told me one day that I was "spending too much time and energy on the pastorate" and that my doctoral work was going to suffer. Since he had expressed his hopes for my future in archaeology, I paid attention. But not only was I still motivated by a decidedly Christian sense of vocation; I was channeling my energies into the renewal movement that was now revitalizing some branches of liberal Christianity. My old hunger for both biblical authority and relevance in faith resonated with this movement. I even managed to introduce into Bethany's church school some of the features of the biblical theology that I had thought in seminary days was making a comeback. I invited Ernest himself (a Presbyterian minister) to speak to a United Church of Christ teachers workshop on the South Shore. He was a great hit. Here we were, he and I, both still churchmen, among other things.

I launched what our senior minister, Banks, might have thought subversive but in fact generously supported: a house-church movement within the larger congregation at Bethany. Soon we had half a dozen small groups

Fig. 16. Bethany Congregational Christian Church, Quincy, Massachusetts.

of parishioners meeting in various homes, first with me and soon under their own lay leadership. They were reading Christian literature, studying the Bible, praying together as they were moved to do, and holding vigorous discussions on faith and ethics. My evangelist father would have been proud of me. But today, an agnostic and secular humanist (not to mention being a Jew), I cannot imagine that I ever did such things. Neither can my children: "Abba, you're making that up!"

Meanwhile, ironically, Norma and I were becoming steadily more worldly—the one thing my sainted mother consistently warned me about. We had season tickets at Boston's Symphony Hall. We went frequently to the Charles Playhouse, other theaters, and avant-garde cinema in Harvard Square (and discovered Ingmar Bergman's films). We even took mini-vacations in New York and indulged ourselves in all the Broadway and off-Broadway theater that we could squeeze in. We saw a couple of operas at the Met. We bought a new car and toured New England on holidays. We ate out in ethnic and historic restaurants in the city. Norma began studying for a MA in history at Boston University. We dressed quite well. After all, we were both making good salaries, we had no children (and no prospects), and Boston was our apple.

We took a big bite.

By 1963, however, general examinations were staring me in the face. That entailed finishing all the required coursework, which by now I had

Fig. 17. Our house at 41 Homer Road, Quincy.

done. Having switched my major to archaeology, I had gotten out of at least one of the language requirements. I passed off the Latin and Greek requirements by transfer, then the French and German requirements by oral examination. So I had only to demonstrate a comprehensive knowledge of all the inscriptions in the major Northwest Semitic languages: Ugaritic, Aramaic, Phoenician, Moabite, Ammonite, Edomite, Punic, and so on. I dropped out of Akkadian after one year, and I escaped Arabic altogether. As for Hebrew, I had to be prepared to read the entire Hebrew Bible by sight, without any aids. My fellow students and I carried around Hebrew flashcards all the time, and well before the exam we had memorized every Hebrew word that occurred more than five times in the Bible. We could guess the rest, we hoped.

For more than six months, I worked hard preparing for the generals. I was terrified: all the hopes I had built up, the career that I envisioned, hinged on passing those exams. They were as bad as I had feared, each of the majors and minors a three-hour, closed-book written examination. For the Northwest Semitic exam, I drew the ninth-century BCE Phoenician Kilamuwa royal inscription, on which, happily, I had written a paper. For part of the Hebrew exam, Cross gave us photographs of unpublished Dead Sea Scrolls fragments. We were supposed to translate them, locate them in the Masoretic Text of our Hebrew Bibles, compare the Greek version in the Septuagint, do a thorough exegesis, and discuss the relevance of these fragments for biblical criticism. All this without anything except our Greek and Hebrew Bibles—and our wits. Mine nearly failed me, but somehow I passed. It was the first time I ever actually expected to get a Harvard doctorate. I called to congratulate a classmate, but he said that he had failed. No one ever heard of him again.

Hebrew Union College—A New Home

Shortly after the April exams, in the spring of 1964, Norma and I were preparing to go to Jerusalem for the following academic year. Ernest had been appointed the second annual director of the new Hebrew Union College-Jewish Institute of Religion (HUC-JIR) in Jerusalem (after Frank Cross the previous year), where Nelson Glueck wanted to launch a Biblical and Archaeological School. Ernest had again gotten me the Pfeiffer

Fellowship, and HUC-JIR had offered us housing on the campus for $150 a month. There I intended to work more closely with Ernest, completing the research for my dissertation. He hinted that we might also begin an excavation project in Israel, along the lines he had discussed with me at Shechem in the summer of 1962. But first, the 1964 season at Shechem, in Jordan on our way to New Jerusalem on the Israeli side.

Again we bought a VW microbus in Germany, and several of us drove it across Eastern Europe and through Syria to Jordan. I would then keep

Fig. 18. Hebrew Union College, Nelson Glueck School of Biblical Archaeology, Jerusalem.

the car for the upcoming year at HUC. Darrell Lance was to be the other Fellow for the year at HUC, and we shared the vehicle. That summer I worked in Field VII, excavating Iron Age and then Late Bronze Age levels. My supervisor was the venerable Seventh-day Adventist archaeologist Siegfried Horn, a Dutch scholar who was, however, more Teutonic than Dutch. He strode masterfully about the balks, issuing commands and meticulously recording whatever he thought important. But down in the deep trench, I had scarcely a clue as to what I was doing. Our Arab workmen cheerfully whacked away. One day they churned up a nearly intact Late Bronze Age bronze Baal figurine (ca. thirteenth century BCE). It was a great find, but when I examined it, I could see a fresh break where an upraised arm had been. We hurriedly sifted the dump and found the arm.

We really couldn't reconstruct the context *postfactum*. Such a thing would never have happened later at Gezer, where student volunteers worked under the close scrutiny of trained area supervisors and the recorded context was everything. Darrell Lance and I were learning by doing, and later we would undo the system at Shechem, when we wrote the first draft of the Gezer *Manual of Field Excavations* (1978) during our year at HUC.

On weekends we grad students at Shechem spent time exploring the Old City and touring archaeological sites. I still wouldn't stay at the American School, however. I preferred the cheap but somehow exotic Christian hostels in the Old City—the Knights' Palace, the Dom Polski, the Franciscan Fathers—or the more refined hostel at Saint George's Anglican Cathedral outside the walls. But I deigned to eat occasionally (when I could afford it) at the American School. One Saturday evening in the dining room I ended up by chance seated between Ernest Wright and James B. Pritchard of the University Museum at the University of Pennsylvania, then excavating at biblical Gibeon. During the animated conversation, Ernest leaned over the table, looked across me at Pritchard, and remarked, "I think Dever here ought to do his dissertation on MB I pottery. What do you think, Jim?" Pritchard nodded, and that was that. I hardly knew what MB I pottery looked like (now EB IV), and I certainly had never handled a piece of it at Shechem. But I had a dissertation topic—not to mention a research focus that has stayed with me for these fifty plus years and has even been passed on to my students. As it turned out, together we revolutionized the field. Did Ernest foresee that? He had written some seminal ideas on that period himself in his 1937 dissertation, but the rest was his uncanny intuition.

After the dig ended in late August and Ernest had relocated with his family at HUC in West Jerusalem, I set off in the VW for the port of Beirut. There I was to meet Norma. We had rented our Quincy house to a fellow graduate student at Harvard (Michael Novack, later renowned as a media political commentator) and had listed our nearly new Fiat 2400 for sale. Norma had packed a trunk full of personal effects, collected Darrell Lance's trunk, and set out for the Middle East. This was Norma's first trip out of the United States, and she was brave to do this alone. With some friends she went to the World's Fair in New York, boarded the Italian liner *Leonardo de Vinci* for Genoa, and took another Italian ship in Genoa bound for Beirut via Alexandra, Egypt. After some confusion, I found her at the port in Beirut, we cleared customs, and we loaded the trunks into the VW.

We spent several days in Beirut, the Paris of the Middle East. Then we set off for Damascus, Amman, and Jerusalem. We toured sites along the way in Syria (especially Palmyra), delaying our arrival in Jerusalem until after the Jewish High Holidays. Before crossing into Israel, Norma, Darrell, and I made a grueling and memorable trip in the VW to Baghdad, Iraq, and back. While in Iraq, we spent several days driving about Baghdad and visited Babylon, Ur, Mosul, Nimrod, Nineveh, and Hatra in the desert. In Jordan we visited Jerash, the Crusader Castle at Kerak, and Petra.

In early October we crossed the Mandlebaum Gate, a rather stressful procedure, and with relief drove to the HUC campus at 13 King David Street in the New City, near the historic King David Hotel and the YMCA (yes, with mostly Jewish members).

Norma and I had been allotted the gatehouse right on the street, a small, modern stone blockhouse with a tiny bedroom, bath kitchenette, and living-dining room. When we lay in bed at night, our feet at the open window for a bit of air, the Egged buses frequently roaring by shook the whole building, and the diesel fumes nearly suffocated us. But we lived there conveniently for the next nine months while I researched my dissertation topic.

Ernest and Emily, with their high school–age children Danny and Carolyn, lived in one of the two furnished apartments in the main building. Darrell had a room in the dormitory, with kitchen privileges, but he often had dinner with us or went to the YMCA. I remember those winter evenings, after a hard day's work and a good dinner (and a bottle of Carmel wine) behind us, tucked away cozily and dreaming together of an unknown future.

Chasing Macalister's Ghost at Gezer

One of our dreams was really Ernest's: a dig at Gezer. Already in September he had conferred with Glueck and had planned a brief fall season before the onset of the winter rains. Ernest's first published article, following up on his ground-breaking 1937 dissertation under Albright on the pottery of the Early Bronze Age in Palestine, had been titled "The Troglodytes of Gezer." He restudied some of R. A. S. Macalister's badly published Gezer materials of 1912, correctly sorting out what we would now call the Late

Chalcolithic and Early Bronze I pottery. He never forgot his early interest in Gezer, however, and now it was time to visit the site he had never seen.

One day in early October, Ernest, Darrell, and I set out with Macalister's three massive volumes in hand. We followed the map, but there was no road to the tell (mound), only a poorly marked dirt path beyond modern Kibbutz Gezer. Finally, Ernest's little Ford Cortina labored up to the western end of the impressive site apparently near Alan Rowe's 1934 sounding. We got out and looked around at the waist-high overgrowth, but we couldn't get our bearings, even consulting Macalister's plans.

Finally we stumbled over his huge dump heaps on his westernmost deep trenches, dug all the way to bedrock. Nearby, despite the weeds, we could see the partially filled water system dug into the bedrock. We wandered about, Ernest getting more and more excited, gesturing grandly (as he characteristically did) about where we would begin digging. Darrell and I worried about him having a heart attack, but we obviously shared his excitement. A dig in Israel. *Our* dig! That was a modest but auspicious beginning, but Gezer was to occupy much of my energy and attention for the next fifty-plus years.

We dug for three weeks in November–December 1964, a small group of us commuting each day from Jerusalem. We decided that reinvestigating Macalister's huge exposures but poorly understood building phases, our initial goal, was best pursued by opening a long, narrow trench immediately west of his first trench. A sounding to bedrock, this would expose Macalister's enigmatic monumental city defenses, the inner- and outer-wall systems. Characteristically, our biblical archaeology presuppositions focused mainly on *public* architecture: we wanted to reconstruct the great deeds of the great men who made history.

We dubbed this first trench, which was 3 meters wide and eventually 68 meters long (with ten squares), Field I. We laid out and opened three squares at the north end, each of us supervising one area with two or three volunteers. We were not more than a few hours into the first day that fall before Israeli visitors began to arrive at the nearly forgotten site where Macalister had dug in 1902–1909, expecting, of course, to see Wright, the great American archaeologist. I still recall Ernest abandoning his square to tell the visitors the story of Gezer, gesturing grandly over the site. He was in his element! But again Darrell and I feared that he would have a heart attack. Besides, how did Ernest *know* the story so soon?

Fig. 19. The first season at Gezer, fall 1964, Wright in the distance.

When it came time to draw our balks—the well-cut vertical sides of our trenches—Darrell and I proceeded in good Wheeler-Kenyon style, as we had learned (or so we thought) at Shechem. But Ernest, who, amazingly, had not been in a trench of his own since 1932 with Albright at Tell Beit Mirsim, insisted on drawing his own balk. We watched as he banged in a horizontal string as a datum line but noticed that he didn't use a line-level to establish it. Darrell and I gently suggested that perhaps we could help. Ernest was impatient, but we did get a level datum line in for him.

We went about our own drawing, and when we were all finished Ernest proudly showed us his section drawing. Instead of a carefully measured drawing, using numerous plotted points on the graph paper and following the tip-lines precisely, he had put in a few dots and had connected them with straight lines. We looked at each other, nodded, and said nothing. After the dig was over, we went back and drew the section of Area I, Field I, properly. But we kept Ernest's drawing in the files we were now establishing at HUC. In the summer of 2004, Norma and I found Ernest's section drawing, conspicuously labeled "GEW." It is a unique document.

When the winter rains began, we retreated to Jerusalem. Back at HUC, we washed and sorted and read our pottery in the cold basement workroom. Ernest, one of the foremost authorities in the world on the pottery of ancient Palestine, seemed puzzled by some of the sherds with red-painted rims. He would shake his head and say, "It's another world from Shechem." Finally he pronounced these diagnostic sherds "Persian." He was about to write up the very first preliminary field report, when something (not us) prompted him to reconsider. He had simply never seen this typical southern twelfth-eleventh century BCE wares at Shechem, in the north of the country. This time he was right. Later we would come to master Gezer's varied ceramic repertoire on our own and would delight in reading pottery with him on his annual summer visits. We were learning Petrie's essential alphabet of archaeology.

Doing a Dissertation

During the winter, which at Jerusalem's altitude at above 2600 feet can be cold and wet, I plunged into collecting all the published pottery of the EB IV period. It was then an enigmatic period, a sort of dark age in the interlude between the great urban eras of the Early and Middle Bronze Ages, circa 2500–2000 BCE. Ernest had first synthesized the pottery of the Early Bronze Age in 1937. At Harvard he had systematically divided up the remaining pottery into periods that he assigned to all of us as thesis topics. Joe Seger was to do the Middle Bronze Age, based, of course, on the sequence at Shechem; Jack Holladay would handle the Iron Age.

I felt somewhat left out: the EB IV period was a backwater, not even represented at Shechem or much of anywhere else in stratified deposits. Most published pottery was from tombs, and no one had ever studied it systematically except Ruth Amiran in a 1960 article. I soon got to know Ruth, and, although somewhat amused by the hutzpah of these young Americans, she encouraged me. Looking back, all the connections I made that year were due to my hanging onto Ernest's coattails. However, the Israeli establishment archaeologists would in time become close associates and dear friends of my own. Today they are all gone.

HUC did not yet have much of an archaeological library, especially since so many report volumes were out of print and virtually unobtainable. So I worked most days around the corner in the library of the Pontifical Biblical Institute, a huge ancient monastery with no heat, almost no light, and, happily, no one there but me. All but one of the good fathers had died, and he seemed dead, or at least on his way out. It was so cold that I sat at a table pouring over musty report volumes (they were all there) wearing an overcoat, hat, scarf, and even gloves, my breath frosting on the frigid air. By the spring I had traced a drawing of every published EB IV sherd—some 1,200 in all—and this being the precomputer age had pasted them, with Norma's help, on a punch card with holes around the edges. With a knitting needle, you could punch through a coded hole, and all the relevant cards would drop out. (I still don't use computers.) I didn't get any writing done, but with a comprehensive ceramic corpus I had the database necessary for my dissertation.

There was, of course, more to life than dissertation research, and it was necessary to get outdoors to preserve one's sanity. On Sabbath, not being Jewish and with the HUC library closed, Ernest would take his family, Darrell, Norma, and me on fieldtrips. It seems incredible, but, authority that he was, he had never been to Israel except for a whirlwind, largely incognito visit in 1958. After all, he worked in Jordan. Ernest was certainly not anti-Israel (on the contrary), but he had to be discreet. Now openly in Israel, with time on his hands, he was anxious to see all the sites. So were we, and to visit them with Ernest was a rare treat, the memory of which I cherish to this day. A year's leave from Harvard advanced my education in the *real* world of archaeology immeasurably.

Wherever we went with Ernest, we would scour the site, picking up sherds on the surface. Over a typical picnic lunch on the ground, huddled in a circle in the deep mid-winter grass, we would sort sherds as Ernest dated them. An alfresco seminar! Back at HUC, we began to label and shelve all the pottery, the start of a study collection, another of Ernest's passions. Not only did we get to know Ernest and Emily on a more personal basis, but we came to know their younger children. Some forty years later, I recently saw Carolyn while on a Midwest lecture tour. I didn't recognize her, but she introduced herself and then asked if I ever thought of her father. I said, "Carolyn! I think of Ernest *every* single day." And it's true.

Spring Season at Gezer in 1965

In order to have a spring season in March, we had to find some place to live near the tell. This was not easy. We had to plunge in and clean up a ramshackle, dirty kibbutz building that had not been used in quite some time in order to make the place livable. We replaced windows, swept up the dead birds and mice, and cleaned up the three rooms where we made a dormitory, a common room, and a small room for Norma and me. It got cold and damp that spring, raining several days, and even under blankets on the cots we nearly froze to death. I taped over the windows in the bathroom and converted it into a makeshift photo darkroom. We ate in the primitive kibbutz common dining room. There were holes in the screens, and I remember the birds perching on the edge of the bread baskets, pecking away. The kibbutznicks from the dairy barn would tramp in with their muddy boots (and hands). There was bread, soup, salads, eggs, and little else. Ernest stayed in Jerusalem, coming out each day unless we were rained out. Even so, it was a successful season.

A Job!

In late April, when Israel bursts briefly into a glorious display of spring flowers, Glueck came out from Cincinnati. We planned a field trip to the south, with me driving the VW microbus. One day as we were going east from Beersheba toward Arad, Wright and Glueck began to talk excitedly about the Gezer project—especially since in the spring we had just completed a second brief field season that was quite promising. Then the conversation turned to specifics: they would need, of course, a director. I just drove, listening. After the tour, when we got back to the Desert Inn in Beersheba, Ernest whispered to me, "Meet me and Nelson in the bar before dinner. He has something to say to you and Norma."

When we gathered in the bar, Glueck simply said to me, "Ernest and I have talked. I want you to come back to HUC and direct the Gezer project. If you finish your degree next spring, I'll appoint you senior archaeological fellow at HUC, and a year or two later you'll become director."

I wasn't entirely surprised, given Ernest's predictions two years earlier, but I collected my thoughts and then said cautiously, "But Dr. Glueck, I'm not Jewish." To this day I recall Glueck's response, word for word: "I don't care whether you're a Jew, a Christian, or a Hottentot. I want an archaeologist." I replied, "I'm your man." We spoke briefly about salary (only $5,000 a year initially), plus housing and car, but no other fringe benefits. And that was that. Ernest beamed.

Back at HUC, Ernest began to be apprehensive. Would we actually go? He came to Norma one day in the school laundry room and urged her to make every wifely sacrifice and support me in this somewhat risky move. All my other Harvard classmates were stepping into tenure-track positions, some at prestigious universities. To her credit, Norma said, "Of course, we're delighted!" The die was cast, but the future was still very uncertain. There was no written contract, only Glueck's word. Our parents were aging, and it would be difficult to go abroad for an indefinite period of time. Further, Norma and I were still Christians, if not devout at least committed, minorities in Israel and not fully at home there. But we had no children, no obvious prospects back home, and nothing to lose. Why not?

In the summer of 1965, Ernest, Darrell, and I mounted a larger campaign of Gezer, confident now that the project would go. Ernest and Nelson Glueck, with the collaboration of HUC-JIR Dean Paul Steinberg, had looked into the possibility of securing PL 480 Counterpart Funds. These were soft currencies (and Israeli's then was very soft) that had accumulated in foreign currencies as a result of US projects and could not be converted into dollars. American enterprises in countries on the list could apply for these funds, so we did. Over the years HUC received more than a million dollars of these monies, which provided our primary funding from 1966 through 1973. HUC and the Harvard Semitic Museum lent their names when Wright and Glueck became official advisors to the Gezer project, but that was all.

Ernest was my mentor in archaeology, probably more influential in my life than my own father. So it is hard to be objective in assessing his place in biblical archaeology. Still, it is clear that he—not Albright—was the real founder of the movement. Albright, although a legendary scholar, was not a biblical scholar and, in my judgment, not actually a professional archaeologist. He was more an "orientalist"—and an extraordinary one. But Ernest was a distinguished Old Testament scholar, probably the best known such scholar in America in the 1950s–1970s. At Harvard, in his peak years, Ernest was Parkman Professor of Biblical Studies in the Divinity School; in addition, until his death in 1974, he was an active, ordained Presbyterian clergyman.

Fig. 20. Gezer advisors Nelson Glueck (right) and G. Ernest Wright, with me and Associate Director H. Darrell Lance.

Ernest's first widely known publication in 1957, *Biblical Archaeology*, brought his two lifetime preoccupations together in a way that he never really questioned. His only major field project, however, was in 1957–1966 at Shechem, the regular account of which was appropriately entitled *Shechem: The Biography of a Biblical City* (1965). The sponsors were three Protestant divinity schools: McCormick, Drew, and Harvard; the staff was made up almost exclusively of Protestant clergyman (myself included; there were no clergywomen in those days).

It was Ernest who established biblical archaeology as a real institutional *movement*, a school, not merely an emphasis. It can be all traced back to him, as I suggested hesitantly in a critique and appreciation of him in a 1980 *Harvard Theological Review* article. The field was already changing when Ernest sponsored me and others of his students at Gezer beginning in 1964. We were moving away from biblical archaeology's rather parochial (!) approach toward a more specialized, professional, secular discipline that we thought was more appropriately called "Syro-Palestinian" archaeology.

Ernest himself had begun this trend, although unwittingly, but he was never quite reconciled himself to the consequences. For him, the *biblical* orientation, although admittedly embracing only a part of what we all did, was dominant. Ernest's earliest work on Palestinian pottery, in 1938, was brilliant—precocious, useful still today. But he became distracted by theology, and during the war years and into the 1950s he devoted himself more to Old Testament studies. Then ill health (a serious heart condition) foreshortened his Shechem excavations, which he never lived to publish. The Gezer project, his dream, will be his best legacy, even though it marked the demise of biblical archaeology.

In 1974, Ernest founded an excavation in Cyprus at Idalion, where Pamela Gaber, later my second wife, became director (1978–). Ernest's legacy affects us both (and so many others as well). Ernest dedicated his body to medical science, so he is not buried near his beloved summer home in Jaffrey, New Hampshire, where Frederick Bliss, an early pioneer in our field, is buried. There is simply a bronze plaque on the old New England stone wall with the dates of his birth and death and a quotation from the book of Isaiah: "And they shall mount up on the wings of eagles."

Pulling Up Stakes

After the July dig in 1965, Norma and I returned to Boston. We shipped the VW to New York and later sold it for a reasonable loss. I did not resume my duties at Bethany Church because I faced an April dissertation deadline. No degree, no job. Norma went back to teaching, this time at a new school about 20 miles down the South Shore in Hanover, Massachusetts. I stayed home to write full-time; it would be close. By late winter I was well along, but by March I began to panic. As the April 15 deadline approached, we went all-out, working around the clock, sustained by little but caffeine. I struggled to complete not only my handwritten manuscript but also to draw all the innumerable pottery plates by hand. I knew that we had to produce twenty-five perfect copies, and in those days making a single change meant retyping the whole chapter.

A day or two before the deadline, Norma and I were in a state of exhaustion and despair. We were close, but there was no way that we could finish, especially with the required twenty-five copies, before the deadline. It was over. I called Ernest and told him that we were giving up. We actually had the text and plates completed, and I had run off twenty-five copies of each page on the church multilith machine. Copies of all 444 pages were stacked on the church gymnasium floor, but it was nearly April 15, and we were simply too exhausted to collate the pages and deliver the twenty-five finished copies. Hearing this, Ernest replied, "Hold on. The kids and I are driving down to Quincy; we'll help. You can't give up! I'll call Frank and tell him that I have the dissertation and am working on it. That will give us few days." Work on it Ernest did. I still have a picture of Ernest, Carolyn, and Daniel down on their hands and knees on the gym floor, collating copies. Ernest did cover for me, and the dissertation went to the committee more or less on time.

At the oral defense, when I had recovered somewhat, things went reasonably well. The committee included Ernest as chair, Frank Cross, the distinguished Assyriologist Thorkild Jacobsen, and visiting professor Nahman Avigad, a senior Israeli archaeologist and epigrapher (whom I came to know well later). I approached my defense fairly confident. After all, who knew more about the EB IV period than Ernest and I? And I felt that he was in my camp.

Cross grilled me a while on the Hebrew Bible, and I managed to field most questions. Avigad asked me about the Syrian and Phoenician ivories of the ninth-eighth century BCE; I had written a paper on that topic, so I was safe there. Then Jacobsen began to delve into Mesopotamian history; I had only audited his course that year part-time, so I began to flounder.

Fig. 21. Graduation, Harvard, 1966, with my parents.

Mercifully, Ernest broke in after a bit and said, "Well, Thorkild, I think we've exhausted his knowledge on that subject, so let's move on." When he moved to the topic of my dissertation, I rallied, and a lively discussion ensued. I began to be hopeful. Finally, Ernest threw out on the table a bunch of sherds and asked me to date them. I could do that! And so the ordeal ended.

I left the room awaiting the committee's decision. I knew the ritual: if they were all standing with extended hands when you reentered the room, you were a PhD. Then, after a handshake and congratulations all around, my professors would say, "Now you must call us by first names." But it was years before I could say "Ernest," and he finally had to shame me into it. I don't think I said "Frank" for years. Anyway, the dissertation was miraculously awarded "Distinction." Then there were graduation ceremonies for which my mother bought my doctoral gown. Both Mother and Father attended, and they were proud. After graduation I was on my way—four days later, on the plane bound for Israel, HUC, and Gezer. I was thirty-two.

6

THE JERUSALEM YEARS: MY SIXTH LIFE

A mong the great cities of the world, Jerusalem is unique—and a uniquely powerful symbol. As a child of the manse, I grew up with visions of biblical Jerusalem:

> If I forget thee, O Jerusalem,
>   Let my right arm wither.

But Jerusalem remained an elusive symbol, somehow larger than life. Then, in 1957, I unexpectedly encountered the new Jerusalem and fell under its spell all over again. In chapter 4 I recounted that first auspicious visit, when I was a twenty-three-year-old seminary student. Enthralled though I was, I never expected to return. After all, I was going to be a pastor who dealt with Old Testament Israel, not a scholar devoted to the study of modern Israel, much less one of those antiquarian archaeologists I had met. But later in my graduate career, while pursuing a doctoral degree at Harvard, I did return—this time to get into archaeology not as a tourist but as a hopeful professional. That was how I came to dig at Shechem in the summers of 1962 and 1964, spending the weekends in east Jerusalem, then under Jordanian administration. Israeli Jerusalem, on the west wide, where I had spent the summer of 1957, seemed worlds away. But this was the old, biblical Jerusalem of which I had dreamed. Meanwhile, there was the reality of shifting my doctoral major at Harvard from theology (God forbid) to archaeology and by 1966 completing my dissertation on the Early Bronze IV period, 2500–2000 BCE. As noted above, in the spring of 1965 Glueck had offered me a job at the Hebrew Union College in Jerusalem if I finished my degree by the following year.

In the Field at Gezer: Our Dig Now

So it was that I arrived in Jerusalem in early June of 1966, four days after commencement in the Harvard yard (which I scarcely remember), sporting a brand-new PhD and clutching in my hand a mailing tube with some plans of the site of Gezer labeled proudly "Dr. William G. Dever." No longer "the Reverend" but "Doctor," I was too dazed to realize what this turning point meant. That would take years.

The dig at Gezer was to begin in a few days with my first season as director. Norma had stayed behind in Quincy to complete the sale of our house, send some of our possessions to her parents in Virginia, send or bring personal possessions to Jerusalem, and dispose of other things. After all, we were moving to a new life abroad—forever, we thought. Meanwhile, I moved into a large apartment that the college had rented in Jerusalem as a headquarters for what we were calling the Gezer core staff: me and eight other carefully selected professionals in archaeology and related disciplines. In typical American style, together this team would oversee the new multiyear Gezer project all the way through fieldwork and publication. It was a noble ideal, but we were young and somewhat naïve.

During the winter and spring, Professor James Ross, an old friend from Shechem and visiting director at HUC that year, had done a masterful job of building a tent dig camp for up to 140 people on the western spur of the mound at Gezer. The site was then only about 2 miles inside the border with Jordan, isolated and scarcely reachable via a dirt track from Kibbutz Gezer. But we had our own generators for electricity, a pump at the reservoir down the hill and a water tower, tent latrines and showers, a kitchen and large eating pavilion, and even an airconditioned photo darkroom in the dighouse (which quickly became a bar for predinner meetings of the core staff).

When, however, the core staff arrived and we all went out to Gezer to settle in, we discovered that the camp was not yet in working order. There were tents to put up; endless supplies of food, bedding, and tools to be laid in; and a kitchen to equip. We all worked frantically for several days, hoping to be ready by the time the student volunteers arrived. But as the Egged buses from the Lydda airport toiled up the dusty track to the mound the evening before the dig was to begin, we were still trying to get one of the Lister diesel generators up and running so the camp on the

Fig. 22. The dig camp at Gezer, established in 1966.

hilltop would be lit. We succeeded just as the buses pulled up at the camp gate and disgorged their passengers, as exhausted as we were. So this was what field archaeology was like!

All the concern with logistics seems quaint today, when Israeli and American archaeologists and student volunteers simply move into a rented kibbutz or moshav guest house with air-conditioned rooms that have telephones and TV, grassy lawns and swimming pools for leisure time, and excellent meals in the communal dining room. But we had no choice except to build a dig camp on the mound. And camp life at Gezer in the years from 1966 to 1971 was memorable.

Pioneering Field Schools

Student volunteerism was a novel experiment in 1966, tried only once before, by Yadin at Masada in 1964–1965, and as a former chief of staff he had the Israel army at his disposal. Consequently, most of our colleagues were skeptical. American college students were not only untrained; they were spoiled and undisciplined. You couldn't run a dig with a work force like that—but we did, and within a few years all the American and Israeli digs in Israel and Jordan (some in Cyprus) had adopted the Gezer model of summer field schools in archaeology.

The students, mostly American, were highly motivated, quick studies, curious to learn about every aspect of what we were doing, and hard workers in the heat and dirt. However, conducting a seminar in the field with nonspecialists who did not necessarily share our presuppositions and professional commitments forced us to confront new questions. The core staff were nearly all seminary graduates, Protestant clergymen (not clergypersons; there were no women clergy in those days). After all, this was the heyday of American-style biblical archaeology, and we were its emissaries to Israel. But the students were not impressed.

Typically skeptical, they always wanted to know, "Why?" More disturbing, they would ask, "What do you expect to find?" I remember drawing myself up with the full assurance of a newly mined PhD and declaring: "We have no expectations; we'll take whatever is here." We had never heard of the sort of research design common in other branches of archaeology, but we soon would. In any case, working with bright, young students, rather than the genial but uninquiring Arab workers we had known at Shechem, proved to be revolutionary in more than one way.

Not the least of its benefits was that student volunteerism provided a training ground for a new generation of American archaeologists who would work in the Middle East, especially in Israel. That had been one of the original aspirations of Wright and Glueck for the Gezer project. It was to be a showcase for American methods, practical know-how, and above all the exploration of the Holy Land, *our* holy land, too. If all this sounds a bit naïve, it was. Yet student volunteerism *worked*, as Dame Kathleen Kenyon conceded in reviewing *Gezer I* (Dever et al. 1970), saying, "The proof of the pudding is in the eating."

Today, having celebrated the fifty-fifth anniversary of the start of the Gezer project, we take pride in the fact that perhaps several thousand people discovered a lifelong love of archaeology at the site. A woman who began in

Fig. 23. Me instructing the Gezer volunteers on balk-trimming.

the 1960s as a student in the dirt at Gezer (Norma Kershaw) recently endowed a university chair in archaeology at UC San Diego for a professor who also began there as a student in 1971 (Tom Levy). In addition, more than twenty-five dig directors in Israel, Jordan, Egypt, Cyprus, and the United States received their first training at Gezer. Many of the successive presidents of the American Schools of Oriental Research since the late 1960s have come out of Gezer. Finally, Gezer methods, once experimental, have become nearly universal (below). Of course, we didn't foresee any of this that night in 1966 when the buses pulled up to the gate of our newly lit dig camp, all of us exhausted but ready for whatever adventures lay in store.

The Gezer Project: Firsts

A full-fledged summer field school to train American and other students both practically and academically was not the only innovation at Gezer. For one thing, Gezer was the first large, entirely American-directed excavation in modern Israel. Gezer was also the first American (or any other) excavation to employ modern three-dimensional stratigraphic methods, featuring the careful analysis and drawing of sections following the pioneering development by Kenyon at Jericho and Jerusalem, which were then in Jordan (the Wheeler-Kenyon or balk-debris layer methods). Gezer was the first dig to employ a large multidisciplinary staff, beginning with geologists and geomorphologists, then extending to include paleoethobotanists and zoologists, physical and cultural anthropologists, and other specialists from the natural sciences. As a result of our development of a specific research design akin to other modern archaeological projects, far removed from the catch-as-catch-can goals of traditional biblical archaeology, Gezer was able to qualify for the first large secular funding that an American project in Israel had ever received. These monies came principally from the American government through the Smithsonian Institution (above) but also from other nonsectarian sources.

Proud as we were of our pioneering efforts, our Israeli colleagues were underwhelmed. They tolerated me and my young American collaborators because we were proteges of older archaeologists they knew and respected, such as our two patrons, Glueck and Wright, at the time the most prominent biblical archeologists in America. But I recall one day in 1966 when Avraham Biran, director of the Israel Department of Antiquities, came to visit Gezer with an entourage of younger Israeli archaeologists. As they stood on the edge of our large trench, I explained the details in one of the then-novel sections that we had carefully cut, dressed with a trowel, and tagged. Down in the trench I explained, "You see how this tip-line drops down here, and then here you see an intrusive pit." I went on in some detail, whereupon I overheard one of the Israelis whisper to Biran in Hebrew, "But I don't see anything." Biran replied, "Neither do I, but humor the Americans." (I understood Hebrew better than I let on; you learn a great deal that way.)

The suspicion when we began at Gezer was that these well-funded but inexperienced young Americans, with their teamwork approach and fancy new methods, had nothing to teach Israelis. But teach (and learn) we did. When I visit most Israeli digs now, I feel right at home. Stratigraphic methods and interdisciplinary approaches are taken for granted, just as volunteer labor and field schools are. I like to think that we at Gezer helped to set these new trends. However, I was only thirty-two years old when I began as director at Gezer. Today I would do things very differently (and perhaps less pretentiously).

Developing a Program at Hebrew Union College

Glueck—rabbi, explorer, and archaeologist turned college president—was my benefactor and first employer. In 1957 he had secured a strategic but risky piece of property near the King David Hotel, directly overlooking the no-man's land on the border with Jordan and the Jaffa Gate of the Old City beyond that. He later delighted in telling visitors to the magnificent campus of the college that he had rented this land on a ninety-nine-year lease for a dollar a year. As usual, Glueck the visionary saw what no one else did: an American postdoctoral research institute for archaeology in West Jerusalem like the old school in East Jerusalem (the American School of Oriental Research) that he himself had directed in 1932–1933, 1936–1940, and 1942–1947. But there would be a difference: an attached seminary for training American Reform rabbis. Not only did no one else envision that; no one else *wanted* it. The naysayers included Glueck's own

HUC-JIR board of governors, who thought archaeology a diversion and a waste of money, but also the Orthodox religious authorities in Jerusalem. They spoke contemptuously of American "deform Judaism" and vehemently opposed the school from the beginning.

Finally, by 1963, Glueck had raised sufficient money to construct on the land a stunning white limestone building designed by the modernist Israeli architect Hans Rau. But on the day the college was inaugurated, the Orthodox rioted in front of the building, smashed the huge plate glass windows in front, and tried to close down the ceremony. Glueck persisted, however, opening his new institute provisionally with several visiting annual directors. Early appointees were Frank Moore Cross Jr. of Harvard in 1963–1964; G. Ernest Wright, also of Harvard, in 1964–1965 (when I was first a fellow); James F. Ross of Virginia Theological Seminary in 1965–1966; Marvin Pope of Yale University in 1966–1967, during my first year as resident senior fellow and director-elect; and Saul S. Weinberg of the University of Missouri in 1967–1968.

Glueck had always intended, however, to have a long-term resident director, as he had been at the old American school in what was then British Mandate Jerusalem. Against all odds, I was to be the first such director of the Jerusalem school, including the seminary—a rather green young American Christian far from his roots yet filled with dreams of archaeology in the Holy Land. When I took up residence at the college after the hectic summer dig at Gezer in 1966, I began to see the enormity of the task ahead of me.

Vagabonds for Awhile

In mid-August I broke camp, packed all the materials off to Jerusalem for analysis, then flew to Paris to meet Norma, who had been delayed by settling affairs at home. I met her at the airport, and we taxied to the dealer where I picked up the new baby blue Peugeot 404 sedan that we had ordered. That same afternoon we set off on a two-month journey on our way back to Jerusalem, through France, Germany, Austria, Czechoslovakia, Hungary, Romania, Bulgaria, Yugoslavia, Turkey, Syria, Lebanon, and Jordan. The legendary orientalist W. F. Albright, the teacher of all my teachers, had been instrumental in getting me a small grant from the

American Philosophical Society to pursue the research that had led to my dissertation, on the peoples of Palestine in the Middle Bronze I period circa 2500–2000 BCE, a subject on which both he and Glueck had done pioneering work. It was a grand tour (not all work), but when I submitted my report to the American Philosophical Society in 1968, one of my first publications, I had to conclude that the connections were simply fortuitous, and so they came to be.

Settling In

In early October, the transients arrived in East Jerusalem by car, checked in briefly at the American School, stayed a few days at the Saint George Hostel, and proceeded with much trepidation through the no-man's land to the border crossing at the Mandelbaum Gate. The car was loaded with goodies we had acquired to help set up house in Jerusalem (Riedel crystal stemware and a set of Bavarian china). We didn't know what customs formalities might be. Furthermore, we were Americans coming from the Arab countries, with no Israeli work visas and no proof that I was employed in Israel.

We breezed through, however, and with a great sense of relief and high spirits drove to 22 Metudella Street, where I had rented the apartment of the Israeli ambassador posted to Italy, Jonathan Prato. It was located in the garden-like district of Rehavia ("expanses"), where many of Jerusalem's older intellectuals and artists lived, including famous scholars in my own field such as Benjamin Mazar, Yigael Yadin, Avraham Biran, David and Ruth Amiran, Hayim and Miriam Tadmor, Avraham Malamat, Nahman Avigad, and others. The apartment was near the Valley of the Cross, with its eleventh-century Greek Orthodox monastery, and beyond that on the distant hill the sprawling box-like complex of the Israel Museum. The apartment was quiet, spacious, and beautifully equipped with dark, heavy Italian antique furniture (slightly worm-eaten) and oriental carpets (slightly musty). We felt at home and were enthralled by our new setting in the cultural heart of Jerusalem.

At the college, I had to start from scratch, since annual visiting directors had not been commissioned to develop a long-range program, equip an archaeological library and laboratories, or employ permanent specialist staff. I did not yet have much of a budget, but I knew that I had Glueck's ear. There was a large basement room with a sink and some storage cabinets, which I commandeered from Moti the gardener. There I set up some sawhorse tables and put Moshe Levy to work, an incredibly skilled *formatore* who set about mending the innumerable potsherds we had brought back from Gezer. The sink was convenient for cleaning other artifacts, and the cabinets soon housed them.

I had not realized how large an accumulation of material resulted from a mere six-week dig season. Soon the huge furnace room, warm and dry, became a warehouse for row upon row of boxed material marked with the elaborate Gezer code. I had no drafting staff, but before long I hired Yael Avi-Yonah (the daughter of the famous archaeologist Michael Avi-Yonah) to come to the college after-hours and draw pottery in a vacant classroom. I did the photography myself, developing and printing in a bathroom when necessary.

The tiny gatehouse where we had lived as students in 1964–1965 now served as my office; Norma helped as an unpaid assistant. The library's archaeological holdings were scant, and we had only an idiosyncratic old man as a part-time librarian (who used to click his heels and salute when he saw me). Using these meager facilities and part-time staff, I set out to prepare a preliminary report of the 1966 season; appeared in *Biblical Archaeologist* (Dever 1967b), a journal that Ernest had founded in 1938 (with French, German, and Hebrew versions of my report soon to follow). It was the first of more than four hundred articles and chapters that I would write over the course of my career.

My duties as senior archaeological fellow at HUC included offering an introductory course in archaeology for the rabbinical students and, periodically, seminars for the several annual postdoctoral fellows in Judaic and biblical studies who were appointed each year. Glueck's policy from the beginning was typically baffling to those who did not know him: all beginning rabbinical students at the New York, Cincinnati, and Los Angeles campuses were required to spend the first of the five-year seminary program in residence in Jerusalem. There they would learn Modern Hebrew at the college, experience Israel firsthand, and be introduced to archaeology both in the classroom and on field trips and digs. At the same time, Glueck insisted that the college should be a research institute and one as ecumenical as the old East Jerusalem's nonsectarian institute had been.

In keeping with his vision, he funded several postdoctoral fellows each year, usually professors on leave, and made sure that a number were non-Jewish (as all his previous annual directors had been). Thus I was thrown at once into a heady intellectual atmosphere almost as challenging as that at Harvard.

My first year at the college, the annual director was the distinguished Semitics scholar at Yale, Marvin Pope, a specialist in ancient Ugaritic, a sister-dialect of Hebrew. Marvin was one of the world's leading authorities on all the Semitic languages, but, like me, he could scarcely speak a word of Modern Hebrew. Even his own name was a problem. In Hebrew, *p* and *f* are written with the same letter (*peh*), just as another character (*waw*) can represent either *o* or *u*. So Marvin usually became "Professor Foof," a mistake that he could not correct. Frank Cross, distinguished Hancock Professor of Hebrew and Other Oriental Languages at Harvard University, had a similar experience during his year at HUC. Frank was stopped by an Israeli cop for a minor infraction. The cop inquired in Hebrew as to how long he had been in Israel. Frank, forgetting that in Hebrew there are two words for month, replied, "three menstrual periods." The cop asked, "Shall we continue in English?"Not surprisingly, Marvin and I decided to organize an *ulpan*, a crash-course in spoken Modern Hebrew. We hired a terribly conscientious Hebrew teacher and assembled a group of a dozen or so eager students, mostly Christian professors of Bible and theology. Things went along well enough for a few sessions, but we simply could not keep the *ulpan* rule that you do not speak anything but Hebrew. Above all, in this approach you learn inductively by doing; you do not analyze grammar. The teacher would introduce a new Hebrew word to us, and invariably Marvin would interrupt to say, "You see, in Proto-Semitic this root would be X; then it appears in Akkadian as Y, and it becomes Z in Phoenician, Aramaic, and Hebrew." He would toss grammars and lexicons down on the floor, and the whole class would set about to parse the form, forgetting altogether about speaking Hebrew. It was all very learned and entertaining (Marvin could be the funniest man alive, even when doing grammar). But in a couple of weeks the Israeli instructor took me aside and said, "I can't teach these professors anything. I quit." That was the end of the *ulpan*, and I never really did learn to speak Hebrew well.

The class for rabbinical students, who were required to take my survey course in archaeology, fared well enough. I had never taught before, but having just completed my PhD, I knew more than I would ever know again, so I plunged in. I worked very hard on a syllabus and bibliography, beginning the class notes that I would add to over the next thirty-five years of teaching.

Then there were the periodic field trips that I began to introduce the students to the sites we were studying. For each planned trip, I assigned a different site to each student, who was to prepare a handout guide. On one visit to Gezer, I stood on the side of a deep trench and explained patiently what each layer (or stratum) represented, top-to-bottom, until I got down to bedrock. After a respectful pause, one rabbinical student asked: "Well, how did the bedrock get down there?" Astonished, I replied: "God put it there." Another time I went on a flying leap across a wide, deep trench, expecting the students to follow, but when I looked back they had all fallen into the bottom of the trench. Nevertheless, we persisted. A few rabbinical students even stayed on for the summer excavations at Gezer.

The Six-Day War

The academic year of 1966–1967 wore on through the fall, the excitement of being in Jerusalem carrying Norma and me through. By spring, however, there were ominous signs. There were increasingly violent incidents along the usually quiet border with Jordan, some of them in our neighborhood adjoining the no-man's land between the college and the old walled city. The radio (there was no television then) and the newspapers began to carry stories of a military buildup in Jordan, Syria, and Egypt, and the Israel Defense Forces (Zahal) were soon on high alert. In late May, Arab forces threatened to defy the UN peacekeepers and blockade the Straits of Tiran on the Red Sea. Since this would close Israel's port of Eilat, it was regarded as an act of war. Jordanian radio was now broadcasting hours of anti-Israel and anti-American propaganda, predicting that Jerusalem would fall any day and that we would all be massacred. The Israeli army began to commandeer civilian vehicles, including our jeeps and trucks and even the Gezer staff Ford minibus that I had bought. Bread trucks, gas tankers, heavy lorries, Egged buses—all were soon amassed in enormous parking lots awaiting the inevitable. My Peugeot was spared because it belonged to an American.

As the tension mounted in the first few days of June, I tried to keep Glueck informed. I told him that I thought war would break out but that I would telegraph him my final observations on Sunday, June 4. Around midnight on that day, I walked up to the post office on Jaffa Road and sent a cable: "War inevitable, but we will not evacuate. Recommend canceling the Gezer dig."

The next morning things were quiet at first, but it wasn't long until gunfire could be heard around in the distance. I saw that school children were being kept at home, and the streets were already swarming with police and soldiers. But there was little or nothing on the radio. I raced to the college, about a mile away, because some time ago we had arranged with the Israeli police that they would take over our building, strategically located as it was within sight of the Jordanian positions on the Old City wall. When I got there, the police were already dug in.

I gathered staff and some students in the lower corridor, where there were no exposed windows. I had never been shot at before, and I admit that I was so scared I was shaking. The heavy firing did not begin in Jerusalem until after 11 am, and it increased in the afternoon. I could hear shells from batteries in the Old City ricocheting off the stone walls of our building, so I soon felt a bit safer. Actually, I was now more worried about my new Peugeot (all paid for) sitting in the parking lot. Several other cars were hit, and down King David Street later that day I saw some cars riddled with machine gun bullets. Happily, no bullets hit my car. The only casualty I suffered that day was later, when I ran down the street toward the American consulate, darting in storefronts to dodge bullets. I slipped, fell down, and tore my pants.

Norma had volunteered for the war effort on her own, working in the American consulate typing up evacuation forms for the hundreds of American citizens in Jerusalem, including many of the Orthodox, who kept their American passports and could not wait to get out. On the Friday before the war began, she was only up to names beginning with M. There was simply no way that the American officials could have gotten all of its citizens out of Jerusalem. As for Norma and me, we had already decided that we would not evacuate. Although we weren't sure that Israel could win against such overwhelming odds, we had thrown our lot in with our Israeli friends, win or lose. Years later, when we were preparing to come back to the States for other reasons, one of these friends said to us, "We'll never forget what you did for us." When I asked what we had done, she replied, "In 1967 you *stayed*, while other Americans, most of them Jews, fled."

By late afternoon on the first day of the war, I had been able to monitor some of the Hebrew news (with the help of my colleague Ezra Spicehandler and others), and I had peeked out of the front doors of the college to see Israeli tanks and armored cars on the advance toward Government House, the UN headquarters on the border.

Near dusk, I decided to risk going up to the American consulate, about two blocks away on Mamilla Road: Norma was working there. We had not been in touch all day. When I got there, I was astonished to be asked, "Do you have any idea what's going on?" This was American intelligence. But the local staff at the consulate were all Arabs, and no one on the American staff understood Hebrew. I reported what little I had seen and heard. Amidst the confusion, it soon became clear that one of the major concerns at the consulate was what to do about dinner.

At dinner in the elegant dining room of the century-old Pasha's house, Norma and I were seated near the consul general, Evan Wilson, and General Odd Bull, the UN commandant. General Bull had been driven out of his headquarters at Government House (the old British seat of government), and he and his staff had made their way through the firing zone, turning up at the consulate. His major concern was that the nephew of U. Thant, the UN secretary general, who had been in Jerusalem, was unaccounted for. Where could he be? Was he safe? (He was.) The situation was horribly embarrassing. Then Consul General Wilson turned to Norma, who had been working closely with him doing secretarial work, and suggested that she go with him into the fortified communications room, where he would dictate to her the first official communication to Washington and New York. The war had begun twelve hours earlier, the Israelis may already have gained the upper hand, and our consulate had not been able to report much. No wonder we were never evacuated. Norma replied, "No, no, I might get it wrong." Evan said, "Well, I guess my secretary, who has been up since the crack of dawn, can do it." Norma readily agreed.

Dinner was *very* good: cuts of imported beef; our choice of fine French wine, champagne, and cognac; superb service by the white-coated Arab staff. It was a pleasant little interlude, but eventually we had to get home somehow. The consulate offered us beds, but we had had enough.

By now it was pitch dark, Jerusalem under a black-out and a curfew. We got in our car and drove to our apartment in Rehavia. Already the evening before, we had watched as Israeli mortar batteries were dug in down below our apartment in the Valley of the Cross, facing the Old City. Women and children were visiting the soldiers, bringing cookies and words of encouragement.

These were the families of the Israeli soldiers at the front, in their own backyards, as it were. All members of the Jerusalem brigade, they would fight to the last man to defend their homes and their homeland. That was one difference in the opposing forces. After the war we learned that many of the Jordanian soldiers in Jerusalem—mostly West Bank Palestinians who had little loyalty to King Hussein and the East Bank—simply peeled off their uniforms and blended into the civilian populace.

That night we tried to decide what to do. Our building had been hit, but only by light fire on the upper floors. We had filled the bathtub with water; we had some food in the pantry and the refrigerator; we would stick it out. We packed a little bag each with a change of clothes, passports, and all the money we had, just in case. We tried to get some sleep, but that was impossible. We listened as the Israeli mortar shells fired from the valley below went whoosh, then after a long whistling trajectory landed somewhere in the Old City.

We would hear airplanes but didn't know whose they were. The next day we heard amazing reports that early on the morning of June 6, Israel had launched a preemptive strike on Egyptian airbases and had destroyed some four hundred planes on the ground. It also began to appear that a long column of Jordanian tanks and other vehicles, exposed as they inched up from Jericho to Jerusalem, had been hit from the air and wiped out. (We were to see the evidence for ourselves a few days later.) How long would it last? Six days, as it turned out.

The next morning, Tuesday, June 6, after little sleep, I went out to my car; there on the sidewalk was Avraham Biran, director of the Department of Antiquities. I asked him where he was headed, looking so jaunty: "To the Rockefeller Museum in East Jerusalem; it's in our hands." I couldn't believe it, but I asked if I could tag along. Biran, governor of Jerusalem at the time of the 1948 war (and later my successor at HUC), knew the museum well, but then so did I. No such luck. While the Israelis had penetrated the Old City here and there, there was still heavy resistance in some areas. But I knew then that Israel would prevail. I proceeded to take Norma to the consulate, where she continued to work for the consul general until the end of the war and then went back to HUC.

A day later, I watched from our vantage point on the upper terrace at the college as plumes of smoke went up all over the Old City, then white flags appeared sporadically. The Old City had fallen. That day Israeli columns reached the Wailing Wall at the Temple Mount, and Moshe Dayan was photographed tucking paper prayers into the crevices of the wall, as Jews had done for centuries until 1948. I couldn't wait to get there.

On the fifth day of the war, a stringer from *Time* magazine phoned the college and asked whether I knew anything about the Old City. Did I?! I told him I knew it well from before the war. He said that he could get me a fake press pass, and we would sneak into a caravan of cars with permits to get into the Old City. Then we would pull away, and I would show him around on our own. That's just what we did. I made straight for the École Biblique et Archéologique Français on Nablus Road. There I found the legendary Dominican archaeologist and biblical scholar Père Roland de Vaux, his wispy beard still quivering with rage at what he said was the harsh treatment of the Israeli soldiers who had overrun the compound. Yet I saw little evidence of damage, except where the soldiers had taken out a Jordanian sniper in the chapel bell tower.

Fig. 24. Nelson Glueck, end of the Six-Day War, 1967, with Père de Vaux at the École Biblique et Archéologique in Jerusalem.

Then around the corner to my own old stomping ground, the American School of Oriental Research on Salah ed-Din Street. There I found the faithful cook, Omar Jibrin, whom Glueck had hired in the 1930s, standing resolutely in the doorway, as he had all during the war when he single-handedly held off the Israeli soldiers. All of the Americans at the American School, along with Paul Lapp, the long-time previous director, and his family, had fled for Jericho on Monday morning, the first day of the war. Lapp had been shifted by Ernest to the position of professor of archaeology in 1965. He was a brilliant but idiosyncratic (and somewhat irascible) man with a long list of excavations and several promising publications behind him. But he was very pro-Palestinian. All these Americans somewhat foolishly had driven down the Jericho road, across to Amman, and on to Greece. Omar's family was living in Bethany, but Omar stayed at the school and had run up the American flag. The school emerged from the war viable and intact, although deserted except for Omar. Finally, we drove up to the British School of Archaeology in the Sheikh Jarrah suburb; Director Basil Hennessey was still there but badly shaken up. Like de Vaux, he had no use for Israelis and never in his wildest dreams expected to encounter them face to face. He soon returned to Australia.

None of us yet realized the enormous impact that the Israeli takeover of the Old City would have on archaeology, all the foreign schools except HUC being there. But a few months later I published my very first article on the subject for an American magazine: "Archaeology and the Six Day War" (Dever 1967a). A journal that I had kept during the war was also soon published, and by then it was beginning to dawn on me that, except for de Vaux, I was the only ranking foreign archaeologist in Jerusalem and deeply involved in the uncertain fortunes of two American schools. I was thirty-three.

On June 13, about a week after the war, Glueck, who had pulled some powerful strings in Washington, arrived unexpectedly at the airport. He was excited, determined to get at once into the Old City that he had left in 1947 and never expected to see again. I managed to get another fake press pass, and I drove us across no-man's land, even though there was still some sporadic small-arms fire. We went straight to the American School, and I stood aside quietly as two grand old men—Rabbi Glueck and an Arab named Omar—fell tearfully on each other's necks. I shall never forget that moment; this was the old Jerusalem, now reunited.

Every day after that, Glueck would roust me out, saying, "Let's go to the Old City!" or "Let's tour in the West Bank" (the Israeli-occupied territories). It was a great adventure for me, even though a bit risky. One day an Israeli soldier stopped us at a checkpoint and was about to turn us back, since we didn't have a pass. I said to him, "Do you know who that is in the back seat? That's Nelson Glueck." Like all Israelis, he had studied archaeology in school, so he recognized the name. He waved us through. Thereafter, that was my pass.

Glueck and I encouraged Lapp and his family to return to Jerusalem, although he was no longer director of the American School. They had flown to Athens right after the war started. Now they returned to Israel, and in the taxi coming up to Jerusalem his small children asked, "Will they [the Israelis] kill us?" That was the image many Americans living in East Jerusalem had. The taxi driver, who understood English said, "Don't worry, little boy; I won't hurt you." (This story was told to me by Paul himself.) Norma entertained the family while I took Paul to his former home in Beit Hanina. The house was pretty much intact, some glass broken and the like. After a couple of nights in the YMCA in West Jerusalem, the whole family returned safely home. In the weeks to come I helped as much as I could to get the Lapps through the traumatic experience of living in Israeli Jerusalem. In about a year Paul and his family returned to the States. Paul died of a heart attack in the spring of 1970, at the age of thirty-nine. The anti-Israel era at the American Schools of Oriental Research was over.

Melancholy March

A few days after the war, Leonard Bernstein, who had been musical director of the Israel Philharmonic and was beloved by Israelis, was scheduled to give a concert first on the Mount Scopus campus of the old Hebrew University and then at Binyanei Ha-Oomah Hall. We had long had fifth-row center season tickets (right behind Supreme Court Justice Haim Cohen), so we went, exhausted like everyone else but searching for some reassurance. The crowd gathered slowly, people speaking in hushed tones, wondering what would happen since there was no printed program. The prime minister came in a side door, met with stunned silence.

Suddenly Bernstein appeared on stage, but again there was not the usual thunderous applause. The audience simply rose silently to their feet in tribute to "Lennie" and their beloved orchestra, astonished that there could be such an occasion and glad that we were alive to witness it.

The baton was raised, and then began the strains of "Ha-Tikvah" (Hope), surely the most mournful national anthem in the world despite its name. Already as it rose to its climax, the audience was half in tears. We were seated, waiting expectantly. What piece could possibly do justice to this occasion? Then the orchestra began to play what most of us recognized immediately, in part because of Bernstein's well-known penchant for Mahler: the Fifth Symphony.

The tortured cacophony of the first movement ("Melancholy March: Measured Cacophony") rose and fell again and again, first with the trumpets alone, then the percussion instruments, mirroring our own confused feelings. The seventy-minute symphony was performed without a break. The slow fourth movement, the Adagietto, was a single agonizing eleven-minute breath. Then the finale, the Rondo, which gradually rose, tranquilly at first, then driving toward a climax. By the time the last triumphant chords ended, people were transfixed, their eyes glistening with tears. It was the most moving night of my life. (Listening to Bernstein's recording as I write these lines recaptures a moment I will never forget.)

Father William Van Etten Casey of Holy Cross College, an affable Irishman, was now in East Jerusalem, the annual director of the American Schools of Oriental Research (ASOR), and he was making some overtures toward the Israeli establishment. Still at HUC and now the director, I watched all this, pretending a certain detachment but wondering all the time whether Jerusalem really needed two American archaeological schools. Later, in 1968, ASOR opened a new institute in Amman named the "American *Center* of Oriental Research" to distinguish it from the old American *school* in Jerusalem and then renamed the latter the "W. F. Albright Institute of Archaeological Research." What's in a name? A lot, it seems.

Glueck, the only scholar who had ever been head of both American schools in Jerusalem, seemed too preoccupied to think about the question. In fact, he seemed to imagine himself in charge of both again, and he enjoyed the situation immensely. But his real interest lay in exploring the newly open West Bank, terra incognita for most local archaeologists but for him (and me) the place where it had all started. About a week after the war, the Israelis were helping (encouraging?) Palestinians who were apprehensive about Israeli occupation to leave. Glueck, Norma, Ezra Spicehandler, and I went over to the Damascus Gate to watch Arabs being loaded on to old Jordanian buses to depart for the Allenby Bridge on the Jordan River, bound for Amman. One old man in ragged clothes couldn't find a place inside the bus, so he started to clamber up the rear ladder to the roof. But halfway up, one of his plastic sandals fell off. Rabbi Glueck stooped down in the dust, picked up the sandal, put it on the old man's dirty foot, and blessed him in Arabic. That was the way Jerusalem once was—and that was my kind of rabbi.

Another day I drove Glueck and a rabbinical colleague down to the Allenby Bridge to watch the Palestinians crossing over to Jordan. It was a hot June day, and on the steep descent down the Jericho road we passed long columns of Arabs on foot, some going down to the river, other having changed their minds struggling back up the ascent. As we slowed, Glueck became more and more agitated. Suddenly he said, "Stop the car! Give them all our water." As always, I had stocked the Jeep Wagoneer (Glueck's personal car) with food and water for any contingency. I started to unload the water, but my colleague protested that we would need the water ourselves. Glueck shouted, "Shut up! Give them the water."

When we got down to the bridge, blown up in the middle, we saw some Arabs trying to swim across the swift current, a few Israeli soldiers taking pot shots over their heads to urge them on. Glueck stood silently on the jagged edge of the border, gazing across the Jordan at the world he had long since left behind, his face inscrutable. (I will have more Glueck stories presently.)

About a week after the end of the war, a group of Israeli archaeologists asked me to join in planning a day-long excursion to some of the archaeological sites in the West Bank. The older ones could remember them from their twenties, but those my age had never seen them. They knew these famous sites, mostly biblical, only by name. We organized a caravan of cars, senior Israeli archaeologists such as Yadin, Avigad, Avi-Yonah, and Aharoni in the lead. I was the only foreign archaeologist—and also the only one who knew the sites recently and firsthand. That day we went northward to Ai, Gibeon, Shechem, and Samaria—all sites that Americans had excavated or reexcavated in the 1950s–1960s under Jordanian administration. I led the tour at Shechem, where I had started in 1962–1964 before settling in Israel. I was a bit uneasy before this august assembly, but they listened attentively. Elsewhere the older Israeli archaeologists held forth authoritatively on the history of these sights, and I chimed in to update the discussion. It was a sentimental journey for all of us, the Israelis because the heartland of biblical Israel was once again theirs, I because I was returning to my own modern roots.

The 1967 Gezer Season

When I had cabled Glueck the night before the June war canceling the Gezer dig due to start in June, we lost all the American student volunteers whom Associate Director Darrell Lance had laboriously recruited. But since the June war was mercifully brief, we quickly rescheduled the start of the Gezer excavations for late June. Where could we get some 150 or more volunteers on such short notice? As it turned out, Israel was awash in young idealistic American students, mostly Jewish, wanting to volunteer to help. There were, in fact, so many that the Jewish Agency could not absorb them all. So they told us simply to go down to Lydda airport with a couple of Egged buses, meet some incoming flights with placards advertising the "opportunity to be part of the war effort" (i.e., at Gezer), and see whom we could recruit.

Odd though the suggestion seemed and despite the fact that it violated all our strict standards for student volunteers, we did it—and it worked: we enlisted enough last-minute volunteers to add to the returning volunteers to fill out our workforce. Staff members had all changed their plans back at the last minute, so the Gezer dig was on. We were the first dig on the field that summer, despite the logistical challenges facing a foreign excavation. By now, with a successful first season behind us, the staff and I were gaining confidence (some needed it more than others).

Chasing Tomb Robbers (1967–1971)

In September, just as I was settling in back in Jerusalem, planning to work on Gezer excavation reports, I was drawn into what was probably the most dramatic archaeological adventure of my life. I had begun to go now and then to the souks (or bazaars) in the Old City, as I had done before the war—good therapy. Thus I came to renew my acquaintance with the antiquities dealers in the Old City. I revisited Baidun Antiquities Shop near the Via Dolorosa. I had known the old man, Mahmoud, and now I became a confidant of his resourceful son Musa. Another young man, a son of an antiquities dealer, Victor Barakat, audited my archaeology class at HUC and became quite knowledgeable about antiquities, especially pottery. (Little did I anticipate that he would end up years later owning an up-scale antiquities shop on Rodeo Drive in Los Angeles.)

One day the Baiduns came over to HUC and asked that Glueck and I come to their house to see a large collection of Iron Age pottery (eighth–seventh century BCE). They mentioned an inscription they had. Upon later inspection this turned out to be an authentic Hebrew inscription, which I dated about 750 BCE. It read:

(Belonging to) 'Ophai
the son of Netanyahu;
this is his tomb chamber.

Although I was, like all archaeologists, opposed on principle to trafficking in antiquities, this rare Hebrew burial inscription, with good biblical names, deserved not to end up as a trinket on some collector's mantle. So I promised to buy it for HUC, along with the whole collection of associated pottery, if they would tell me where it came from. After all, in archaeology everything is about provenance. Besides, I thought, if I can ferret out of them the find spot, there may be more inscriptions. (There were, as we shall see.)

The Baiduns kept their word and gave me a description of the middleman who had sold them the tomb robbers' inscription: a "one-eyed man from es-Samiyeh" (or so the Arabic name sounded to me). Now, I knew of the site of Khirbet es-Samiyeh northeast of Jerusalem, notorious for having been looted for more than half a century. So I rushed up there, made many inquiries of the wary villagers, and indeed saw then (and later) quantities of fine Iron Age pottery that had been dug illicitly. But no one-eyed man.

Then by chance I began to see vast collections of much earlier pottery on the market, EB IV in date (ca. 2500–2000 BCE). That era had been the subject of my dissertation only a year or so earlier, so, of course, I became interested in the great cemetery where this stuff must be coming from (and in 1968–1971 I excavated it.) But what intrigued me most was the name of the new site, which I finally wormed out of the dealers: Samiyeh.

The similarity of the two names in Arabic is striking. Was *this* the place the Hebrew inscription had come from?

By now, several months after the war, I had discovered the foreman of Philip Hammond's defunct dig at Hebron in the early 1960s, Ali Musa Abu Argoub, languishing in the small village of Samua near Hebron in the remote southern West Bank. I took on Ali as my right-hand man, and we worked together for nearly forty years; my faithful foreman died in 2007. Ali had no sons then, only a daughter named Hope. But when his first son was born, Ali named him William. This is the highest honor a Westerner can ever receive, because Ali now became Abu-William, "Father of William." Today William is a college graduate, a healthcare professional in Ramallah, working with the World Health Organization, serving his own people. Incidentally, since I had no children then, my Arab workmen named me (behind my back) Abu-Mafish, "Father of nothing."

With Ali's unwavering courage and enormous knowledge of local conditions, we began an off-and-on search for tomb robbers in the West Bank that lasted for a year. It became a story of risks, false leads, endless intrigue, and reward beyond all our expectations. We began with the Arab village of Samiyeh, about 12 miles west of Hebron. The first day in October when Ali, my assistant at HUC John Landgraf, and I visited the site, we found nearly everyone from the villages of Samiyeh and nearby Khirbet el-Qôm out in the field. They were frantically churning up a vast, pockmarked hillside cemetery, sending up a cloud of dust, shouting and bargaining over the pots they were finding, triumphantly rolling the skulls down the slope.

We watched helplessly. Even the Israeli army couldn't help; they had stopped us repeatedly, warning us that we were unarmed and didn't even know where we were. (We knew exactly where we were; did they?) And the Israel Department of Antiquities was nowhere to be seen. So the tomb robbers were having a field day, literally. Nevertheless, after persisting we did discover that, yes, there was a one-eyed local dealer (whom we later met), and there had been an inscription found in one tomb, which the villagers even showed us, though it was by now completely back-filled.

Elated but realizing that there was little more we could do now, I promised the villagers the equivalent of $100 if they would dig out the tomb again and show it to me when I came back in a few days. They kept their word, and when we entered the splendid Judean bench tomb (empty,

Fig. 25. Inscription 3 from Tomb II at Khirbet el-Qôm.

of course), we found on the floor the missing last letter of the inscription we had bought. Bingo! We also recovered a second inscription painted over the doorway to the inner chamber, which read: "(Belonging to) 'Uzza, the daughter of Netanyahu." So this was 'Ophai's *sister*—a typical Judean family tomb.

Later, during the 1968 salvage excavations, we recovered a third Hebrew inscription that is now widely regarded as our most significant single datum for reconstructing ancient Israelite folk religion. In late October, as the fall rains were rapidly approaching, I was out in the field one day finishing a tomb drawing. An old man came along with a flat stone tucked under his arm, squatted down to smoke a cigarette, and finally spoke up. "Do you ever buy a *maktub* [an inscription]?" My ears perked up, but not wanting to drive up the price I continued to draw nonchalantly. In due course I said, "Sure." The old man said, "How much do you pay?" I paused, then declared, "We always pay two dinars" (about $7). He hesitated a bit, then said, "Tayeb" ("Good"). I scarcely dared to look at the dirt-encrusted stone but accepted it and laid it on the ground while I finished drawing.

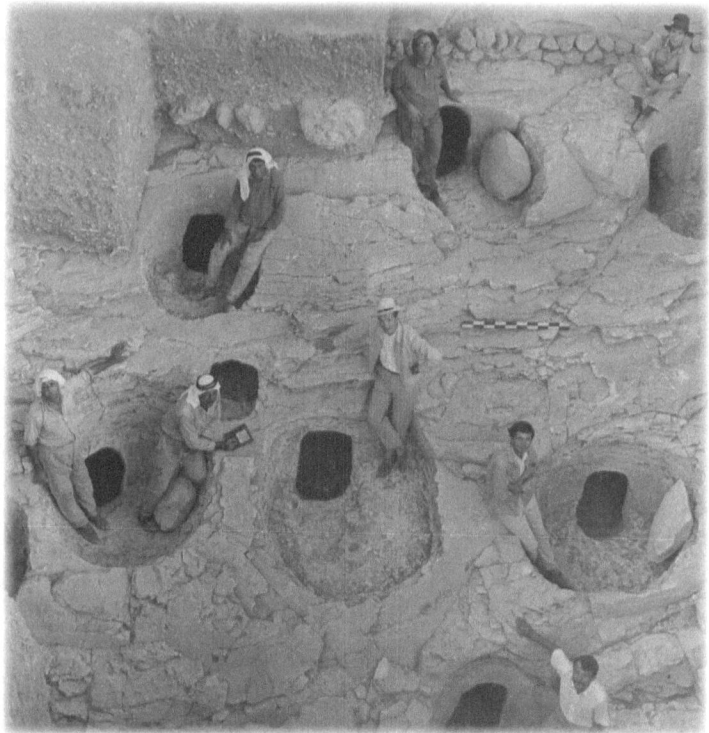

Fig. 26. The staff at Jebel Qaʻaqir in 1971, in Cemetery B (ca. 2300 BCE).

When properly cleaned and deciphered after much difficulty, the inscription read:

(Belonging to) 'Uriyahu the governor;
this is his inscription.
May 'Uriyahu be blessed by Yahweh
and saved from his enemies
by his Asherah.

Asherah is the name of the old Canaanite mother goddess, consort of the principal male deity El. But now we know that Canaanite Asherah was venerated much later in Israel, and in some circles she was even worshiped alongside the Israelite deity Yahweh as his consort.

I published this inscription (no. 3) promptly but hesitantly in 1969–1970. Many years went by before mainstream biblical scholars recognized its far-reaching implications. All three Khirbet el-Qôm inscriptions now reside in the Israel Museum, where they belong. But for us, they would have evaporated into the international antiquities market, their original provenance lost forever, even possibly dismissed as fakes. Was the admitted compromise of principle in acquiring these inscriptions worth it? I think so, although I haven't dealt with antiquities dealers (or tomb robbers) since.

Ethnographic Adventures

During three campaigns at Khirbet el-Qôm and nearby Jebel Qa'aqir (below) in 1967–1971, a small staff of Westerners lived in villages in the Hebron hills. The first year we rented an empty house in Deir Samit. Thereafter we rented a schoolhouse in Samiyeh. We tried to live like the villagers: arising and bedding down with the sun, cooking and eating local foods, drinking from the wells, sleeping on the roof like everyone else when nights got hot. Whole families slept together in thatched mud-brick circles on the roof, open to the sky. We learned more than we wanted to know from the sounds and sighs drifting across the dark night sky above

Fig. 27. The Arab village of Samiyeh, where we lived.

the closely grouped mud-brick houses. At least one of our group got hepatitis from the polluted well water.

We were so preoccupied with the logistics of the dig in 1969–1971 that we did not fully realize that we had a unique (and last) opportunity to do some ethnography. We had the advantage of being long-term residents, familiar and accepted, with access even to the usually hidden lives of women and children. We did interview some people, and we took many photos, but we did not record as fully as we should have the everyday lives of the Arab villagers who lived almost exactly as the biblical Israelites had in the Iron Age. We thought that there was time. But within a few years, the quaint lifestyle of these agricultural villages had been transformed by contact with more modern Israelis. I never went back until 2004, when Ali and I revisited the villages and the excavation sites. I scarcely recognized anything. The picturesque old houses were abandoned, in ruins, replaced by modern cinderblock houses, lit with neon lights and garishly furnished. Progress, I suppose, but that was only one of my many worlds that was lost, gone forever.

Milestones

In the summer of 1968 I directed a third season at Gezer, which had matured into one of the largest archaeological projects in Israel. By now we had Fields I, II, III, IV, V, and VI open, with increasingly promising results. *Gezer I* was soon going to be in press, as the first annual of the Hebrew Union College–Jewish Institute of Religion in Jerusalem (published in 1970). That summer I moved up from executive officer of HUC to become a permanent director, just as Glueck had promised me. Still at least nominally a Christian (I was an elder in the nearby Scottish Saint Andrews Presbyterian Church), I found myself director of a Reformed Jewish institution with an attached theological seminary, giving orientation sessions for each incoming class of rabbinical students, along with my friend and colleague Ezra Spicehandler, the dean of the rabbinical school.

The last visiting annual director, now departing, was Saul S. Weinberg of the University of Missouri, a distinguished classical archaeologist who had been directing his own excavations at Tell Anafa in Upper Galilee. His wife, Gladys Davidson Weinberg, was equally distinguished as an excavator, specialist in ancient glass, and longtime editor of *Archaeology* magazine.

The Weinbergs, whom we saw constantly, were delightful. Saul was soft-spoken, a very domestic sort of man who loved to cook (although his mild manner concealed a mind like a steel trap). Gladys, on the other hand, was a large, angular woman with a brusque manner and a raucous laugh. She would occasionally smoke a big black cigar. She once said jokingly, "What Saul and I need is a wife!" Years later, shortly before they died, I brought Saul and Gladys, who by now had won jointly the gold medal of the Archaeological Institute of America, to the University of Arizona. They mesmerized my graduate students with a joint seminar that was not typical but played them off against each other in a fascinating account of their long and distinguished adventures in archaeology.

In 1967–1968 the Weinbergs resided at the college, where there were two modern (but minimalist) apartments. By the summer of 1968 the Weinbergs were at their excavation site, and Norma and I had moved into the apartment, largely because Glueck wanted his director to be on top of all things at all times. I didn't mind, since it was rather like being the master of a collegiate house, with other live-in colleagues and fellows. For many years thereafter, I was to live where I worked, combining research and publications with consultation, counseling, and an active social life. HUC was, in fact, becoming not only the home base of a large excavation but also a research center with a library and other facilities. In addition, it was a scholarly community of Americans and a kind of ambassador for American relations with Israel. Glueck kept the second apartment for his frequent visits.

In addition to rotating resident fellows, there were endless American and international visitors, and Israeli colleagues became accustomed to our frequent, rather lavish catered receptions. Even the Reform synagogue on the campus, under the tutelage of my colleague Rabbi Ezra Spicehandler, was flourishing, drawing a small but respectable congregation each Shabbat.

The college was now bursting at the seams, so in the summer of 1968, with a generous gift of Mrs. Rosaline Feinstein of Philadelphia, Glueck oversaw the construction of a large fourstory residential building on the back portion of the property. The top floor featured a splendid, airy apartment with magnificent unobstructed views over the Old City. It was intended for Glueck's retirement, but he did not live that long. (I once thought that I might eventually live there, as Glueck had hinted.) In late summer, I went to Dublin for a few weeks in an attempt to find out something more about Robert Alexander Stewart Macalister, who had excavated at Gezer in 1902–1909 (and left a mess). I even hoped to locate long-lost field notes or diaries. But all I found out was that Macalister was a Protestant in Catholic Dublin (and an organist at Saint Adelaide's Presbyterian Church), an irascible fellow who later wrote on such diverse subjects as Irish archaeology, ecclesiastical vestments, and musicology, answering every review with a blistering reply, and a bungling excavator of several Irish national monuments. At the famous monumental passage grave at Knowth, Macalister failed to find the entrance, so he blew off the top with dynamite. His pupil and successor at Trinity College, George Eogan, declared, "He was a buffoon who should never have been allowed in the field." I was sympathetic. In the end, I found no unknown records in Dublin and no surviving family I could interview, since Macalister was a bachelor. So the ghost of Macalister lingers on. Later I did discover some of his correspondence in the files of the Palestine Exploration Fund in London, his sponsor, but they were uninformative and uninteresting except for the gossip.

In the fall of 1968, I followed up the Gezer dig with a long salvage campaign back at Khirbet el-Qôm, or, more precisely, at nearby Jebel Qa'aqir, the source of the EB IV pottery that we had acquired. This was a full-scale excavation of the partially robbed cemetery, plus some areas of seasonal occupation by the ancient pastoral nomads who had frequented the site in summer. The tombs were particularly interesting because of the completely disarticulated secondary burials, as well as the exceptionally well-preserved bones, pottery, and copper implements. The final report was finally published only in 2014.

Already in the fall of 1967, Glueck had responded enthusiastically to my initial request for college funds to do a salvage dig. He continued his support in 1968, since he had done pioneer work himself in exploring EB IV sites in the Negev in the 1950s (claiming in his popular report that he had found the "age of Abraham" in the desert). He even visited the site, congratulating us on our results. We both knew that salvage digs, while logistically difficult, can sometimes produce spectacular results for a modest investment. Moreover, now HUC had two major excavation projects and fieldwork extending over several months a year.

Furthermore, I had several part-time staff members: John Landgraf, already mentioned, and a talented young photographer, Theodore A. Rosen, who came from Gezer with me. We also took with us some of the Christian resident fellows at the college, providing them with the hands-on field experience that Glueck had envisioned. Also with us was Fellow Seymour Gitin, later director at the American School in East Jerusalem, now the W. F. Albright Institute for Archeological research. The dig was the kind of ecumenical experience that Glueck liked in another way. We employed two old friends from Shechem in 1962–1964, well-known Arab technical men of the kind said to be essential, Abu Issa and Jabber, from the village of Balatah near Nablus.

After the 1968 seasons at Gezer and Jebel Qaʻaqir, one night at dusk Norma took me aside and asked me to go out onto our terrace at HUC overlooking the Old City. At first I was reluctant when Norma said hesitatingly that she had something to tell me. Umm ... *mysterious*. She said, "I'm pregnant." That would have been stunning news in any case. But we had been married sixteen years (since we were nineteen), had been told after consulting with medical experts that we would never have children, and had given up birth control at least ten years ago. We simply forgot about children—because we had to and also because we were so preoccupied with our busy and exiting life in Jerusalem.

For once in my life, I was speechless. But when I came to my senses, I was overjoyed. We even joked a bit about it. Norma had told me about the "most charming man" she had met while I was in Dublin, who turned out to be a fast friend, the noted biblical scholar David Noel Freedman. I said, "This kid better not look like Noel!" But we calculated that Norma must have conceived at Gezer the previous July. Noel died in 2008, long since among my closest friends.

Sean William Dever was born at the Misgav Ladach hospital, which was an old Arab house in the German Colony in West Jerusalem, on March 9, 1969. He came into the world of archaeology in which we now moved amidst appropriate fanfare. The legendary American archaeologist and mentor to us all, Albright, was in Jerusalem at the age of eighty (for what turned out to be his last time). He was to be made a Yakir Yerushelayim, which is like being presented the honorary keys to the city. Everyone had come to celebrate with Albright, especially his many students, among them my teachers at Harvard, Cross, and especially my own mentor Ernest.

Ernest was having a late lunch with us in our apartment at the college, and afterward we were enjoying conversation when Norma suddenly said, "I think I had better go to the hospital." Ernest left, and after a short time off we went. I went back home to await news of the baby's birth. I couldn't sleep, so I put the finishing touches on an article in a volume of the Hebrew Union College Annual honoring Nelson Glueck's seventieth birthday, the final publication of the Khirbet el-Qôm Hebrew inscriptions described above. Just as I was finishing the final footnote, at about 4:30 am, the phone rang: "You have a son." I rushed to the hospital to find Norma and baby doing well. Norma was beaming, and Sean was bright-eyed and alert.

Fig. 28. Sean's christening at St. Andrew's Presbyterian Church, Jerusalem, May 1969.

There are some parallels with Glueck that as a father I find uncanny. When Norma first consulted a gynecologist at Hadassah Hospital, it was a Dr. Rosen, who as a young internist had been Helen Glueck's doctor. Our son Sean, an only child, was born in Jerusalem almost exactly thirty years to the day after Glueck's only child Charles had been born there. When we spoke a few months later in Cincinnati, Glueck said to me, "Don't be the kind of father I was; I never saw much of Charles until he was eight." Glueck had sent his family home in 1939, as the war was drawing on in Europe, and he remained alone at the school in Jerusalem until 1947, when

Fig. 29. Albright's visit to the high place at Gezer, April 1969.

he was called home to become (somewhat reluctantly) president of the Hebrew Union College–Jewish Institute of Religion (HUC here). Charles followed his mother Helen into hematology and never returned to Israel. Sean rests there forever.

Three days after Sean was born, I brought Norma and baby Sean back to the college, where I had organized an elegant champagne reception. So Sean was introduced immediately to the crème de la crème of archaeological society, including Albright and Wright. (We still have the baby blue sweater Yadin gave him.) A bit later, Sean was dedicated at the St. Andrew's Presbyterian Church (aka Scots Memorial Church), with Ezra and Shirley Spicehandler his Jewish stand-up godparents. They accepted the responsibility to look after him if anything happened to us. But that was unthinkable: our prince, he would lead a charmed life.

Several events other than Sean's birth stand out from Albright's visit to Jerusalem. First, he wanted to see the famous Gezer high place, which we had reexcavated the previous summer. With Joe Seger, who would be my successor at HUC, I went next door to the King David Hotel to fetch him. His wife, Ruth Norton Albright, met me in the lobby, a little wisp of a woman. She warned me, "Young man, if you harm a hair of his head, I will kill you!" I took notice. At Gezer, with Joe and me guiding him, Albright stumbled a bit going up the slope and apologized, saying, "I'm no longer seventy-five." He was almost blind, but we stood by reverentially as he went up to one of the enormous standing stones (the biblical *māṣṣebôt*), embracing the monolith and stroking it.

Albright had been one of the few non-Jews to learn Modern Hebrew in the 1930s—indeed, from its creator, the legendary Eliezer Ben-Yehuda. On his visit now, he was scheduled to give a lecture in Beersheba to an audience of Israelis, who, of course, thought of him as a god, especially since no one could remember ever having seen him in modern Israel. We all went along, and to our astonishment Albright lectured for over an hour in flawless Modern Hebrew! Unfortunately, it was the Hebrew of the 1930s, and while everyone admired the tour de force, few understood the Hebrew. It was like some of us listening to Chaucer.

One evening there was a reception at the president's house for Albright (it was during the term of Zalman Shazar). It was at this gala occasion that Albright was presented with the certificate honoring him as a Yakir Yerusa-layim. It was one of the few times that a non-Jew had been so honored, but Albright was a well-known and staunch supporter of the modern state. Ernest had carefully prepared a brief speech in Hebrew (not to be outdone by Albright), but his Midwestern American *goyische* accent was enough to bring the house down. Fortunately, I had not been asked to speak.

Another evening we were all invited to the house of Benjamin Mazar, the doyen of Israeli archaeologists. Since I had just completed the article on the Asherah inscription, I took along photographs and tracings. I showed them to the leading epigraphers in the world, including Albright and Cross, but no one supported my reading of a key phrase as Asherah, the goddess. So in my revised article I downplayed the reading, which is still in my notes, in favor of something less heretical. I have always regretted that, but these were the world's leading authorities, and who was I? Scared is what I was.

A final evening we went over to the director's house at the old American School of Oriental Research in East Jerusalem, now the W. F. Albright Institute of Archeological Research. Albright had helped to build that house in 1931 and had lived there in 1933–1936, as had Glueck in 1932–1933, 1936–1940, and 1942–1947. There sat in that grand house Albright, Glueck, Cross, Freedman, Wright, and other notables—and me. In a nostalgic and celebratory mood, Frank, Noel, and Ernest began to tell stories about each other. Before long they turned their attention timorously to Albright, who sat quietly, tall and erect as usual, looking rather bemused like one of the

Fig. 30. Mrs. Albright, on one of her visits after her husband's death.

gods on Mount Olympus. It was a remarkable display of affectionate, filial piety. I was entranced—especially since by now, two years after the war, I had begun to entertain secretly the thought that perhaps I would shift over to the older American school myself. It was in July of 1971 that I would move into the director's house myself—the house that Albright built.

After Albright's death in September of 1971, Mrs. Albright came to visit us in Jerusalem, staying as an honored guest in the institute bearing her husband's distinguished name. She would reminisce, telling wonderful stories that we all treasured. While they lived at the school in the 1930s, she began to go down the street to the École Biblique, where she fell under the spell of the Dominican fathers and eventually converted to Roman Catholicism. When I asked her how Albright felt about this, she said "We almost got a divorce." One of their four sons, Hugh, became a Roman Catholic monk. Albright, the son of Methodist missionary parents in South America, was never quite reconciled to his wife's conversion—or to some other realities.

Mrs. Albright told us that Albright (only *she* said "William") had always been convinced that at Johns Hopkins, where he taught for all of his career in the States, there were two kinds of PhDs: the ones he gave, for which there were real standards, and all the rest. She had completed her own PhD there with a brilliant dissertation in Sanskrit studies. She was about to launch what would undoubtedly have been a fine career when they met and married. She abandoned her career for him and devoted herself to rearing their four sons. I was so impressed that I asked if they had ever discussed this sacrifice. She hesitated a moment, then told me the story. They had never spoken of it, but when he was literally on his deathbed, he turned to her and said, "But yours wasn't a real PhD, was it?" That says more about Albright and the fact that he lived in a world of his own than any scholarly analysis I have ever seen.

On another occasion I asked Mrs. Albright how Albright had dealt with his associate director at Tell Beit Mirsim in the 1920s, Melvin Grove Kyle, who was a well-known fundamentalist ideologue. She simply remarked, "William was oblivious." He was oblivious to other things as well. One of his sons had twins who were visibly disabled, but she said Albright ignored the fact and treated them as if they had no disability. In his view, Albrights could never be less than brilliant. At an occasion in Baltimore honoring him, another one of his sons gave a long tribute to Albright and his work. I couldn't help but notice, however, that he never once said "my father" or even "my dad." It was always "Professor Albright." Albright's contributions to archaeology and ancient Near Eastern studies were magisterial, but they came at great price.

Orientalist Extraordinaire

William Foxwell Albright was undoubtedly the most prolific and influential ancient Near Eastern scholar of our times, with an extraordinary range over Assyriology, Egyptology, Semitic philology, and especially the history and archaeology of the southern Levant. The latter was a discipline that Albright really founded with the first true mastery of the pottery of ancient Palestine at Tell Beit Mirsim (biblical Kiryat-Sefer) in 1926–1932.

It is noteworthy that Albright originally called the discipline *Syro-Palestinian archaeology*, but later (in the 1950s) he adopted and popularized the more specific term *biblical archaeology*. Then his many students continued its use and its fundamental biblical orientation when they came to dominate the field in America. Notable among Albrights students was Ernest, my own teacher. In turn, most of our senior American archaeologists now working in Israel and Jordan were trained under Ernest and have their own students now. So Albright is often regarded as the father of biblical archaeology, with a fourth generation of students now perpetuating his original coupling of archaeology and historical/biblical sources.

But as I have shown, the new archaeology had undermined any simple, essential biblical connection by the late 1960s, and today little actually remains of the house that Albright built except its partly ruined foundations. In retrospect, Albright's positivism—his conservative bias in favor of the historicity of the Bible—has not been borne out by continuing research in either Levantine archaeology or biblical studies. Yet all of us working in the field—Americans, Europeans, Israelis, and Jordanians—stand on the shoulders of this twentieth-century giant. I feel particularly fortunate to have been schooled in the Albright tradition, to have known him somewhat in his last years, and to have directed the Jerusalem institute bearing his name after his death.

Albright died in September of 1971, just after I had begun as director of the institute. I draped the whole entrance in black, placed an ad in the *Jerusalem Post* with the dates of his life and the simple statement "Orientalist Extraordinaire," then planned a memorial service for him across the street at St. George's Cathedral.

Archaeology in the 1960s: A Golden Age

Looking backward a bit, the 1960s constituted a golden age for Israeli archaeology, thanks to the flourishing of the new State of Israel and the foundations laid so courageously and presciently by the first generation discussed above. Now a second generation, well trained and eager to further a national school, was in place, mostly in their thirties or early forties, both at the Hebrew University and in the Department of Antiquities. In addition to those discussed above, trained principally at Hazor, I would mention Michal Artzy, Gaby Barkay, Pirhiya Beck, Itzhaq Beit-Arieh, Eliot Braun, Avi Eitan, Rudolph Cohen, Ram Gophna, Ze'ev Herzog, Aharon Kempinski, Amos Kloner, Moshe Kochavi, Ze'ev Meshel, Avraham Negev, Ora Negbi, Eliezer Oren, Avner Raban, Ronny Reich, Yoram Tsafrir, and others (some not on an academic track but in the Department of Antiquities).

There were now many more Israeli projects in the field, including the beginnings of a national region-by-region survey intended to eventually cover the entire country. The emphasis was partly on big sites, following the style of Hazor, among them the excavations of Avraham Biran at Dan, on the Syrian border. The project began in 1966 (and ran until Biran's retirement as director of the Nelson Glueck School of Biblical Archaeology in Jerusalem in 1993). Yadin went on to Megiddo (1960–1971) to follow up his investigations of Solomon's City Gate at Hazor, seeking parallels there. Then he moved on to explorations in the Qumran area (1960–1961) and finally to his legendary exploits at the fortress of Masada (1963–1965).

Ruth Amiran excavated the vast lower Early Bronze city at Arad, near Beersheba, from 1962 to 1984, while Yohanan Aharoni cleared much of the Judean fortress on the upper mound (1962–1964). Moshe Dothan led the joint Israeli-American excavations at Philistine Ashod under his direction and that of David Noel Freedman (1962–1972); this was the first American project, even before Gezer.

The scope of excavation projects was expanded during this time as well, for instance, to sites with hitherto poorly known Persian period levels (Shiqmona and 'Ein-Gedi) and sites in the Negev (such as Tell en-Nagileh), until now almost terra incognita. This expansion reflects something of the confidence of the burgeoning national school. Complementing the emphasis on big cities and sites dug previously (above), some of these were small, virgin sites. Overall, however, Israeli archaeology was beginning to focus more on Iron Age sites, that is, on ancient Israel and Judah, in keeping with the biblical archaeology then still in vogue.

A notable Hebrew University project of the early 1960s was the Judean Desert Survey, headed jointly by Yadin, Aharoni, Avigad, and Bar-Adon in 1960–1961. This survey was undertaken south of Qumran along the Israel shores of the Dead Sea, hoping to find more Dead Sea Scrolls there. Instead, in the Cave of Horrors, they found remains of the Bar Kochba revolt in 132–135 CE, and in the Nahal Mishmar they recovered astonishing copper hoards of the fourth millennium BCE, along with several papyri and coins relating to Simon Bar Kokhba.

The 1960s also saw the first joint digs (such as Ashdod; above). One of the most remarkable was the Japanese-sponsored excavation at Tel Zeror, on the Sharon Plain, directed by Moshe Kochavi (1964–1966, 1974). I recall visiting this excavation with Ernest and seeing a procession of men dressed in white lab uniforms carrying all sorts of the most modern scientific instruments, all working in methodical silence. When we asked about their intentions, they replied that all the Jews and Christians had obviously been biased; being Buddhists, *they* could be objective. How Kochavi—Kookby to his friends—managed, I will never know, but he did publish three volumes of final reports (1966–1970).

The 1960s also witnessed the first large-scale, completely American excavations, notably Gezer, which began in 1964 (through 1973; again in 1984 and 1990), on which I have commented above. This was the *American Hazor*, a training ground for the first generation of American archaeologists to work in Israel, self-consciously experimenting with newer (and, we thought, more advanced) theories and methods. Significantly, Gezer marked a deliberate shift of American interests from Jordan to Israel—and this well before anyone could even have imagined the 1967 war and the access it gave to the West Bank (below).

In the West Bank, only a few new excavations supplemented Shechem (1955–1968). James B. Pritchard, of the University of Pennsylvania, excavated Tell el-Jib (biblical Gibeon) in 1957–1962. In principle, however, American institutions were opposed to any new excavations in the occupied territories. Nevertheless, I carried out salvage excavations on behalf of Glueck's School of Biblical Archaeology in Jerusalem at Jebel Qaʿaqir, west of Hebron in 1967–1971. They revealed pastoral nomadic campsites and vast cemeteries of the EB IV period (ca. 2500–2000 BCE) related to other EB IV campsites in the Negev. Excavations at Tell el-Farʿah (North) continued through 1960 under the direction of deVaux. Shechem and el Jib would be among the last American excavations in the West Bank (due to the 1967 war; above) and Tell el-Farʿah was the last French dig there.

The Albrightian paradigm and biblical archaeology now prevailed in Israel, even among the younger Israelis who were coming into their own, and Iron Age sites still attracted the most attention in historical archaeology (called biblical archaeology by Israelis to this day). The only other American excavations in the 1960s, however, were the projects of Saul Weinberg at the Persian-Hellenistic site of Anafa in the upper Jordan Valley (1968, continued by Sharon Herbert) and the excavation of a unique glass factory in Lower Galilee, at Jalamie, by Gladys Weinberg. Notable exceptions in the 1960s were a few excavations of later-period sites, such as Avraham Negev's work at Nabatean/Byzantine sites in the Negev: Avdat (1959–1964) and Kurnub (1965–1972). One should also mention the great coastal medieval/crusader and later Phoenician harbor site at Atlit (Elisha Linder and Avner Raban, 1963–1976).

In 1968 the picture changed suddenly (and for the better) when Yadin's old rival Yohanan Aharoni left the Institute of Archaeology in Jerusalem and launched the New Institute of Archaeology at Tel Aviv University (now the Sonia Nadler Institute of Archaeology). The major thrust was Aharoni's long-time interest in surface surveys and what was coming to be called regional studies, in this case specifically the Negev Desert. Other somewhat younger archaeologists soon joined the Tel Aviv faculty, among them Pirhiya Beck, Ram Gophna, Moshe Kochavi, Ze'ev Meshel, and Itzhaq Beit-Arieh. Soon excavations were underway at Arad (Aharoni, 1962–1964); Beersheba (Aharoni, 1969–1974); Tel Esdar (Kochavi, 1963–1964); Yeruham (Kochavi, 1963–1964); the Negev (Benno Rothenberg, 1964); Tel Malḥata (Kochavi, 1967–1971); and, later, Tel 'Ira (Beit-Arieh, 1971–1981); Tel Masos (Kempinski et al., 1972–1975); Kuntillet 'Ajrud (Meshel, 1975–1976); and Ḥorvat 'Uza (Beit-Arieh, 1982–1988).

Over the years since, the Tel Aviv institute has provided a healthy alternative to the Jerusalem institute. I should add that the younger Tel Aviv archaeologists (later including Aharon Kempinski, David Ussishkin, Israel Finkelstein, Shlomo Bunimovitz, and Rafi Greenberg) have been especially innovative, even though for the most part they did not make pioneering contributions to more recent advances in archaeological theory and method. Ussishkin claims to have been influenced at Lachish by Gezer methods, including section drawings. But the final publication volumes in 2006, although admirable, belies that claim. There are few section drawings, none adequately detailed, in my judgment.

A much more significant development in the 1960s was the Six-Day War in 1967 (above). For the first time in the living memory of young Israeli archaeologists, the Old City of Jerusalem and indeed the whole of the West Bank, the heartland of ancient Israel, was open to survey and excavation. Even the older archaeologists could scarcely remember this region. Within a short time after the war, Benjamin Mazar began extensive excavation south and west of the Western (Wailing) Wall (1968–1979). Before long, Nahman Avigad, long in the shadow of Yadin, emerged as a leading excavator in his extraordinary salvage work in the soon to be rebuilt Jewish Quarter (1969–1982, the latter year his death).

The major excavations were soon complemented by the dozens of smaller salvage excavations (which continue to this day). It must also be noted that the most remarkable excavations in Jerusalem during the summer of 1967 were not Israeli at all but the final season of Dame Kathleen Kenyon's work, with special permission now of the *Israel* Department of Antiquities.

Soon after the war, Tel Aviv University, principally under the leadership of Aharoni and Kochavi, launched a hurried survey of the Golan Heights (also some of Judea and Samaria) in 1968. They also instigated the Land of Geshur project, which investigated several Golan Heights sites such as the Leviah Enclosure, under the direction of Kochavi and Pirhiya Beck. A unique Stonehenge-like site, Rujm el-Hiri, excavated by Yonathan Mizrahi in 1988–1990, proved to be a megalith originally dated to the Early Bronze Age, with a reuse in the Late Bronze Age. These were all later excavations of the Tel Aviv Land of Geshur project. (Golan Heights digs of the 1970s–1980s will be covered below.)

In the West Bank after 1967, the only major American project continued in the field was Shechem (1956–1973). Lapp, director of the American School of Oriental Research in Jerusalem (after 1968, the W. F. Albright Institute of Archaeological Research), had mounted several small digs, in caves in the Wadi ed-Daliyeh (1963–1964) and at Saul's Fortress at Tell el-Ful (1964). He also directed excavations as Ta'anach in the Jezreel Valley (1963–1967). But although he remained in Jerusalem, Lapp did not excavate under Israeli authority and simply worked on publications. He returned to Pittsburgh and died in 1970, at the age of thirty-nine. Three years younger than me, he might have become the leader of the field.

There were no other postwar American excavations in the West Bank except those of Southern Baptist Seminary under Callaway at Ai, which had begun in 1964 and continued until 1970. Callaway bought a flat and moved to West Jerusalem, one of the few foreign excavators to make such a transition. In 1968 the American Schools of Oriental Research opened a new school in Amman, named (for political reasons) the American Center of Oriental Research. American excavators whose sympathies remained with Jordan soon transferred there. Although they have flourished, that story is both known to others and beyond my purview here.

Back Home?

After another eventful season at Gezer in the summer of 1969, it had been agreed that Norma and I, now with Sean, would spend an academic year on leave at the Cincinnati branch of the HUC-JIR. We arrived there in late August and settled into rented quarters, fellow-Gezerite Joe Seger having replaced me in Jerusalem as temporary director. I took up teaching responsibilities at the college, already familiar with rabbinical students and their needs, as well as with President Glueck (although in another venue, where he was much more relaxed and congenial).

Among my students was a personable young man who was an ordained rabbi and now assistant director of student affairs at the college, Seymour Gitin. He had wanted to do archaeology, but Glueck—who liked to be sui generis, the only American Jewish archaeologist—gave him no encouragement. I did, and the next summer Gitin returned with me to Jerusalem, and he remained at the college as a fellow until he completed his doctorate with me in 1978.

Fig. 31. Sy Gitin in the garden of the Albright Institute.

Gitin was unanimously elected director of the Albright Institute in 1980, and he recently completed his thirty-fourth year—a worthy successor of Albright and Glueck and the best director the school has ever had. Without Sy's selfless dedication, through budget crises and a worsening political situation, the school would never have survived—and a whole generation of younger American archaeologists, including most of my students, would never have gotten a start in Israel.

I often think that finding, training, and helping to place Sy in Jerusalem was probably the best thing I ever did in a long, adventuresome career. But it was fortuitous—not so much virtue as good luck: being at the right place at the right time and seizing the opportunity, plus a bit of hard work. That is the story of my life.

During my year on home leave, I traveled widely and gave papers at national meetings of the American Schools of Oriental Research, the Archaeological Institute of America, and other professional societies at which I had never had any exposure. Glueck encouraged me because it publicized the college's burgeoning program in archaeology. On one of these trips I met a young, smartly dressed Long Island housewife who had a love affair with archaeology. When she asked me how she could pursue her interests, I suggested that she come to Gezer the next summer and begin in the dirt. She did. Today Norma Kershaw is a widely admired trustee of both the Archaeological Institute of American (at whose annual meetings I met her in 1970) and the American Schools of Oriental Research. Recently she endowed a chair in the archaeology of Israel at UC San Diego—for Thomas E. Levy, another Gezer graduate (1973). Fortuitous again?

During home leave, after three continuous years abroad, I also saw my parents, now retired in East Tennessee, several times. They loved seeing their grandson Sean, the miracle child. I was the solicitous (and slightly guilty-feeling) long-absent son. But my father's health was failing, a victim of bone cancer. I remember that, on a visit during spring break, we were wandering around his front yard looking at a tree that needed to come out. I took a few swings at it with an axe, but Dad said, "Here, let me try it." And, bent over as he was from recent back surgery, he chopped the tree down.

Father was a strong, proud man, and he took a long time to die. As the June exams at HUC drew near and the starting date of the Gezer dig loomed large, I tried desperately to get everything done in order to move back to Jerusalem and still see my Dad one last time. But by the time I got to Johnson City, he was in the hospital in a coma. I never got to tell him how much he had meant to me. I hung on as long as I could, watching his silent suffering and wishing that he could just die peacefully. I couldn't wait much longer and still get back to Jerusalem in time. Finally, I went to his funeral with my mother and sister. That afternoon, at the last possible moment, Norma, Sean, and I boarded the plane for Israel. Gezer called. My father would have understood, because for him, too, duty was everything.

In my rapidly expanding world, all new to me, I had almost unconsciously begun to expand my horizons—physically, intellectually, and emotionally. I was no longer a small-town boy from Middle America, Mark

Twain's "innocent abroad." I was certainly abroad but not so innocent. Among other more worldly people I had now met were some attractive and even fascinating women. I had been engaged at eighteen, married at nineteen, a virgin. Norma and I had a stable but conventional marriage and now a baby for whom I was totally unprepared.

I began to realize that at thirty-six I was undergoing the dreaded midlife crisis. That year in Cincinnati my career, so auspiciously begun, was at a turning point. Glueck, my employer and mentor, was obviously failing. Ernest had approached me with the possibility of my moving over from HUC to the older Jerusalem school. My father was dying. After a long and totally faithful marriage, I was thinking about other women I had come to know—one in particular, whom I saw off and on despite crushing guilt. In the face of increasing stress, I was drinking heavily and, although I didn't realize it, showing signs of clinical depression. I was thirty-six and hugely successful, it seemed. What was *wrong* with me? Only years later, in my fifties, was I properly diagnosed as having Bipolar Type II disorder. But I didn't know that back then, so I sought no help. I thought that, as always, duty would see me through.

I repressed what we would now call my "inner self" and went back to Jerusalem, determined to remake myself once again. I saw the other woman now and again over the next few years, but there was no way for us to be together. It would have taken me away from my marriage and my son, and it would have ruined both our careers. Today she is an accomplished professional, well known to my wife, and one of my dearest friends and confidants. This woman, a deeply spiritual person, had a profound and beneficial impact on my life. Maybe duty *is* best.

In the spring of 1970, Ernest called me one day in Cincinnati and told me that I was to be the next director of the Albright Institute in Jerusalem, not a total surprise. He said that there was no need for a job description or a search committee. As ASOR president, he had arranged it. (In those days the old boys club was the reality.) What should I do? Glueck was my first employer, but he was ill. Furthermore, as a Christian director of a Jewish institute, I was soon to be a lame duck. Ernest, however, was my *Doktorvater*, my mentor, without whom I would not even be in the field. Yet HUC had a thriving program in Israel that I had been instrumental in establishing, and HUC sponsored my dig, now among the largest and most prestigious in Israel. How could I leave all that—and for a nearly bankrupt old school in East Jerusalem, with little left but its past reputation in Jordan and a highly uncertain future in Israel?

Duty again. I accepted Ernest's off-the-record offer. But how to tell Glueck? In May I walked reluctantly up to his office and told him in a few words that I would likely be moving over to the older American School in Jerusalem, where he had been director in 1942–1947. He listened silently, his hands folded over under his chin in the usual thoughtful posture. His eyes misted over. After a long pause, he observed briefly that I was doing exactly what he had done as a young man. Then he said, "God bless you."

Rabbi and Archaeologist

Glueck died on February 12, 1971, just after *Gezer I* appeared. Back at the Jerusalem school in 1970–1971 in my last year, I gave a eulogy for Glueck in the campus synagogue. It was widely praised, but there was no manuscript and no recording. I don't remember much of what I said; It was too painful. I admired and loved Glueck, and, unlike so many others, I never had a bad experience with him. "Of blessed memory," as we say of Jews who have departed this life, because their memory lingers on. Nelson Glueck's certainly does.

Fig. 32. Nelson Glueck, cover of *Time* magazine.

Glueck's place in biblical archaeology has been much disputed. Ernest hailed his extensive surface surveys in Transjordan in the 1930s, then little-known, as "the greatest one-man achievement in the history of Palestinian archaeology." But more recent and extensive fieldwork has revealed, not surprisingly, flaws in the changes in large-scale settlement patterns that Glueck thought he could discern from surface surveys. Glueck's forte was the love of pottery that he had learned as a protege of Albright (and successor as director of the American School in Jerusalem). Moreover, these surveys suited Glueck's temperament; he was always a loner, an adventurer at heart, with a romantic attachment to the land of the Bible. He was not really patient enough to be a good field excavator.

Glueck was more an archaeological personality than a professional field archaeologist and publishing scholar, a protege of Albright in the 1920s and his successor as director of the then American School of Oriental Research in Jerusalem (1932–1947). Glueck's major achievement was his pioneering field survey of Transjordan in the 1930s–1940s, amply published in several volumes. But his excavations at Khirbet et-Tannur in Jordan (1937) and Tell Tell el-Kheleifeh (Solomon's seaport of Eziongeber, 1938–1940) were characterized by inadequate methods. In 1970, he was president of a Reform Jewish seminary, the HUC-JIR, with campuses in New York, Cincinnati, Los Angeles, and Jerusalem. It was at the latter school, beginning in 1964–1965, with Wright as visiting archaeological director, that Glueck made his comeback, envisioning the school as the counterpart in Israel of the old American School in East Jerusalem that he had directed long ago. With the launching of the long-running Gezer field project that year, Glueck's dream was beginning to come true. And like Ernest, he connected archaeology in Israel with the Bible—the *Hebrew Bible*, at an American Reform Jewish seminary. That the school came to be directed by a non-Jew—and a Christian clergyman at that—was a tribute to Glueck's ecumenical spirit. I was fortunate to have worked so closely with this larger-than-life man.

The Winter of Our Discontent

The year back in Jerusalem (1970–1971) was difficult. We could not move back into our convenient apartment at HUC and lived instead in a cramped flat on Sinai Street, in a building complex thrown up hastily after the war in the former no-man's land in Ramot Eshkol. To me, it felt like the wilderness wandering in the Sinai. We missed our support staff at the college. Now a lame duck, I could only try to finish up my duties at the college. In Cincinnati, Glueck was ailing; he died in February. I went to the office every day, and Norma was understandably preoccupied with our son Sean, now going on two. We both knew that our marriage was troubled, me more so than Norma, but we persevered. We were in no position to take any further risks. We had no real home and very little money. I was beginning to see that professional success can be poor compensation. But I still thought that I was on the fast track—if I could hold out. After all, look

Fig. 33. Moshe Dayan and I, circa 1970.

at my mentors and supporters: Albright, Wright, and Glueck. During the total of six years at HUC, because of my position I had gradually become acquainted with many Israeli archaeologists and others—especially senior people such as Benjamin Mazar, Yigael Yadin, Yohanan Aharoni, Avraham Biran, Trude and Moshe Dothan, Ruth and David Amiran, Miriam and Hayim Tadmor, Na'ama and Avraham Malamat, Miriam Rosen-Ayalon and David Ayalon, and others. All these had become my dearest friends (all of them gone now), and over the years I have been immensely grateful for their kindness to Norma and me when we were unknowns, trying to find our place in Israel.

I also began to see the younger Israeli archaeologists who later became close friends and colleagues, although at first most of them were still graduate students. These include especially the Jerusalem folk: Yigal Shiloh, Amnon Ben-Tor, Ephraim Stern, Dan Barag, Avraham Negev, and others (now all retired or deceased). There were also the Tel-Aviv archaeologists: David Ussishkin, Itzhaq Beit-Arieh, Ora Negbi, Pirhiya Beck, Ram Gophna, Moshe Kochavi, Anson Rainey, and others (most also retired or deceased now). We were all "young Turks" together.

I also came to know the ranking foreign excavators, especially after the Six-Day War: de Vaux and Kenyon. This maybe the right place to include my personal impressions of some of these famous figures.

Soldier, Scholar, Statesman

Yigael Yadin dominated archaeology in Israel in the 1960s and 1970s, world-renowned as the excavator of Hazor (1955–1958), the Judean Desert Caves of Bar Kokhba (1961), and especially the spectacular site and national shrine of Masada (1963–1965). Furthermore, as long-time head of the Department of Archaeology at the Hebrew University of Jerusalem, he trained almost the entire generation of younger archaeologists working in Israel. Yadin was Israel's equivalent of Albright and Wright in America, of Kenyon in Britain, and of de Vaux in France. He was a brilliant organizer, intuitive, charismatic, multitalented, and possessed of boundless energy.

Yigael Yadin was, quite simply, a genius. A brilliant, charismatic archaeologist for most of his career, he had also been chief of staff of the Israel Defense Forces in the 1948 war still in his twenties, then in his later years was deputy prime minister of the State of Israel. He headed the Institute of Archaeology of the Hebrew University of Jerusalem for many years and trained most of the present generation of senior Israeli archaeologists. He was the only internationally renowned superstar of Israeli archaeologists and in that capacity has no successor, even though many of his proteges are better technicians in the field and even superior scholars.

Yadin's exploits at Hazor, in the Judean Desert Caves, and at Masada made him legendary. Nevertheless, it must be said that the fact that he always had to be center stage: he left many of his deserving colleagues in the wings, and most of his students did not come into their own until he left the scene. Even with all his restless energy, Yadin did not live to complete the final publications of most of his field projects. Finally, his public quarrels with his only rival—Yohanan Aharoni, who founded the Tel Aviv Institute of Archaeology—did him no credit. Yadin may have been more brilliant (and certainly more arrogant), but Aharoni was the better person.

Nevertheless, Yadin founded the distinctive Israeli school and inspired two generations of Israeli archaeologists. On a more personal note, even though he was a formidable personage, he was very supportive of me when I was beginning, my own career in Israel—especially in our excavations at Gezer. In 1984 when we were producing further corroboration of

Fig. 34. Yigael Yadin (center) at Gezer, flanked by me and Magen Broshi on the left and Darrell Lance and Nelson Glueck on the right.

his masterful 1958 reconstruction of the Solomonic Gate at Gezer, I called him to invite him out to see the results. He was excited and promised to come, but the next day he died of a massive heart attack. He was sixty-four. My obituary for him in a major journal was entitled "Yigael Yadin: Soldier, Scholar, Statesman." Fortunately, Neil Asher Silberman later wrote a full-scale biography (1993), but even that may not have been adequate tribute to a man larger than life.It was a rare opportunity for a neophyte in archaeology such as me to get to know Yadin. In fact, I had an advantage over his own students in some ways, most of them my own age. Yadin often overwhelmed them, but he was always cordial toward me—probably because his famed nose for opportunity sensed that I was already head of a significant institution. I had also confirmed his famous identification of Solomon's City Gate at Gezer. No matter: Yadin was a memorable influence in my life in my thirties.

Once I proposed that we younger archaeologists should collaborate on a textbook in Syro-Palestinian (or biblical) archaeology. We divided up the various periods according to our special interests, and we even had the participation of some young Jordanian archaeologists. But Yadin got wind of our scheme, and he literally summoned me to his house one Saturday morning. "You cannot do this!" he said. We didn't.

Yadin was legendary for his high-handedness—but then, why not? He was one of a kind, and he was fully aware of his celebrity status. Once I was sitting next to him at the annual professional meetings of ASOR in Toronto, and we had listened to several rather boring slide presentations. When Yadin's turn came, he said to me, "Now watch this." And we all did, spellbound. Upon returning to his seat, where I was next to speak, Yadin leaned over and said, "Go get 'em, Dever!" But his act was a hard one to follow.

Yadin acceded only to one person, his wife Carmella, who efficiently managed their everyday lives and helped with his publications. If you phoned the house, you got Carmella, and unless you could explain your quest to her satisfaction, she is the only person you got. One day Yadin called to say that on Saturday he and Carmella would be on their way to their weekend place at Caesarea and would like me to give him a private tour of our current excavation at Gezer. We were not in the field on Saturday, of course, but I gladly agreed. *Any* conversation with Yadin turned into a lively seminar. I met them and was in the process of giving Yadin the grand tour, but Carmella, restless, soon broke in and declared, "Yigael has to go now." And so he did.

Pioneering the Regional Approach

I also got to know Yadin's principal rival, Yohanan Aharoni. Aharoni was a modest, unassuming man, a product of the idealistic kibbutz movement and later a leader of the nationalistic Land of Greater Israel movement. A true patriot, he was also a believer that the Hebrew Bible was Israel's real constitution. Thus his fieldwork from the earliest years focused on historical geography, based on extensive regional surveys. That focus became programmatic when he broke away from the Hebrew University in Jerusalem (and Yadin's overwhelming influence) in 1968 and founded the Institute of Archaeology at Tel Aviv University.

Despite Aharoni's tenacity, however, his fieldwork at Arad and Beersheba was flawed, and the publications that have appeared (mostly after his untimely death in 1978 at the age of fifty-three) leave much to be desired. The larger picture may be clear, but the details will probably always be disputed.

Kathleen Kenyon: Jericho and Jerusalem

I got to know some of the prominent foreign archaeologists only after the Six-Day War, of course, among them Kenyon. Dame Kathleen Kenyon was the counterpart of America's Albright, France's de Vaux, and Israel's Yadin, all of whom she overlapped in her career from Samaria in the 1930s, Jericho in the 1950s, and Jerusalem in the 1960s. She was a formidable presence, admittedly more so in fieldwork than in scholarship, and she trained and placed two generations of British archaeologists, first as director of the venerable British School of Archaeology in Jerusalem (1951–1961) and then as principal of St Hugh's College at Oxford (1962–1978).

At Gezer, we modeled our field and recording methods self-consciously on Kenyon's methods, and in that permutation these methods are found in use on the majority of excavations in Israel and Jordan, particularly American projects. Kenyon's nose for stratigraphy was celebrated, as I saw firsthand on her visits to Gezer and on frequent fieldtrips around Israel with her. I was fortunate to have known her quite well and honored to have been invited to write a recent brief biography and critical assessment. Like Albright, she was unique and has no real successors. Certainly no one would dare to imitate her. (More on Kenyon below.)

Beginning to Publish

I published several things in those years: *Gezer I* (1970), a long chapter on the EB IV period in a Festschrift for Glueck (1970), the Khirbet el-Qôm inscriptions (1969–1970), an article on vestigial features in EB IV pottery (1970; I thought it brilliant, but few ever quoted it), and a piece on the peoples of Palestine in EB IV for the *Harvard Theological Review* (1971; as close as I ever got to theology). I also published several tributes to older colleagues in Festschrift volumes: for Noel Freedman (1983), Olga Tufnell (1985), Joe Callaway (1988), and my own teachers Wright (1976) and Cross (1987).

One piece I published, in 1973, was a brief article in *Christian News from Israel* entitled "'Biblical Archaeology'—or 'The Archaeology of Syria-

Palestine'?" It was my first shot across the bow in what would become a long war, attempting to secularize our branch of archaeology. It was becoming increasingly clear that, in order to move beyond our amateur status, we had to separate archaeology from theology. We had already begun the divorce in our work at Gezer, sponsored entirely by nonsectarian funding and with a staff that was far removed from the typical clerical staff at Shechem. Norma warned me that this was a topic too hot to handle, but I replied, "It's in a semipopular, Christian-oriented magazine published in Israel; no one will ever see it." But Ernest saw it, and he wrote an anguished letter to me as though I were the prodigal son. Ernest was the father of biblical archaeology (even more so than Albright). In the last sentence of his letter, Ernest warned me, "You've got to get right with Albright!" With all due respect, it sounded like a toothpaste commercial to me. Within a few months, I was drafting the upcoming 1973 Winslow Lectures at Seabury Western Theological Seminary, published in 1974 as *Archaeology and Biblical Studies: Retrospects and Prospects*. The die was cast.

As I look back on these early publications, I realize why I was becoming prominent. They were well researched and written, but most of all, these publications had *ideas*, as well as a nascent vision for the field. I had the native talent, the training, the focus, the capacity for hard work, the right teachers and mentors, the best connections, an enviable institutional base. Why wasn't this enough? I don't know, except that I was too restless. But the manic energy that fueled me (which I still didn't comprehend) was about to run out.

The Last Season at Gezer: Moving On

The 1971 season at Gezer went as planned, even though it would be the end of Phase I, and I was scheduled to transfer over to the Albright halfway through the season. We finished the large exposure in Field VI on the acropolis as well as our work in the so-called Solomonic Gate in Field III. Among the student volunteers that season was a young graduate student in my old department at Harvard, Pamela Gaber. I had met her earlier, in the spring of 1969. I advertised the April dig in a flyer sent around at the Hebrew University, where she was doing her junior year abroad. She showed up one day on the front steps of the college, inquiring about the

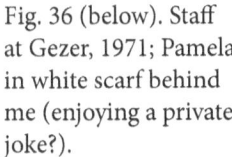

Fig. 35. Pamela (left) at Gezer, spring 1969.

Fig. 36 (below). Staff at Gezer, 1971; Pamela in white scarf behind me (enjoying a private joke?).

dig. I recall saying to her, "My dear, I'm sorry, but we don't take undergraduate students." She flashed an electric smile, tossed her dark hair, and said, "But I'm a quick study." So she was.

I discovered the spring volunteer list when going through the college files in 2004, and there is listed a certain "Paula Garber" with a question mark after her name. The question remained for twenty years. But in 1971 I got to know Pamela better, and we became close friends—as close as the distance between us in the Gezer staff picture that year (the outtakes are even more suggestive).

Before leaving the HUC era, I cannot refrain from a few more stories about Glueck. Once when I went down to the airport to meet him (it was like meeting royalty), I found him at customs, furious. He had brought a Torah scroll for the synagogue at the college, forgetting that imported Torahs are not kosher. I tried to explain: "But this is Nelson Glueck." Nothing doing. Up to Jerusalem we went, but no Torah scroll. A few days later, the Christian fellows at the college wondered whether, since it was Christmas, they could have a Hanukkah bush. So I went to the Jewish Agency with two requests from HUC, already under suspicion. One was a petition to get Glueck's Torah scroll out of hock; the other was for a Christmas tree from the Memorial Forests. (The latter was not as outrageous as it sounds: the Jewish Agency does provide a limited number of Christmas trees as a gesture of goodwill toward non-Jews.) We got both!

Another day we were on a field trip to the Negev. On the way from Beersheba to Arad, we stopped near a makeshift shanty town where Arab Bedouin had been settled by the army. As we approached some traditionally robed bystanders, Glueck began to remonstrate with them. "What are you doing living in galvanized tin shacks? Don't you have any pride? Be a *real* Arab!" (The word *Arab* means a true "son of the desert," not a despised *fellah* or town-person.) I will never forget that spectacle: an American rabbi lecturing Bedouin on how to be real Arabs—in fluent Arabic. (After all, Glueck had spent years in the 1930s and 1940s living among Arabs and exploring Transjordan).

At the Albright

The first weekend in July of 1971, Norma, Sean, and I moved into the director's house at the Albright Institute in East Jerusalem. The move was so carefully coordinated (and staged) that by the afternoon of Saturday we had transformed the elegant three-story wing of the old building. The drab institutional furniture was gone, replaced by the elegant Danish modern furniture, oriental carpets, antique copper, new lighting fixtures, and dramatic crimson drapes and valances that we had preassembled. That night Norma and I hosted a formal reception for the Gezer staff, with an open bar, the women in long gowns. I was determined to change the dowdy image of the Albright (although Albright himself was probably turning over in his grave). It was the first of many grand dinners and parties that we gave during the next four years, often doing part of the cooking ourselves. I suppose that's how many remember the Dever era.

The truth of the matter is that we had no choice: there was little else that we could do. We had a budget of less than $40,000 a year, barely

Fig. 37. The director's house at the W. F. Albright Institute of Archaeological Resarch in Jerusalem.

enough to pay staff. There was nothing for field trips or even for the library the first year or so. There were only a few resident fellows, the hostel and dining room often almost empty except for the three of us. The trustees, in their infinite wisdom (or self-interests?), had forbidden me to excavate, so with increasing frustration I watched Joe Seger across the city at HUC, with a staff, a real archaeological institute, and an excavation—my excavation! Already I was beginning to question the wisdom of Ernest, whose influence and health were now declining, leaving me to fend for myself with a board of trustees that seemed to be rivals rather than supporters.

That fall was ominous in another way, far more significant than my growing discontent. In September, de Vaux, at the École Biblique around the corner, whom I had looked forward to knowing better as a colleague, died suddenly at the age of sixty-eight. I had always thought that a Frenchman should die either in the bedroom or the kitchen. De Vaux, a Dominican monk, died, as it were, in the kitchen. He had been cooking something, slipped on the floor, developed a thrombosis that moved to his heart, and died in the French Hospital in Sheikh Jarrah.

His funeral was a celebration of his life. All the clergy and the diplomatic corps of Jerusalem were there, many elegantly robed. Père Benoit, de Vaux's longtime colleague, played the organ, led the prayers, and gave the eulogy. De Vaux lay in the chancel in a plain wooden box, looking composed but a bit green since there was no embalming in Jerusalem, and

Fig. 38. Père Roland de Vaux at Gezer.

it had been several days. At the close of the service, several Arab staff came up to the box with a hammer, nailed the lid on, and carried the coffin out through the garden, the crowd following. At the back of the compound was the underground crypt where the good fathers of the École, far from home, had been buried for nearly one hundred years. There we interred de Vaux, just above the crypts of his distinguished predecessors in archaeology, Père Marie-Joseph LaGrange (1855–1938) and Père Louis-Hugues Vincent (1872–1960). Dame Kathleen Kenyon, a close friend of de Vaux's, had come out from Oxford, and with her and others we had tea and cookies in the churchyard. It was not a funeral as much as a celebration of a life lived in purest devotion to a great cause.

I remember one night when we gave a dinner at the director's house for a number of guests, including de Vaux (just a few weeks before he died) and the director of the British School, Crystal Bennett. Scarcely had dessert been served when Crystal announced that de Vaux was not feeling well, so she would walk him home. Much later, as I was delivering other guests to their homes, I spotted de Vaux and Crystal walking along a side street, talking animatedly.

By strange coincidence, Albright died within ten days of de Vaux. What should I, a young scholar only now getting settled in as his successor at the institute bearing his name, do to commemorate this giant of a scholar? Above, I have described my all-to-modest tribute, including a memorial service. It was the second of several memorial services that I would come to lead, as I had recently done for Glueck and now for his teacher and, by extension, mine.

In late December of 1971 I was brought to the States for trustees' meetings, held at the Harvard Club in New York City. However, I was excluded from the major meetings and not even informed of the results. When the trustees emerged from their breakfast meeting, I was hanging around, so I asked if I might know their decisions. I was told that "matters had been taken care of." I gave a brief, admittedly downbeat, report at another meeting, but no action was taken. Norma and I spent New Year's Eve in Times Square with Darrell Lance, pretty well frozen all around.

I was granted a two-month home leave in the winter of 1972–1973 (no vacations were in my contract). Having no home to go to, I volunteered my time to do a promotional tour on behalf of ASOR. Philip King arranged the tour, on which during five weeks on the road I gave forty-five lectures coast to coast. There was no remuneration, and if there was a thank-you letter I don't recall it. But it was on that trip that I made many of the connections that would stand me in good stead later. I also delivered the Winslow Lectures of Seabury-Western Theological Seminary, which helped to focus my growing suspicions about traditional-style biblical archaeology (published in 1974). I also saw both women who by now loomed so large in my consciousness, confused as it was.

To be sure, back at the Albright in 1970, there were a few fellows with whom it was a pleasure to work. One year the only hostel residents were Larry Stager and Jim Sauer, both working assiduously on their dissertations so that we often saw them only for meals in the dining room. Larry, who had begun his field experience under me at Gezer, did a small dig that year in the Buqeiah wilderness, east of Bethlehem. As his dissertation on that topic was nearing completion at Harvard, he was called to a position at the Oriental Institute of the University of Chicago. From there he went on to the Dorot chair at Harvard, as well as to excavations at Carthage in Tunisia, Idalion in Cyprus, and, finally, more than twenty years directing the excavations at Ashkelon. Larry died in January 2018 at the age of seventy-five. Jim finished his dissertation on Islamic pottery, went on to direct the American School (ACOR) in Jordan, then to a professorship at the University of Pennsylvania, and, finally, to the presidency of the

American Schools of Oriental Research (1982–1988). Unfortunately, Jim died of Huntington's disease at age forty-one.

Another year we were fortunate to have in residence the codirectors of the great Bâb edh-Dhrâ project in Jordan, Walter Rast and Tom Schaub. Although they worked in Jordan, they were warmly welcomed by Israeli colleagues and had a very productive year. Both are deceased now, but they published the site fully.

One year the only resident fellows were two women scholars. One was Suzanne Richard, who had done her Hopkins dissertation on the end of the Early Bronze Age under my direction, and now we coauthored an article on Albright's old Stratum J at Tell Beit Mirsim. Suzanne went on to Drew University, then to Gannon College (her alma mater). She has also carried out major excavations at Khirbet Iskander in Jordan since 1981, one of the few sites in the country directed by a woman, directing long-running excavations that have revolutionized our understanding of the EB IV period.

One young archeologist with whom I met regularly for a seminar was not a fellow of the Albright at all but had remained behind at HUC to coordinate the ongoing Gezer publication effort. Sy Gitin finished his dissertation under my guidance on the Iron Age, Persian, and Hellenistic pottery of Gezer in 1978, then became (as noted above) my successor as director at the Albright in 1980.

We also saw a great deal of our younger Israeli and British colleagues—often, I confess, at rather rowdy dancing and drinking parties that went on well into the wee hours. We were all at turning points in our careers, frustrated at being held back (so we thought), and in some cases struggling with personal relationships. There was a certain air of desperation at these parties that gave them a frenzied vitality. We danced away the night as though there was no tomorrow. I began to think that maybe there was none for me.

Yet I did manage to do some fieldwork, under the guise of two brief salvage campaigns back at Shechem, with the connivance of Ernest. In the fall of 1972 and again in 1973, I reexcavated (and duly consolidated) the famous Northwest Gate at Shechem, untangling the old German stratigraphy to reveal a Middle Bronze Age Palace, temple, and barracks. I had a workforce of only a half-dozen hired Arab laborers from Balaṭah, among them Abu Issa and Jabber, who had worked with me at Shechem in 1962–1964 and again at Khirbet el-Qôm in 1968–1971. I did all the surveying, drew all the plans and sections, took all the photographs, and washed and registered all the pottery. After being the CEO of a large excavation such as Gezer, this one-man show was delightful—and a boost for my sagging ego. A born dirt archaeologist, not a hostel keeper, I was in the field again. For the most part, however, the trustees (and Ernest as well) saw the director in Jerusalem as a facilitator, someone to enable other archaeologists to do their work. During my tenure I was expected to support, help to coordinate, and keep the books for several ASOR-affiliated field projects—most of them, ironically, staffed by the very people I had helped to train at Gezer. These included the work of James Strange at Sepphoris in Galilee; Carol and Eric Meyers at Khirbet Shema and Meiron, synagogue sites in Galilee; John Worrell, L. E. Toombs, and others at Tell el-Ḥesi near the Gaza Strip; and Robert Bull and others at Tell er-Ras and Caesarea (below). The directors were all friends, and I did my best to make them at home at the Albright. But those budgets that came from Smithsonian counterpart funds were sometimes mismanaged, and at least once I refused to sign the audit. I never had any real input, and I visited the digs in the summer with only my own credentials as an experienced field archaeologist to give me any authority. It was very frustrating.

War Again

The Saturday after I returned from the brief fall 1973 season at Shechem, while I was taking a nap, I was awakened by air-raid sirens going off. It was Yom Kippur, the holiest day of the Jewish year. What fool had set the alarms off? But as I got up and joined Norma and Darrell Lance (the annual professor) in the courtyard, the Arab staff informed us solemnly: "We're at war." Who is *we*? And *what* war? As it turned out, the Yom Kippur war lasted some three weeks and was nearly a disaster for Israel. For us, now in Arab East Jerusalem, with an all-Arab staff, it was not only our second war but one filled with ambiguity and uncertainty.

We were under a strict curfew, all lights blackened out after dark. Not having much to do, I built a harpsichord from a Zuckerman kit that I had imported some time ago. (When I left Jerusalem, I gave it to the synagogue at HUC, and there for some time it played to the glory of Yahweh.) At night, after an early dinner and the Arab staff's departure for home, we all sat outdoors in the quiet garden, listening in the dark to music I had piped out from the director's house. Sometimes I played sad songs, full of *Weltschmerz:* Mahler's "Das Klagende Lied," "Lieder eines fahrenden Gesellen," "Das Lied von der Erde," and even the unbearable "Kindertotenlieder" (Songs on the Death of Children). So we got through the 1973 war. Once again, Israel, with last-minute American help, miraculously prevailed.

I was losing my own war. By now I was increasingly withdrawn, often working all night in my study upstairs in the director's house, sleeping much of the rest of the time, leaving the day-to-day oversight of the institute to Norma. I confess that I neglected my son, now four turning five. Work was the only therapy I knew for my malaise (surely not an illness!), but I drank too much while on these all-night vigils. When I reviewed the fervid scribbled pages in the calm light of day, it was obvious that some of the brilliant stuff was nonsense. Nevertheless, by the sheer force of the output I produced some of my best early work in these years. In 1974 there appeared the Winslow Lectures at Seabury-Western Theological Seminary, *Archaeology and Biblical Studies: Retrospects and Prospects*, and the same year a large final dig report, *Gezer II*. In 1972 and 1973, publications on EB IV continued my original interests there but expanded now to a new concern: methodology, especially where biblical archaeology was concerned. Excavation reports of Shechem and Khirbet el-Kirmil also appeared (1974, 1975).

In addition to writing voluminously, I was also able to teach some (despite its name, the Albright *School* was only a research institute). I taught now and then in the summer school for overseas students of the Hebrew University of Jerusalem. Since I had no proper academic title, I had also been appointed as adjunct professor (*in absentia*) at my old alma mater, the Christian Theological Seminary in Indianapolis. On home leave I would give a few lectures there, but often a Freudian slip gave away my real feelings. I would inadvertently speak of "theological cemeteries." This Christian boy was a long way from his roots. I no longer went to church at all. Although I didn't know it, I had relapsed.

I was alienated from the board of trustees and their policies, from the biblical traditions of most of our constituents, from everything that was happening in America in those years, alienated even from my family. I still thought about the other woman, although the relationship was obviously doomed. Nowadays we would say that I was in denial, but I had never heard that term. I continued to drink heavily. I neglected my appearance. I became so volatile that the slightest thing might set me off. I frightened even myself. I became suicidal.

Finally, friends and family urged me to see a psychiatrist. Once I did, he listened but said nothing (at $80 an hour). I left thinking that he was crazier than I was. I resolved to grit my teeth and just try harder. Duty once more, this time with a capital *D*. There were those who might have helped me, including Norma, but we were now largely estranged. There was talk of a divorce, and at one point Norma almost packed up to go home to her parents' house in Virginia. I asked her to stay and soldiered on, perhaps bravely, but certainly foolishly.

In 1974 several events intervened to shock me into reality. We were sitting at dinner one evening in August when Omar the cook came in to say I had a telephone call in the kitchen. It was the president of the Albright Institute, Phil King: Ernest was dead, at the age of sixty-four. I was stunned. Ernest was my mentor, a father figure, my last connection with anyone in ASOR who sympathized with my dreams. A few days later, I gave a eulogy for him in a service I arranged at St Andrew's Scottish Presbyterian Church, where we had both been elders and where our son Sean had been dedicated. Halfway through I choked up and could barely continue. People may not believe me, but not a day goes by that I do not think of Ernest. Without him, I would never have been in this field. But I never dedicated a book to him until 2001, because I never thought I had done anything worthy. Finally, my 2001 book *What Did the Biblical Writers Know and When Did They Know It?* was dedicated to him. The dedication reads simply:

For Ernest Wright (1909–1974)
My teacher

When Ernest Wright died, I knew that it was over, at least for me at the Albright in Jerusalem. Sure enough, a few weeks later some of the trustees came to Jerusalem and informed me in so many words that I was fired. They forced me to resign even though I had another year on my contract. When they got back to the States, they used Norma's unwitting private plea of desperation to one of them that our marriage was on the rocks. They threatened me with a scandal if I did not resign immediately. Beaten, and psychologically unable to resist any longer, I capitulated. I had no home, no job, no money, no mentor, no connections back in the States, and apparently no family. Although I didn't realize it until much later, I was in a deep clinical depression. There seemed no way out. I was forty years old and alone, or so it seemed.

In early December, I received a phone call from the University of Arizona. Rabbi Albert Bilgray, head of the fledgling Judaic Studies program, asked me to come to Tucson for a job interview. I said I didn't even know where Arizona was, and I wasn't in the mood to go prospecting. Besides—Judaic Studies? But Bilgray said to come at their expense and give a lecture or two. I had no choice, since nothing else was on the horizon. (Later I would learn that Arnold Band at UCLA, together with my friend from Gezer days, Eric Meyers, had cooked up this scheme.)

While I was planning reluctantly for this trip in December, another phone call came, this time from my sister Myrna, telling me that Mother was in the hospital in a coma, dying. I discussed this with Norma and Sean, now five. Sean thought about this for a minute, then asked if Grandmother (he hardly knew her) would die. I said that she was a strong woman but that she was very ill and might die. Again Sean took that in quite solemnly. Then he said: "Well, tell her that if she dies and sees God, she should tell him that I'm okay." As though God had nothing else on his mind.

In early January I flew to the States for the interviews, stopping over for a few days in Johnson City and hoping to see my mother before it was too late. But she never recovered consciousness. I stayed until the last minute, taking turns at the hospital with my sister. My mother was sixty-four. The day after the funeral, I flew to Tucson and gave the first of two lectures, one public and the other for the famed Department of Anthropology. I have no memory of what I said. The morning I was to leave, I had breakfast with President John Schaeffer and Dean Paul Rosenblatt. They said they wanted me to come to Arizona and offered me an associate professorship. Since I didn't want to come in any case, I answered recklessly, "No—a full professorship." I had never held any academic position except the sort of sham adjunct professorship at Christian Theological Seminary. Suprisingly, they agreed, and we talked briefly about salary and shook hands. That was it. A new life was about to begin—my seventh. I went back to Jerusalem, and we started making arrangements to leave at the end of June.

Fig. 39. The living room of the Albright Institute director's house during our time.

The Better Days at the Albright

I do have some good memories of the Albright. I have already mentioned the American fellows whose early progress I was privileged to share. There were also the acquaintances with Israeli colleagues that deepened during those years. With the younger archaeologists there were those parties (!), but we also shared more serious social activities and joint projects of sorts. Our families spent many pleasurable times together, and to this day these archaeologists are among the closest friends I have. I grew up with the second generation of Israeli archaeologists, most of whom became directors of their own excavations and leaders in the field. During summers, since I was not excavating, I was free to visit Israeli digs, and I have the most pleasant memories of field trips.

Usually I would call up Israeli biblical and Semitics colleagues such as Jonas Greenfield, Avraham Malamat, and others, and off we would go in the Albright station wagon for a day or two. The gossip in the car was memorable, and often I learned more from the academic chitchat than from the trenches. The major Israeli projects in the early-mid 1970s were Akko, Arad, Ashod, Beersheba, Dan, and Second Temple sites (more below), as well as many salvage excavations in Jerusalem. I saw them all frequently. The first-hand knowledge (and the slides) from these excavations made me the American who was best informed on Israeli

Fig. 40. Reception in the garden of the Albright Institute, with Omar at the table and Ernest and guest at the far left.

archaeology, later enriching my teaching of graduate students for twenty-five years.

The highlight of the summers was always the visit of Ernest, who was president of ASOR until near the end of my tenure as director in Jerusalem. I would meet Ernest at the airport and install him at the luxurious American Colony Hotel around the corner from the school (which was too spartan for a man with a heart condition). We would tour digs as Ernest was able, where he was always received with the respect reserved for the grand old man of American archaeology. I was delighted to chauffer him around, and along the way the two of us would talk.

Ernest was too reserved to be as close as I was later to my graduate students. (It took me forever to call him by his first name.) But one day, in his last visit in the summer of 1974, he seemed to want to talk more personally, apparently sensing his own mortality. He said to me, "You know, the tragedy of my life is that my biblical colleagues dismissed me as an archaeologist, and my archaeological colleagues dismissed me as a biblicist." I listened quietly, saying to myself, "Ernest, you should have chosen." I *did*, as most of his other students also did. By that time, no one, not even an Albright, could have combined archaeology and biblical studies. But Ernest was Parkman Professor of Divinity at Harvard, a widely published Old Testament theologian, *and* the most prominent archaeologist of Jordan and Israel in North America. When I and others of his early students, all clergymen, defected from theology to archaeology, we always explained: "Not defrocked, just unsuited." But Ernest died a believer. (Sometimes I wonder if I ever really was.)

I recall most vividly the receptions we gave for Ernest in the lush garden of the Albright. We would invite up to two hundred people, including Israelis, the directors of all the foreign schools, and Arabs and Christians from East Jerusalem; the Albright was one of the few neutral places where such an ecumenical group could gather. Omar and the staff would work for days, preparing Eastern and Western delicacies, and we always had an open bar (even though that threatened to break the budget). I would have Mozart playing in the background, the tiled fountain in the garden with its cascade of pumped water providing an accompaniment. Norma and I would stand with Ernest at the entrance to the garden, greeting guests by name (and prompting Ernest as necessary). Even the Israelis would dress up.

Norma and I were always decked out, I in blue blazer and white flannels, she in a long gown. After the older guests began to trickle away late in the evening, I would change the music, and the younger people would begin to dance in the now-darkened garden. That last summer evening, Ernest finally had to sit down, after an exhausting appearance on stage. Norma asked him to dance, but Ernest, an unsophisticated Midwestern boy at heart, declined. "I don't know how to dance," he said apologetically, "but if I did, I would want to dance with you." A few days later, I took him to the airport. We never saw him again. Shortly thereafter, we learned of his death. I don't think I've danced much since.

I have already introduced some stories about Ernest. He had been Albright's most promising protege, with brilliant publications on the pottery of ancient Palestine in the late 1930s that quickly established him as the leading authority of that essential archaeological discipline. But his only

Fig. 41. G. Ernest Wright at Harvard Divinity School.

opportunity for fieldwork came with participation in Albright's excavations at Tell Beit Mirsim in 1934. He began teaching at the McCormick Presbyterian Theological Seminary in Chicago as an ordained clergyman. During the Second War he turned his attention more to biblical studies, having founded and continued to edit the journal *Biblical Archaeologist*, followed by a 1945 biblical atlas with Floyd Filson, and a best-selling handbook, *Biblical Archaeology* (1957). Indeed the name *biblical archaeology* that soon defined the field, at least in America, was due more to Ernest's influence than Albright's, who often continued to speak of *Syro-Palestinian archaeology*. But Ernest then began to publish articles and books on Old Testament history and theology, such as *The Challenge of Israel's Faith* (1944), *The Old Testament against Its Environment* (1950), and particularly *God Who Acts: Biblical Theology as Recital* (1952). He became a leading spokesman for the neo-orthodox theology movement that was sweeping Europe and America in the uncertainties of the postwar years, especially active in worldwide ecumenical affairs.

It was not until 1956 that he mounted the Drew-McCormick expedition to biblical Shechem, near Nablus (continuing as director through 1966). But the next year, in 1957, he had a serious heart attack at the age of forty-eight, and he was never again in vigorous good health. Distracted by his new duties at Harvard as Parkman Professor of Divinity after 1958, and especially his presidency of ASOR in 1966–1974, Ernest never returned to the field. Nor was he able to publish any major archaeological works, not even any of the final Shechem report volumes. He authored only a popular book in 1965, *Shechem, The Biography of a Biblical City*. Yet Ernest's finest achievement during the 1960s–early 1970s may have been as the teacher and mentor of nearly the entire generation of the now senior American archaeologists in the field, many of them trained further at Gezer, which had, after all, been his own brainchild. His legacy lives on, even though his vision of biblical archaeology has been radically altered—and mostly by his own students. To his credit, in his last few years Ernest foresaw the challenge of the new archaeology and even seemed to welcome it in a few articles such as "What Archaeology Can and Cannot Do" (1971) and another on "The New Archaeology" (1975; published posthumously). Ernest was unique; he has no successor, though many admirers, not least of all me.

We made other friends from the American consulate and among *New York Times* reporters. Also while at the Albright we had many family times with Sean and took several memorable trips—to Turkey, England, Italy, Greece, and to the United States and back. Sean was a wonderful traveler, tireless and interested in everything. I remember when driving along the southern coast of Turkey toward the end of the day Sean would say, "Dad, it's time to look for a cheap, decent little hotel." And we would, usually overlooking the sea, eating in the hotel's tiny restaurant, enjoying the catch of the day.

Other summer visits were also memorable. Dame Kathleen Kenyon, whom I have already introduced, was the doyenne of British archaeologists and excavator of Samaria, Jericho, and Jerusalem. But she had retired as director of the British School in Jerusalem just around the corner before I became director at the Albright, decamping to St Hugh's College at Oxford to become principal there. Crystal Bennett was now the director, but summers she was off to direct her own digs in Jordan, so as the ranking foreign archaeologists it fell to me to tour Kenyon around digs in Israel. We would also host a reception for her at the Albright, where she could hold court for the Israelis, with whom she had a rather distant relationship. One day we visited her protege Père Jean Prignaud from the École Biblique, who had been her doctoral student at Oxford. He was directing a dig at Tell Keisan in northern Israel, and he had worked heroically to have his balks—the sides of his trenches—dressed and tagged in proper Kenyon fashion. She listened with growing impatience as he explained down in the square how various features in the section went. Finally she bellowed, "Nonsense!," jumped down into the area, opened her purse to grab her fabled Marshalltown No. 5 trowel, and began slashing away at his balk. "You fool—don't you see? It goes this way!" I thought poor Prignaud was going to break into tears. But knowing Kenyon, he had put out on the lunch table a full bottle of Gordon's gin (her favorite), and after lunch she and I went merrily on our way.

Fig. 42. Dame Kathleen Kenyon's visit to Gezer in 1967.

In fact, I had seen Dame Kathleen in action similarly a few years earlier, when she visited us at Gezer in 1967. We expected to give her a polite celebrity tour, but she leapt right down into one of our deep squares and proceeded to show us how our section should be interpreted. She was right, of course.

That summer I invited her to dinner at our apartment at HUC, the first of several social occasions I enjoyed with her. I became bold enough to ask her whether the influence of her father, who was a distinguished scholar of ancient papyri and a director of the British Museum, had influenced her to go into biblical archaeology. She drew herself up to her formidable bulk and harrumphed, "Absolutely not!" In fact, her real mentor was the legendary British archaeologist Sir Mortimer Wheeler, and she had become well known for field excavations in Britain and in North Africa before turning to Palestine in the 1930s (at Samaria).

The 1970s: Coming of Age

At this point, let me summarize some of the principal trends in archaeology in Israel in the 1970s, both Israeli and American. First, excavation projects grew further, in both numbers and scope, especially as the second generation discussed above came into their own, with their own first digs. Hebrew University's Amnon Ben-Tor was doing a regional project in the southern Jezreel Valley, excavating several sites: Tel Qiri (1975–1978), the great mound of Yoqneam (1977–1988), and nearby Tel Qashish (1978–1980). Also for the Hebrew University, Ephraim Stern would soon begin long-running excavations at Dor on the Carmel coast, a major Phoenician site (1980–1991), and Mevorakh on the coast north of Tel Aviv (1973–1976). Yigal Shiloh, a rising star and Yadin's protege, began work in the City of David that would occupy him for the rest of his life (1978–1987, the latter the year of his death at age fifty-one). Finally, two grand old men of the first generation of Hebrew University began large-scale excavations in Jerusalem: Benjamin Mazar around the Temple Mount (1968–1979) and Nahman Avigad in the soon-to-be-restored Jewish Quarter (1969–1982, the latter the year of his death). Another veteran of the Hebrew University, Trude Dothan, was excavating Deir al-Balah, an outpost in the Gaza strip (1972–1981).

A younger Hebrew University archaeologist, really of the upcoming third generation (below), was Amihai Mazar, a nephew of Benjamin Mazar. He began almost annual excavations for the first time at Philistine Tel Qasile (where the elder Mazar had worked) in 1971 (through 1974), then moved to Philistine Tel Batash (biblical Timnah, 1977–1989) and to the early Israelite site of Giloh, in the suburbs of modern Jerusalem (1978–1982). Finally, Ehud Metzer and Lou Levine carried out further exploration at Caesarea (1975–1979).

The rival Institute of Archaeology in Tel Aviv now launched larger projects: that of Israel Finkelstein and Moshe Kochavi at Shiloh (1976–1978), of Kochavi at Tel Aphek at the head of the Yarkon Valley (1972–1985), of Aharon Kempinski at the Iron I site of Tel Masos in the northern Negev (1972–1975), and of Itzhaq Beit-Arieh at Tel 'Ira, also in the Negev (1977–1981), the latter following Aharoni's long-time focus on Negev regional projects. Eliezer Oren directed excavations at the northwestern Negev site of Tel Sera' (possibly biblical Ziklag, 1972–1979), the first field project of the recently established Ben-Gurion University of the Negev—now the third Israeli university with an Institute of Archaeology. Steve Rosen, an ex-American prehistorian, joined the growing faculty in Beersheba and later became dean.

Although affiliated with none of the universities, Rudolph Cohen, district officer for the Negev, conducted extensive surveys at Early Bronze IV and Nabbatean/Byzantine sites in the Negev Highlands, as well as at Yeruham (1973–; see also Be'er Resisim below).

For Tel Aviv University, we should note David Ussishkin's long-running excavations at the massive Judean fortress of Lachish (1973–1987), Ze'ev Herzog at Tel Michal (1977–1980), and another rising star, Israel Finkelstein, at the early Israelite site of 'Izbet Ṣarṭah, near Petah Tikva (biblical Ebenezer?, 1976–1978). Although not affiliated with any university, Shmaryahu Gutman's clearance of the Jewish settlement and synagogue at Gamla, on the Golan Heights (1976–), revealed dramatic insights into the period of the First Revolt in 66–70 CE.

There were also several foreign excavations in the 1970s. Gezer continued through 1973 (directed in 1972–1973 by Joe D. Seger). Two American offshoots of Gezer, the senior staffs trained there, now launched projects of their own. Eric and Carol Meyers, with James Strange, began a long-running project focused on Galilean synagogues with excavations at Khirbet

Shema near Safad in Upper Galilee (1970–1972; see further below on other projects of the 1980s), and John Worrell and other Gezerites began work at Petrie's old site of Tell el-Ḥesi, in the northwestern Negev (possibly biblical Eglon, 1970–1983). Another Gezerite, Joe Seger, excavated at Tel Ḥalif in the Shephelah between 1970 and 1989. After my work at Gezer (1964–1971), I moved on to carry out joint salvage excavations with Rudolph Cohen at the large EB IV campsite of Be'er Resisim, in the Central Negev Highlands (1978–1980). Work at Shechem in the West Bank ended with brief campaigns in the Middle Bronze palace and temple that I directed (1972–1973), and the old excavations of Callaway at Ai ended with brief campaigns in 1971 and 1972. At Tell el-Ḥesi, excavations begun in 1970 continued until 1983 (now under Glen Rose). The Joint Excavations at Caesarea began in 1971 (through 1980) under the direction of Robert Bull and Lawrence Toombs, old Shechem hands. Finally, Gus van Beek of the Smithsonian Institution resumed Petrie's old excavations at Tell Jemmeh (1970–1990). All these American excavations in the 1970s were affiliated with the Albright Institute in Jerusalem, which I directed 1971–1975, so their staffs and excavations results were quite familiar to me.

The American excavations at Anafa (above) continued under Sharon Herbert, with Saul Weinberg (1978–1981). The only other foreign excavations in Israel in the 1970s were those at the large mound of Keisan on the Plain of Akko, directed by proteges of Kenyon, Pères Jean Prignaud, Jacques Briend, and Jean-Baptiste Humbert (1971–1980).

The excavations of the 1970s, both Israeli and American, revealed several clearly established trends. These included renewed excavations at older sites, particularly among American excavators (Gezer, Shechem, Ai, Caesarea, Ḥesi, Jemmeh), but also Israeli projects (Jerusalem, Aphek, Qasile). There were, however, some excavations begun at virgin sites (Mevorakh, Batash, Michal, Sera'). Smaller sites now began to attract more attention, as resources became scarce (Kitan, 'Ira). One-period sites, although small, showed their potential ('Izbet Ṣarṭah and Giloh, both early Israelite; and Be'er Resisim). Regional and survey projects were now better established (those of Ben-Tor in the Jezreel Valley and of Meyers and others in Galilee; in addition, the growing volumes of the Archaeological Survey of Israel, now in the dozens).

I would argue that it was not until the 1970s and 1980s that newer archaeological theories and methods, such as those pioneered at Gezer in the 1960s in the spirit of the new archaeology elsewhere, began to have an impact. *Gezer I* was published in 1970, and although it was a preliminary report, it demonstrated what we were doing (or thought we were doing). Then in 1973 both Yohanan Aharoni and I published side-by-side articles in the Israeli periodical *Eretz-Israel* (appropriately, the Dunayevsky volume), sharply contrasting American and Israeli methods. I then followed up with the publication of *A Manual of Field Excavations: Handbook for Field Archaeologists* (1978, with H. Darrell Lance), then a long, fully documented article on the new archaeology and its impact in the *Bulletin of the American Schools of Oriental Research* (1981).

Thus the dialogue, such as it was, began. Nevertheless, the impact on actual fieldwork was minimal. We Americans preferred smaller, more meticulous excavation of debris layers, typically in 5-meter squares, illustrated by copious and detailed measured section drawings and paying close attention to sherds. Teamwork was emphasized, with core staffs (as at Gezer) or several codirectors. The Israelis persisted in large-scale exposures and architecturally defined strata, with the recovery of larger quantities of restorable pottery. Few sections were drawn, and fewer still were published (some merely photographs).

Neither the Israelis nor the Americans were yet publishing prompt final reports, but brief reports of nearly all digs appeared in "Notes and News" of the *Israel Exploration Journal* (1950–), as well as in *Hadashot Arkhelogiyot* (Hebrew 1982–; later in English), and *Atiqot*, a periodical of the Israel Antiquities Authority, in both Hebrew and English versions, had reached more than forty volumes by 2000. A new series of excavation reports launched by the Hebrew University of Jerusalem in 1975, *Qedem*, was particularly instrumental in the prompt publication of dig reports. Finally, in 1973 the Institute of Archaeology at Tel Aviv University began publishing its own journal, *Tel Aviv*.

The increased pace and scope of publications did, of course, facilitate some degree of conversation on method per se, since we could now see results—what really counts—much better. Theory, however, remained virtually off the record. The Israelis typically regarded theory with suspicion, as though it were merely speculation, usually unbridled, an American affectation. Even today, some Israeli archaeologists remain skeptical. They are admittedly pragmatists, for whom theory is largely irrelevant. Good technicians, they are not given to introspection. One of my closest colleagues remarked to me when I tried recently to discuss theory with him: "Nu, Dever.... Once you were an archaeologist [i.e., a digger], but now you've become a philosopher!" In other words, epistemology is not our concern; we *know* what we're doing. Another close colleague, Ephraim Stern, remarked in an article in 1987 that Israelis "connect directly and emotionally" with their past. Perhaps that's the problem.

Going Home

Norma, Sean, and I left Jerusalem in July of 1975. I had bargained for a buyout: ASOR had to pay for shipping our effects (and us) home. When the director's house was empty, we tried to furnish it as well as we could for our successors, but it was sad. We did sell a beautiful rosewood dining suite, with two breakfronts, table and chairs for ten, and a large buffet to the school. The night before we left, I stayed up until 3 am putting the finishing touches on the manuscript of the Gezer *Manual of Field Excavations* that was later published (see above). At dawn the Arab staff gathered to see us off, including faithful Omar and our housekeeper Rose. Edward, the majordomo, drove us to the airport.

That afternoon we were ensconced in a bed-and-breakfast on the island of Mykonos, exhausted and in a state of limbo. A few days later we arrived at Johnson City and my sister's house, also visiting Norma's parents in southwest Virginia. We had stored some things there, so I had a U-Haul to pull all the way to Arizona. Our furniture would arrive in Los Angles several weeks later, so we had nothing much with which to set up a household. I had no idea what lay in store for us, but it had to be better.

When I saw my Arizona University photo ID a few days later, I looked like Howard Hughes toward the end: long straggly hair and beard, sallow complexion, dull, sunken eyes. Now I would have to invent myself once again. I was forty-one.

7
THE DESERT BLOOMS, AND SO DO I: MY SEVENTH LIFE

For the next twenty-eight years I was to be Professor of Near Eastern Archaeology and Anthropology at the University of Arizona in Tucson. The title sounds a bit grand, and I did invent it. I had to, because my position was brand new and had been created especially for me; there were no precedents. Anyway, I actually did have a courtesy cross-appointment in the anthropology department.

The University of Arizona in the 1970s was well known worldwide for new-world archaeology, with a top-rated anthropology department. It also had a forward-looking administration that wanted to expand into other areas of archaeology. It was decided, therefore, to fund four positions in a new program of Judaic Studies: two in modern studies and one or two somewhere in the ancient world, as it turned out in biblical (or what I was now calling SyroPalestinian) archaeology. Since it was assumed that the other appointees would probably be Jewish scholars, a state university ought to seek balance by searching for a non-Jewish archaeologist—preferably someone with long experience in and a close connection to Israel. Now who might that be?

Starting a New Program

The external advisors were Arnold Band, of the program in Comparative Literature at UCLA and an authority on modern Jewish literature; and Eric Meyers, a Second Temple–period archaeologist at Duke who had trained with me at Gezer. They agreed that I fit the bill uniquely. That was how the position at Arizona was created for me, and I accepted it. The mandate was simple: establish a world-class program in the archaeology of Israel and put Arizona on the map in that branch of archaeology. It was a challenge I couldn't resist and needed in my depressed state.

Heading for Tucson in August 1975, driving cross-country by car towing a U-Haul trailer with what little we had, Norma and I felt like the original pioneers headed for a new life in the wild West. Norma and Sean had never seen the desert, and I had only been in Arizona for a few days in January. But Tucson and the Sonoran Desert looked very much like Beersheba, so we soon felt right at home. We camped out in a rented apartment for a week or so before we were able to buy a house in the suburbs, with a down payment from my mother's small estate.

Never before having taught at a university, I scrambled to prepare for undergraduate classes in archaeology and biblical studies. One of the students in my first-year archaeology class was Tom Levy, who later was assistant director at both my old schools in Jerusalem and now holds an endowed chair at UC San Diego.

Reinventing Myself

Looking back at that momentous fall, I recall my mixed feelings. I really didn't want to be there; I didn't even want to be an academic. I belonged in Israel, in the field, where I had intended to spend the rest of my life. I was resentful of the treatment I had experienced at the Albright Institute and chastened by the thought that at forty-one I might have been on the street had it not been for other colleagues. I felt alone and isolated, aware that I was on the edge psychologically, pretty exhausted but determined to begin again. I vowed never to have anything to do with ASOR in the future—except perhaps by showing them that I could survive on my own. Perhaps I could even flourish in my reluctant new career.

We began to lay the foundations for a new life. For some ten years we had lived in institutional life, but now we began to enjoy being private citizens in our own rather cozy house (swimming pool and all). Norma busied herself with graduate work at the university, finishing an MA, then teaching again. Sean, now six, started first grade in an environment totally new to him. After a few weeks I asked him how he liked school and Tucson.

He thought a moment, then blurted out, "I miss being the director's boy!" I replied, "Son, I miss being the director."

Staying busy, getting acquainted (mainly in the Jewish community), establishing a household, exploring the desert and nearby Mexico, daring to dream of a life after Jerusalem—all these things gradually provided some much-needed stability and security for our uprooted family. I resolved to make up for my past vacillation, and I concentrated on building a future together for my family. We had barely enough money to live on. After all those years of professional success, I was only now beginning to have any social security and retirement benefits. It would be a long haul—if I could remake myself. Where I got the strength to do so, I honestly don't know, because I still had never sought the professional help that I now know I needed. Perhaps it was simply my Irish stubbornness. Or providence? Norma was supportive, but she, too, was unaware of how debilitating clinical depression can be.

Within three years I was heading the Oriental Studies Department with more than thirty faculty members, continuing as a trustee of ASOR, and serving as editor of ASOR's prestigious journal founded by Albright: *Bulletin of the American Schools of Oriental Research*. In 1978 I was also invited to take Pritchard's chair at the University of Pennsylvania and a curatorship at the University Museum. I declined and then bargained for what I really wanted at Arizona: to get out of the headship and administration and to have a graduate program in archaeology with adequate financial support. In retrospect, it was a good decision. Pennsylvania to this day has not succeeded in mounting a program or even permanently filling the chair. Soon I accepted my first doctoral students (eventually there would be twenty-eight PhDs), emboldened by the fact that Harvard offered no competition, not having replaced Ernest upon his death in 1974 (his chair went vacant for eleven years).

Back in the Field

In 1978 we also launched Arizona's first field and training project, the Central Negev Highlands project, with generous support from the university and from the National Endowment for the Humanities. This was, like Gezer, an interdisciplinary project, the first in the exploration of the enigmatic Early Bronze IV sites of the Negev Desert (2500–2000 BCE). It would continue for three seasons (through 1981), with the collaboration of Rudy Cohen and his colleagues. The pioneer field work we did back then has never been equaled, much less surpassed. I published annual full preliminary results in *BASOR*, but the distractions of my new life delayed the final report for many years (until 2014). However, I had come a long way in three years, and by now my old confidence was restored. I almost forgot about my troubles.

Fig. 43. Rudy Cohen and I.

The excavations at Be'er Resisim were logistically difficult but the most satisfying of my long career in the field. In 1978 the small staff lived at the field school in Sde Boker (Ben-Gurion's old desert research institute and burial place), and we commuted to the site cross-country by jeep, two hours each way. Results were necessarily limited but sufficient to justify the continuation of a National Endowment for the Humanities grant.

In 1979, now with a larger staff, we tented at Be'erotayim, on the Egyptian border, in the ruins of Lawrence and Woolley's old camp when they did research for *The Wilderness of Zin* (1915). The fleas were as big as grasshoppers, but the sunsets, filtered by the soft desert haze, were glorious. Finally, in 1980, with the support of the Israeli army, we built a camp for seventy at the foot of the site.

Fig. 44. The camp at Be'er Resisim in 1980; site in background.

Our staff were mostly Israelis (Rudy's people, all "desert rats") or my graduate students from Arizona (desert rats, too), so we were used to the desert and relished its vastness and emptiness, its harsh contrasts, its silence. Volunteers came mainly from students and friends of Elmo Scoggin of Wake Forest University, who had been with us for years at Gezer, and again at Jebel Qa'aqir. Norma was with us, as well as Sean, now eleven.

Our camp was primitive. We hauled water constantly by jeep from an army camp near Beersheba, 40 miles away. Each person was allotted three gallons a day: two for drinking (enforced) and one for all other personal uses. Food was minimal. One night we had boiled spaghetti seasoned with cinnamon. We all lost weight, but it was exhilarating, in part because this was the first of the dozens of enigmatic EB IV nomadic camps in the Negev to be properly excavated with modern multidisciplinary methods. A dark age was being dramatically illuminated.

Settling in (Again)

Back home, although still department head for a while (until 1981), heading a burgeoning graduate program and busy with editorial duties, I was also publishing regularly. The Gezer *Manual of Field Excavations* (with Darrell Lance) appeared in 1978. Major articles and chapters in Festschrift volumes soon appeared, one in 1976 in the volume for Ernest. Now, better known back home, I was beginning to be invited to contribute to handbooks in biblical studies (as in *Israelite and Judean History*, 1978) and to speak at international symposia in Germany (1977), Japan (1979), and back in Israel (1981).

In 1977, apparently settled in for the duration in Tucson, we moved into a rambling 1920s Spanish-style hacienda, which we dubbed Casa de la Paloma Blanca (the House of the White Dove). The house had been designed and built by a famous Santa Barbara and Tucson architect named Josiah Joesler. It was the first of several dozen distinctive houses that Joesler built in Tucson, of which only a few survive. But this one was derelict, empty, and in very bad repair. Nevertheless, it featured five wings with varying rooflines, a tower, thick adobe white-plastered walls, a heavy red-tile roof, extensive grounds with a pool and pool house, and several exquisite Mexican tile fountains.

Fig. 45. Casa de la Paloma Blanca.

I managed to buy the house from the discouraged owner for very little and then spent several months of my spare time making it livable enough to move into. Over the next twelve years I lovingly restored the old house, replacing termite-ridden oak floors, making mesquite kitchen cabinets, refinishing everything, and doing never-ending repairs to the mud-brick walls and tile roof. The old pool and the fountains were once again functional. We gave parties for dozens of people in the garden. It was not unlike the splendid 1930s director's house at the Albright in Jerusalem, and it was furnished with the same antique copper and carpets.

Once again, we lived rather grandly, with an active social life (but, unfortunately, no servants). I was getting my revenge on those who had ended my life in Jerusalem and nearly ended my career. I was now forty-three and well on my way to a new career in archaeology. And I would soon go back to Israel—this time on my *own* terms.

My First Sabbatical

We were due for my first sabbatical in 1981–1982. I applied for, and, to my surprise, won, a John Simon Guggenheim Memorial Foundation Fellowship, America's most prestigious award in the humanities. I was invited to spend the year in Jerusalem as visiting professor of archaeology at the Hebrew University of Jerusalem, where the archaeologists I had grown up with were now in the ascendancy. We bought an old VW bus (again!), and Norma, Sean, and I camped for two months across Europe on our way to Jerusalem. There we settled into a lovely rented apartment in Abu Tor, near the St Andrews Scottish Church I knew so well and within walking distance of HUC. Sean could lie in his bed and see the Dome of the Rock. At the college I worked assiduously on a large excavation report, *Gezer IV*, which Norma typed; it appeared promptly in 1986. We socialized frequently with former Israeli colleagues and friends and took frequent field trips, revisiting old sites and seeing more recent excavations. Sean was twelve that fall and went to the seventh grade at the Anglican School on Prophets Street.

We went back to the Albright Institute almost the first night we were in Jerusalem, for dinner in the director's house. I felt almost like McArthur returning triumphantly to the Philippines, because a new long-term director had just been appointed: my student and protege Sy Gitin, who has now recently completed his thirty-fourth year as director of the Albright. Sy really *is* my revenge, because he has been able to carry out all the programs I envisioned that the trustees would not support. Somehow, the circle seemed complete now.

My advanced seminar in the spring at the Hebrew Union University went well enough at the beginning. But soon the 1981–1982 Lebanon intervention loomed, and well before the end of the term nearly all my students, men and women, disappeared. They had been called up as reserves in the army. The nightly news from Lebanon became frightening. Shortly before the war actually began, I had gone to Syria to join an ASOR trustees field trip (a truce now). One evening at a reception at the American embassy in Damascus, the ambassador asked me, "What do you think about the war in Israel?" *What* war? My family was there! I pushed him for information and made hasty plans to get back to Jerusalem via Cyprus. But by then Beirut was being invaded by the Israeli government under Sharon (earlier, in April, the last of the Sinai settlers had been forcibly evacuated). The year ended on a frustrating and sad note. The Israel I once knew was beginning to seem remote. But much worse was to come: the Palestinian uprising, the intifada, had not yet reared its ugly head.

Despite the worsening political situation in Israel in the 1970s, a number of Israeli digs were in the field; some started then. There was a

Fig. 46. Frequent visits to the excavations in Israel, here with David Ussishkin (left) and Israel Finkelstein (right) at Megiddo.

great deal of salvage excavation in Jerusalem, under Benjamin Mazar and Nahman Avigad, as the restoration of the Old City proceeded apace. Most of the other projects I have already summarized above.

These excavations were generally much better than those of the era when I had resided in Israel. At Lachish, for instance, Ussishkin openly praised Gezer's three-dimensional stratigraphic methods and claimed to have adopted them. Younger Israeli archaeologists such as Ami Mazar (Benjamin's nephew, now in his seventies) had indeed learned more meticulous field methods. Aharoni's work, however, has remained unpublished, since he died, unfortunately, in his fifties. The less said about Dan, HUC's replacement for Gezer, the better. For the most part, *truly* interdisciplinary archaeology was still the exception. Publication for the Israelis, as for us Americans, lagged behind—and we Americans had fewer significant field projects. Nevertheless, on annual summer visits beginning in 1976, I visited all the above (and many other) digs each summer, trying to maintain my edge as an absentee archaeologist. In 1981–1982, on sabbatical, I saw the sites in more depth.

The 1980s: A National School

The 1980s saw an emergence of a third generation of Israeli archaeologists (the second generation were now in their late seventies or early to mid-eighties), although a few (Ami Mazar, Israel Finkelstein) had already gotten a precocious start earlier. Relative newcomers in the 1980s would include Yoram Tsafrir at the Hebrew University, a Byzantinologist who worked in the Negev; Shlomo Bunimovitz at Tel Aviv University; Dan Bahat, district officer in Jerusalem and later at Bar-Ilan University; Ayelet Gilboa and Michal Artzy at Haifa University (now with its own institute, Israel's fifth); Steve Rosen at the Ben-Gurion University of the Negev; and Eilat Mazar (Benjamin Mazar's granddaughter), an independent scholar in Jerusalem excavating on the Temple Mount and at David's Citadel from 1985 onward and also working at Achziv. Only somewhat later, however, were these younger archaeologists able to direct their own field projects. The overlapping generation, Mazar and Finkelstein, had directed their own excavations for some time previously (since 1971 and 1976, respectively).

Meanwhile, prominent archaeologists of Israel's second (and even first) generation continued their long-running projects at major sites. The Hebrew University's excavations at Dor under Stern continued throughout the 1980s. The university also continued Amihai Mazar's excavation at Tel Batash well into the 1980s (1989).

Tel Aviv's project at Lachish, under Ussishkin, went on until 1983, and perennial Dan, under Biran, which had been in the field since 1966, persisted throughout the 1980s (and into the 1900s), now under the auspices of the Nelson Glueck School of Biblical Archaeology, which Biran had directed for some time after I had left the directorship in 1971.

There were also new Israeli excavations in the 1980s: the Hebrew University's long-term work at Beth-Shean starting in 1999 under Ami Mazar; the Ben-Gurion University at Tel Haror (biblical Gerar, 1982–) under Eliezer Oren, a member of the second generation; Tel Aviv's work at Tel Michal under Ze'ev Herzog (1977–1980) and at Shiloh under Israel Finkelstein (1981–1984).

One sign of Israel's national school coming of age in the 1980s was a growing rivalry between five institutes of archaeology, as well as personal rivalries now that the first generation had lost its dominating position. Aharoni (who died in his fifties in 1978) and Yadin, the last of the generation of great men, were the chief protagonists, and the quarrels were public and vitriolic. At annual symposia, each would interrupt the other's lecture, and once I recall the chairman giving up in despair and calling the session off. Yadin even drastically (and gratuitously) reworked Aharoni's stratigraphy of Arad and Beersheba.

But Yadin's own exploits at Masada came under investigation when the bones of the Jewish defenders were reexamined and turned out to be in all probability those of Roman soldiers. With Yadin's tacit approval, the fortress of Masada had become a symbol of resurgent Jewish nationalism. It was the scene of the dramatic induction of all new army recruits, the cry "Masada shall never fall again!" ringing across the desert dawn. But Masada did fall: the induction ceremonies became such a public scandal that they were moved elsewhere. Yadin never admitted to any duplicity, and he went on to become Israel's deputy prime minister (a larger stage, it seems).

In Jerusalem, the big salvage excavations of Avigad and Mazar continued, supplemented by dozens of smaller digs here and there—and, of

Fig. 47. Yigal Shiloh and I at the Ciy of David excavations, 1982.

course, by Shiloh's City of David excavation, now at its peak. Here, too, archaeology became involved with more than one Jewish identity crisis.

On the one hand, many Israelis saw the Israeli archeological establishments' unhindered operations in the Old City as a vindication of the state's proclamation of *all* Jerusalem as its capital, ancient and modern. (For the United States and virtually every other country in the world, Israel was simply an occupying power: the embassies were located, at that time, in Tel Aviv.) Archaeology was thus a powerful component in shaping a Jewish past and vindicating a present state.

On the other hand, the Orthodox community in Jerusalem (the *haredim*, or Godfearers) became increasingly incensed over all excavations, claiming that they were desecrating Jewish graves. Shiloh's large-scale clearance of the City of David on the spur of the Ophel became a flash point in the early 1980s. Gangs of bearded Orthodox young men broke into the excavation storehouses and destroyed archaeological materials. They even mobbed the excavation one day in broad daylight, attacking Shiloh personally. But Yigal, a big ex-paratrooper, took several of them out before the police rushed the mob on horseback and dispersed them. The Orthodox called Shiloh's home and threatened to kill his wife and children. Mazar and Yadin, along with many Israeli archaeologists, paraded in the streets of Jerusalem themselves, demonstrating against these hoodlums and calling for the government to halt their attempts in the Knesset to ban all excavations. After Yadin died in 1984, they broke into the military cemetery on Mount Herzel and desecrated his grave, and when Shiloh died in 1987, tragically early at the age of fifty-one, they held rallies in the streets of Jerusalem calling for celebrations.

The mutual hostility that began in earnest in the 1980s continues today, exacerbated now by the post-Zionist leaning of some younger archaeologists who want to remove archaeology from all nationalistic influences, one way or another. That, if it happens, would be a further sign of the national school's maturity.

Meanwhile, American archaeology began to lose its once-secure position. Older excavations from the heyday of the 1970s continued in the 1980s at Tell el-Ḥesi (until 1983) and as part of the Meyers and Strange Galilean Synagogue Project (Nabratein, 1981–; Sepphoris, 1983–, with the Hebrew University after 1985). The only new American projects, however, were those at Tel Miqne (biblical Ekron of the Philistines, 1981–2006) and at Philistine Ashkelon (1985–2017), along with a small Iron I site in Lower Galilee, Tell el-Wawiyat, directed in 1986–1987 by my students Beth Alpert Nakhai, J. P. Dessel, and Bonnie Wisthof.

Some American excavations were exceptionally large, well-funded, long-running projects at major sites, but these excavations were hardly the wave of the American future. Miqne was codirected by Sy Gitin of the Albright Institute and Trude Dotham on behalf of the Hebrew University. This was a joint project, which from this point on all American excavations were to be by Israeli law.

The Ashkelon excavations were directed by another senior American archaeologist, Lawrence Stager, Dorot Professor of the Archaeology of Israel at Harvard. This was a big-money project (thus exempt from the law) funded by the Wall Street financier Leon Levy. Again, it was hardly typical.

In the future, fewer and fewer young American archaeologists would be able to begin a project in Israel or even to continue fieldwork with others. American universities were finding the Middle East a dangerous place, archaeological fieldwork a luxury, and jobs something to be channeled into science and technology. The Israeli national school, now in its third generation, had all the advantages. The colonial era was over.

As vice president for archaeological policy of ASOR from 1982 through 1988, I had the responsibility for coordinating all the American projects in Israel (and Jordan), and I visited most of the Israeli digs as well each summer. Eventually I published some of the rather pessimistic impressions in a 1995 article entitled "Death of a Discipline?" Maybe.

The hesitant dialogue on theory and method begun in the 1970s now continued apace. In 1981, I published a major article on the new archaeology, now well established elsewhere in the world. It made little impact on the Israelis, in their ascendency more pragmatically inclined than ever. It was working for them. The biblical-archaeology paradigm, which we Americans had long given up, still prevailed, although it, too, was scarcely examined critically. That would come later (below).

Eventually, however, the first Israeli articles dealing self-consciously with the history of the national school finally appeared (after the new archaeology was passe), although still not concerned with what we meant by *theory*. In 1982 Amihai Mazar and the eminent prehistorian Ofer Bar-Yosef (long since at Harvard) published a résumé in the journal *World Archaeology*. It is a useful statement but almost entirely descriptive. Then in 1987 Magen Broshi published an incisive critique entitled "Religion, Ideology, and Politics and Their Impact on Palestinian Archaeology," but it appeared in the obscure *Israel Museum Journal*, and few people appear to have seen it (I have cited it often). Ephraim Stern contributed a short article on the Israeli approach in the Glen Rose Festschrift, almost entirely uncritical. In 1988, in the Joseph Callaway Festschrift, Ami Mazar returned to the scene with a more astute survey, though still not very reflective. Finally, in 1989 I offered a friendly but hortatory critique of Israeli archaeology. (For all these publications, see the bibliography below.) Despite those publications, there was no real dialogue. We were talking past each other, and Americans were no longer equal partners.

The Middle Years

We sold the old VW camper to an Israeli colleague and returned from sabbatical to Tucson in the summer of 1982. The ensuing years until 1989 were incredibly eventful, both professionally and personally. The doctoral program had now reached maturity, with more than a dozen students in residence—the largest graduate program in Near Eastern archaeology in the world. Between 1985 and 1987 Arizona graduated five PhDs, several of

Fig. 48. With graduate students University of Arizona, here Michael Hasel.

whom had been trained in the field at Gezer and in the Negev. Let me look only at one class, the 1987 one: Tom Davis has been the long-time director of our American School in Cyprus (CAARI); Steve Falconer is a full professor in the anthropology department at Eastern Carolina University, excavating in Jordan and Cyprus; and Bonnie Magness-Gardiner is with the FBI as an advisor in forensic and cultural properties in archaeology, traveling all over the world.

These were exceptionally productive years in terms of publication: two books (including *Gezer IV* in 1986) and thirty articles and chapters in books. In these publications several of my long-running interests were more closely focused, especially folk religion and the cult of Asherah in ancient Israel (1983–1987), theory and method in American and Israeli archaeology (1983, 1985, 1988, 1989), and what was to become the age of Solomon crisis (1983). I wrote the first of many Festschrift articles honoring my older colleagues, including Menahem Mansoor (1982), Noel Freedman (1983), Yigael Yadin (1984), Olga Tufnell (1985), Joe Callaway (1988), and my own teachers Ernest Wright (1976, 1980) and Frank Cross (1987).

In the spring of 1982 I won the Percia Schimmel Prize of the Israel Museum, the youngest honoree up to that time and the first American. And that sabbatical year of 1981–1982 I had held a John Simon Guggenheim Memorial Fellowship, concurrent with an appointment as visiting professor at the Hebrew University,

In the wider world, I continued as editor of *BASOR* (1978–1984) and was also vice president of ASOR (1982–1988), charged with the oversight of the Committee on Archaeological Policy and more than forty excavation projects in the Middle East. In 1985 and again in 1986 I helped conduct NEH-sponsored Summer Institutes for College Teachers at the University of Pennsylvania. These were designed to enrich their teaching of archaeology. I organized six weeks of back-to-school training for all twelve hundred US Navy chaplains, traveling to naval bases at home, in Hawaii, and in Japan and Okinawa. I came to respect our dedicated and disciplined servicemen and women. (I also liked being called "sir" and being saluted.) Finally, I gave the Samuel and Althea Stroum lectures at the University of Washington, published in 1989 as *Recent Archaeological Discoveries and Biblical Research* (1989b). On the international scene, I gave invited papers at symposia in Germany, Rome, and Israel. It all seemed too good to be true, and it was.

Mortality Intervenes

While Norma and I were attending ASOR's Annual Meeting in San Francisco in November 1985, a phone call came from Sean, who was now sixteen. We had known that there was to be a biopsy of some lymph nodes in his neck before we left. Norma had talked to the doctor, who said that she was going to prepare Sean for the test on Friday, but there was no reason to cancel our trip. Sean saw the doctor while we were away that Friday, and the doctor said that most likely the test would be positive and would show he had cancer. On the phone, Sean said simply: "Mom and Dad, I think I have cancer." Norma flew back to Tucson as soon as she could on Saturday, and I returned the next Tuesday. Sean's biopsy showed he had Hodgkin's disease, cancer of the lymphatic system, which is now curable except in its later stages. Sean was in Stage 1/2, with perhaps a 40–50 percent recovery rate. Incredibly, Sean said, "Don't worry; I went straight to the library and read up on Hodgkin's disease. I can beat this." We all thought that maybe he could, but for the next nine months we were secretly terrified.

Our lives came to revolve around five weekly radiation sessions for many months. Through it all Sean was heroic—with that unshakable sense of immortality that the young often have. Norma and I tried to cope, silently, each in our own way (there is no blueprint for this), but in the end we were of little help to each other. My world was beginning to fall apart again. I had been in Arizona for ten years; I was fifty-one.

Eventually Sean was in remission. I was, of course, enormously relieved but also badly shaken. This crisis had been by far the worst of my life, and I wondered what was next and whether I would have the strength for it. Would Sean's remission *last*? By now, professional prowess, which had driven me relentlessly through everything, seemed hollow. This turned out to be the beginning of my second midlife crisis.

Fig. 49. Sean at sixteen, a few weeks before diagnosis.

Still One More Transition

In 1985, while in Philadelphia for the NEH workshop mentioned above, I had renewed contacts with Pamela after several years. She had gone on from Gezer in 1971 to Harvard to study with several of my old teachers. She graduated in 1982 with a PhD in Fine Arts under George Hanfman and others, writing a dissertation on Cypriote sculpture. She was by now also excavating at Idalion in Cyprus, where some of the most magnificent British Museum sculpture had been found long before. Pamela became the director of Idalion in 1987 and has continued there until the present. By 1985 she had two little girls, Jordana, aged five, and Hannah, aged two. I knew the girls, having seen Pamela off and on over the years. One time in Cyprus, when Hannah was three, she said, "Unca Bill, how come everywhere we go you're there?" I said, "Ask your mother."

By the summer of 1985, Pamela was separated and trying to continue teaching at the University of New Hampshire, excavating at Idalion, and struggling to rear two children as a single mother. Pamela and I talked, somewhat guiltily, about her deteriorating marriage and mine. But when Sean became ill, I knew that this was no time to be thinking of anything else. We both went on with our lives.

In 1986, when I was in Washington to confer with Rear Admiral McNamara on the U.S. Navy tour (see above), Pamela and the girls came to Washington to visit her sister, and I saw her again. By now the girls knew Uncle Bill well.

The next year, in Boston for the ASOR Annual Meeting, I was campaigning openly for the presidency. I had the manic energy for the job, and I needed the diversion. The professionals supported me, but some of the laypeople on the search committee put out the word that "Dever is not convenient," meaning, I suppose, that I could not be bought. If that was the price of principle, I paid it gladly. In Boston in 1987, I saw Pamela again, and this time long-suppressed dreams surfaced. But I went back to Tucson, still trying to hold things together, to plan confidently ahead, and to sidestep emotional turmoil. It was a life-long habit, and it had gotten me this far.

I was to be on sabbatical for the spring semester of 1989, and Norma and I planned a trip around the world, to end up in Israel. In order to make some more money for this trip, I went to Andrews University and the University of Michigan for several weeks. I called Pamela, now divorced, every night. One night, Hannah, then five, seemed a bit sad. Suddenly she blurted out, "Unca Bill, we are lonely. Will you marry us?" I said, "Sweetie, put your mother on the phone." That's how we got engaged, at least provisionally. A few weeks later I flew to Boston with three rings, and we were formally engaged. The question mark after "Paula Garber's" name on the volunteer list for the spring dig at Gezer in 1969, exactly twenty years earlier, was finally removed.

It would be easy to blame the divorce on one party or the other, but that would be a vast oversimplification. It is true that it was I who initiated the divorce, and Norma was willing to go on trying to patch things up. But the truth is that we had grown far apart in those thirty-six years. (Or as Norma could say, "Bill, I never knew you."). We were engaged at eighteen, Norma the only girl I had ever really dated. We got married at nineteen, when I had just completed my sophomore year in college. Neither of us had seen anything of the wider world: Norma from the tiny hamlet of Jonesville, Virginia, and I a skinny, dreamy kid from small towns in Tennessee and Ohio.

For many years we were happily married, good companions, sharing growing adventures that we never expected (and sometimes were not prepared for). But by the time Sean had come fortuitously into our lives, after sixteen years, I was increasingly restless, although still absolutely faithful. The way I was raised, divorce was literally unthinkable. But I did think about it, and I felt so guilty that I simply denied the reality that I was beginning to be estranged from the wife of my youth.

Norma had done nothing wrong, was, in fact, a devoted wife. Norma was one of the last normal people I know: uncomplicated, loyal to a fault, exactly what she appeared to be, a genuinely good person with many friends. But I tried to make her into someone else. That was wrong, and, of course, it didn't work. I admit that for many years I stayed at first out of a sense of duty, then largely to see Sean past his illness and safely into college. But duty is a cold, hard taskmaster. If I had remained in the marriage, Norma and I would have ended up hating each other. As it turned out, neither of us could save Sean, and for a long time Norma was my best friend. Summers we would sit in the garden of the Albright Institute in Jerusalem, remembering our son Sean playing there as a child. Norma died in June 2019. Life is very strange.

In June of 1989, Pamela, the two girls, and I went to Israel together. Old friends looked puzzled, especially when we said that we were engaged to be married in the fall and that I might convert. Their comments varied. Jonas Greenfield, an immigrant from America, a distinguished professor of Semitic languages, and a dear friend, said, "Nu? What took you so long? Welcome to the tribe!" Avraham Biran, a senior Israeli archaeologist who by now had succeeded me as director of HUC, was the best. He said, "Dever, you're crazy! I was born a Jew, but you had a choice!" To my Christian friends, I simply said, "I have it on the best authority that Jesus and all the disciples were Jews. That's good enough for me." One Christian friend, David Noel Freedman, one of America's leading biblical scholars who had converted to Christianity in his youth, said, "Dever, it's a wash. The Christians got me, and the Jews got you."

In July I flew back to Tucson, finalized the divorce, and settled some affairs. When I went back to Concord, I consulted with Pamela's Reconstructionist Rabbi. I told him, "I want to convert to Judaism. What do I have to do?" Knowing something of my history, he said, "You have to know the history of the Jewish people." I replied, "Rabbi, do you want to begin at the beginning?" "No," he said, "You'll do." Then he said, "You have to identify personally with the Jewish people." I noted that I had risked my life with them in 1967, 1973, and 1982 and that most of my colleagues and friends were now Jewish. Finally, we got around to the miqveh, ritual immersion. I said that, although I had been baptized once, it hadn't taken, but we could try again.

I was baptized in Walden Pond. One of the three officiating rabbis was a woman. As I came up out of the water, she said, "Some people are born by accident into the wrong tradition. You were supposed to be Jewish." That felt right then, and it still does. (But Henry David Thoreau would have turned over in his grave.) We got married on August 1, 1989, the girls standing with us under the *huppah*.

Fig. 50. Pamela and I at our wedding in Concord, with Jordana Lee Gaber (now Saletan) and Hannah Susan Gaber, August 1, 1989.

Divorce and the Aftermath

I knew the divorce would be difficult (that's why I had put if off), both emotionally and financially. It was. I left Casa de la Paloma Blanca, the villa in which I had invested so much, with a bit less than half of my worldly goods. For a while I lived in our old motor home in a trailer park, commuting to the university on a motorbike, since I had no car. Agreeing with our lawyers, we made a financial settlement that gave Norma half of the equity in the house, half of our savings and retirement, and alimony until I was seventy. I was also to cover Sean's college expenses (he was now a junior in college). When Pamela and I told her father Martin, a practical businessman (I actually asked for her hand), about our plans, his response was, "What are his obligations?" They were considerable, and I knew it.

The divorce settlement left little for us to live on, and now I had a wife and two little girls to support, although there was some child support from their father. Pamela wasn't employed at first, because soon she was expecting the boy we wanted. I took the headship of Near Eastern studies largely for the raise it gave me. At first we rented, since my name was still on the old mortgage and I couldn't qualify for a loan on my income. On the very last day that our lease was to run out, I managed to get a loan, and we bought the tract house in which we were living. That first year Pamela searched for used clothes for the girls in thrift stores, and I juggled utility bills to see who would get paid that month. Pamela, a big-city girl, hated Tucson.

Sometimes I thought, "What have I done?" But this was the new beginning I wanted (again), and why should it be easy? Evan Jacob Gaber Dever ("Zeb," for a frivolous suggestion, "Zebulon") was born on April 16, 1990. I had originally thought that Pamela and I would at least be able to dig at Gezer again, this time as man and wife. But Zeb was only a few months old by summer, so in June I went alone for the 1990 season. Pamela remained in Tucson. It was a long, hot summer.

Archaeology (and I) Flourish

I was to remain at the University of Arizona from 1989 until my retirement in 2003. Despite the difficulties of starting all over again, these were productive years. The second generation of Arizona PhDs was launched, now fourteen in all. They included students who are now major figures in evangelical circles, hold important university positions, and are working in the science of archaeology. I published or edited eight books, among them the Hebrew edition of a popular work, *Gezer: At the Crossroads of Ancient Israel* (1998), and the first of several bestselling semipopular books, *What Did the Biblical Writers Know and When Did They Know It? What Archaeology Can Tell Us about the Reality of Ancient Israel* (2001) and *Who Were the Early Israelites and Where Did They Come From?* (2003).

The first book was a broadside attack on the European revisionists (or minimalists/nihilists), radical leftist biblical scholars who beginning in the 1990s had attempted to write ancient Israel out of history. At first this appeared to be the typical postmodern crisis in historiography (Can we *write* "histories" at all"?) that had affected many humanistic disciplines, and now biblical scholarship. But when scholars such as those at

Copenhagen and Sheffield began to abuse archaeology, about which they obviously knew nothing, I knew I had to enter the fray. I am still the only archaeologist who has written extensively on revisionism, but most share my concerns. Not the least of the damage done by these super-skeptics is the fact that, if they have their way, there will be no dialogue between archaeology and biblical studies—our only hope for writing new and better histories of ancient Israel. I no longer subscribe to Wright's notion that faith depends upon taking the Bible's historical claims literally, but history still *matters*.

To make things worse, books such as Keith Whitelam's *The Invention of Ancient Israel* (1995) and Thomas Thompson's *Biblical Archaeology and the Myth of Israel* (1999) have been translated into Arabic and have politicized Middle Eastern archaeology, especially in Jordan. If there *was* no ancient Israel, then archaeologists like myself are frauds. I have been called worse: crypto-fundamentalist, McCartheyite, and, by one scholar, both a Zionist and a Nazi at the same time. The only antidote to such escalating rhetoric is a steady focus on facts—the facts that archaeology establishes every day about the past, a past from which we can learn. The revisionists always declare that archaeology is mute. So is the Hebrew Bible, if you don't know Hebrew, as the German biblicist Ernst Axel Knauf has observed.

The 1990s: Archaeology in Israel Changes and Remains the Same

The 1980s saw the maturation of the third generation of Israeli archaeologists, but also the death of several remaining members of the second generation. Aharoni had died in 1978, Yadin in 1984, and even the far younger Shiloh in 1987. Nahman Avigad had died in 1982, while his Jewish Quarter excavations in Jerusalem were still underway. Now Moshe Dothan, another of the founding fathers, succumbed to neurological problems. Benjamin Mazar outlived them all, active to the end. No one really knew how hold he was because his birth certificate had been lost to pogroms in Europe, but he was into his nineties.

The 1990s saw a great proliferation of new, often long-running projects, mostly directed by the third generation of Israeli archaeologists. The Hebrew University launched projects at Bronze and Iron Age sites:

Hazor, under Amnon Ben-Tor (1990–); Beth-Shean (1989–1996) and Tel Reḥov (1997–), under Amihai Mazar; Dor, under Ephraim Stern, continuing under Ayelet Gilboa and Ilan Sharon (1990–). The prehistoric site of Shaʿar ha-Golan was excavated by Yosef Garfinkel (1996–2003). There were also excavations at the classical period sites of Herodion, under Ehud Netzer (1997–2007), and Sepphoris, under Netzer and Zeʾev Weiss (1990–1995).

Major Tel Aviv University Bronze and Iron Age projects begun now included Kabri, under Aharon Kempinski (1975–1993); Megiddo, under Israel Finkelstein and David Ussishkin (1992–); Jezreel, under Ussishkin (1990–1995); and Beth-Shemesh, under Shlomo Bunimovitz and Zvi Lederman (1990–). Haifa University excavated at Tel Nami, under Michal Artzy (1992–1997); Bar-Ilan University at Tell es-Safi/Gath, under Aren Maier (1992–); and Elusa, under Ben-Gurion University (1997–2002).

Other major projects of the 1990s, most under the auspices of the Israel Antiquities Authority, included Gamla (1997–2000), Akko (1992–), Mount Gerizim (1982–2003), Caesarea (1992–1998), Maresha (1989–2001), and Nessana (1987–1995). Many excavations continued in Jerusalem, notably those of Ronny Reich and Eli Shukron in the area of the Siloam spring and water tunnel (1995–2004).

The 1990s saw several foreign excavations continuing, notably the large long-running American projects at Ashkelon, under Lawrence Stager (1985–), and the joint expedition at Tel Miqne/Ekron, under Seymour Gitin and Trude Dothan (1981–1996). Eric and Carol Meyers continued their Galilean Synagogue Project at Sepphoris, near Nazareth (1990–2002; see also the separate work of James Strange). American excavations also continued at the New Testament site of Bethsaida, under Rami Arav (1987–). A small early Iron Age site near Nazareth, Tel Zippori, was excavated by J. P. Dessel (1993–2000). New long-running American digs were begun now by Joe Seger and others at Tel Ḥalif/Lahav (1992–1999) and at the small Judean mound at Tell Zayit, under Ron Tappy (1999–, possibly biblical Libnah).

Other foreign excavations of the 1990s would include those of the French at the great Judean Early Bronze site of Tel Yarmut, under Pierre de Miroschedji (1992–1999); of the Japanese at En Gev, on the eastern shores of the Sea of Galilee (1990–2005); and, later, of the Italians at Jericho, under Alphonso Nigro and others.

A recent subdiscipline of archaeology in Israel, maritime archaeology, explored along the coast under Avner Raban and others of Haifa University in the 1990s. Numerous ancient harbors and a number of early shipwrecks were found, the latter some of the most important discoveries in the Mediterranean to date.

Finally, the pace of salvage digs picked up at dozens, if not hundreds, of small sites all over the country, many scarcely reported but all important, and some with unique surprises.

With such a wide-ranging variety of excavation projects now in Israel, it is difficult to generalize, that is, to identify trends. A notable effort to do so, however, had already occurred in 1984, repeated in 1990: the convening of a session of the International Congress of Biblical Archaeology. This was by far the most ambitious effort to date to define our field, significantly still called biblical archaeology. Dozens of scholars from all over the world were invited to speak, although Israeli scholars easily dominated the sessions. In both cases, the papers were published. The latter volume (1993) included my own paper entitled "Biblical Archaeology—Death and Rebirth?" But there was no consensus, no obvious harbingers of the future. All that was clear was that the colonial era was over, and with it American ascendency.

One welcome sign of the Israeli national school's coming of age was the appearance, for the first time, of several excellent handbooks. In 1990 Ami Mazar produced a textbook that is still widely used, *Archaeology of the Land of the Bible 10,000–580 BCE*. (When I saw the manuscript, I urged Ami to drop "Land of the Bible," but that sells books.) Following that in 1992 came a volume edited by Amnon Ben-Tor, *The Archaeology of Ancient Israel*, with chapters by experts on each period. This was necessarily an eclectic work, varying in style, but most of the chapters are authoritative and well documented.

In 1993 a much more ambitious four-volume compendium appeared, masterfully edited by Ephraim Stern and lavishly illustrated: *The New Encyclopedia of Archaeological Excavations in the Holy Land* (updating the earlier Hebrew edition, a fifth volume in 2008). Then in 1994 and 1996 we saw two entirely new biblical atlases replacing several older works but much expanded: the first was *The Illustrated Atlas of Jerusalem*, edited by Dan Bahat (with C. Rubenstein and S. Ketco); the second was *Carta's Historical Atlas of Israel: A Survey of the Past and Review of the Present*.

Not to be outdone, although now beginning to be marginalized, we Americans produced our own distinctive synthesis, superbly edited by a young Gezerite (and once an Arizona student of mine): Tom Levy's *The Archaeology of Society in the Holy Land* (1995). This was a much more explicitly anthropological treatment than either of the two Israeli handbooks, with a strong socioeconomic thrust. Levy's textbook has become a standard reference work and will likely remain so for many years.

With all these new and authoritative reference works at hand, biblical and Levantine archaeology could at last purport to be serious academic and professional disciplines, accessible to specialists and laypeople alike. No longer can biblicists excuse their neglect of the archaeological data by saying, "But you people don't *publish*."

Alongside these convenient handbooks, there continue to appear a series of final report volumes. Beginning in the 1990s, Israeli (and a few Americans) began to improve their publications dramatically, now all in English. As of this date, Ben-Tor has published five final reports, Stern five, Ussishkin six, Mazar seven, and Finkelstein five; even Shiloh's Jerusalem excavations have produced six posthumous volumes.

Meanwhile, on the American side, Gezer has issued six final report volumes, under the authorship and editorship of Dever, Lance, Seger, Gitin, and Garth Gilmore (1970–2010). The Joint Expedition to Caesarea Maritina has published (somewhat belatedly) several volumes, and Tell el-Ḥesi has published five volumes. (American excavations in Jordan have also published well, with the Madeba Plains Project an astonishing twenty-three report volumes thus far, but that is beyond our view here.)

In the years between 1989 and 2002, I published more than seventy articles and chapters in books. Some of them were technical studies, but others were synthetic studies focusing on larger issues such as the history of Israel, the rise of the Israelite state, religion and cult, ethnicity in the archaeological record, and the future of biblical and Syro-Palestinian archaeology. A popular book on Gezer appeared in Hebrew in 1998. In addition, I wrote dozens of articles for standard dictionaries and encyclopedias, for several of which I also served as a section editor for archaeology (*Anchor Bible Dictionary*; *Oxford Encyclopedia of Archaeology in the Near East*; *Eerdmann's Dictionary of the Bible*). Other editorial positions were on the boards of journals such as the *American Journal of Archaeology*

(1989–1996), *Archaeology* magazine (1993–2000); *Archaeological Odyssey* (1999–2004), and the *Annuals of the American Schools of Oriental Research* (editor, 1989–1997).

In promoting our discipline in other ways—now a major concern of my mature years—I lectured widely at dozens of colleges, universities, seminaries, and church and synagogue groupings. I gave the Stroum Lectures at the University of Washington. Twice I gave the Norton Lectures for the Archaeological Institute of America, their senior award, traveling nationwide. I discovered anew the enormous interest of the American public in what we do. Now a more visible figure on the international scene, I read invited papers at symposia in Canada, England, Ireland, France, Austria, Denmark, Switzerland, Italy, and Israel. I was even invited to Jordan, although the symposium did not materialize due to the illness of the convener.

Approaching my late fifties and early sixties, I kept my early vow to be out of the field by sixty. This may seem strange, since by this time one ought to have learned finally how to do it. But history shows that archaeologists who do extensive field work after about sixty are unlikely to live to publish their final reports. The 1990 season at Gezer was my last, except for one summer as associate director with Pamela at her dig at Idalion in Cyprus. Despite similar training and many of the same teachers, we discovered that husband and wife professional teamwork can put a lot of strain on a marriage. We published a couple of joint articles, but that was it.

Other things worked out well enough, much of our energy focused now on raising two girls (who were often a handful) and our little guy Zeb. Although a bit old to be a father again, I found that it was a rewarding challenge, and I was probably a better father to Zeb than I had been with Sean, preoccupied as I had been at that time with career. Sean was still around, however, finishing his degree at the university, and we saw a lot of him. Our blended family worked exceptionally well. Pamela not only pursued her fieldwork in Cyprus, but she taught for a time as an adjunct professor in my department, then served as principal of the Religious School at Congregation Emmanu-El in Tucson, a Reform synagogue. We were now both educators, attempting in one way or another to bring the past to life and to find meaning in it.

Cyprus Looms Large

My third sabbatical was soon due, so in the spring semester of 1996 we all went to Cyprus, where Pamela had won a Fulbright Fellowship. I was by now vice president of ASOR's institute in Nicosia (the Cyprus American Archaeological Research Institute or CAARI), so we could both pursue our interests. Pamela worked on her field reports, and I finished the manuscripts of eight articles. The girls were in a British school in Nicosia, and Zeb began kindergarten. Life in our old rented house in the village of Dhali was relaxed and pleasant. We had no heat, no TV, not even a telephone at first. It was like living in a small town in America a half-century ago.

We got coarse bread loaves early in the morning from the bakery across the street, still hot and sweet smelling from the oven. We shopped every day at the village farmers' co-op and the local butcher shop. Late in the day Zeb and I would chop some wood, and we would build a fire to ward off the night chill. While the children gave homework a good try, we all sat around the fire, Pamela sewing or knitting, I telling stories. It was a simple but satisfying life. I think it was then that Pamela and I knew that our long-time dream of retiring in Cyprus must not be forgotten. We even explored some abandoned mud-brick houses in the village, excited about how we might restore one. That part of the dream would eventually come true. But another part of the dream would shatter.

When we came back from the sabbatical in the fall of 1996, life returned to normal (whatever that meant for us). The whole family had spent two months camping out across Europe in our old VW van. We took the boat from Cyprus to Athens with the car, then set out for a long tour of many archaeological and other sites, beginning at Delphi in northern Greece and ending up with Stonehenge and sites in England. Camping was the only way we could afford such a trip, but it was a marvelous adventure abroad. That is not to say that two teenage girls were easily managed.

Back home, the children returned to school, enriched by their experiences abroad. Pamela, hired by telephone while we were in Cyprus, began as principal at Temple Emmanu-El and continued there for the next five years. But she still hated Tucson. I resumed the supervision of my graduate program, having gotten out of the NES headship on my sabbatical. But then in 1997 a relatively recent dean in her infinite wisdom decided to eliminate all graduate programs that produced fewer than six

PhDs a year. My program was obviously threatened, so I quickly solicited more than two dozen letters of support from colleagues from all over the world. The responses were prompt and almost embarrassingly laudatory. I sent them all to the president, naïvely supposing that presidents still were academics. Several months went by with no response, not even an acknowledgment. Finally I called the president, who said, "I'm not in the loop."

I had heard the business lingo before. Already when I was still department head, the dean had informed all the heads that we would need to do an inventory. I was puzzled, but she meant that we were to measure the floor space in the offices, list the university-owned furniture, and describe the classroom and facilities (and count the books, I suppose). That was bad enough, but then the dean instructed all heads to do a consumer survey. The administration wanted to know, she explained, what it cost "to deliver the product." I said, "You mean interview students? And the product is education?" Shortly thereafter I submitted my resignation, partly as a threat, but it was immediately accepted. Now, three years later, the dean's revenge would be complete.

I was hauled before a review committee made up of people I had never heard of; there was not a single archaeologist or anthropologist among them. I was given ten minutes to defend a program that had taken me twenty years to build. Finally the dean said, "Well, you know, your program doesn't bring in much money. Every student you recruit we have to subsidize." I hesitated only a moment before saying, since I knew the cause was lost, "Madame, follow out the logic of that. If what you really want to do is save money, close the university. That'll do it." I have no idea why she didn't like me.

That was the end of my program. We still had ten doctoral students in residence, and I wasn't about to leave them stranded. So I went to an attorney friend, who said, "Don't worry. The university lawyers are hacks. I'll do a pro bono letter threatening them if they don't grandfather your students out." I sent the letter to the administration, and in twenty-four hours they capitulated. The students would all finish their degrees—but things had changed irrevocably for me.

The heady early days at Arizona were over, and along with them the program to which I had given more than twenty of the best years of my life. I didn't see how I could start over, and my discipline was tired as well. I published a rather dour article in the *Biblical Archaeology Review* entitled "Death of a Discipline?" (1995). Few appreciated such pessimism, but it turned out to be well founded. Meanwhile, Pamela was discouraged as well. Her rabbi and superior did not seem to share her high ideals in Jewish education, and she was increasingly dissatisfied. She spoke of looking for other employment. The girls were now in, or about to be in, college and would soon leave the nest. Zeb was flourishing in local grade schools, but they did not provide the challenge that he needed.

Mortality Intervenes—Again

In late summer of 2000 we took Zeb to camp in Malibu, and then Pamela and I drove the old motor home up the California coast for a brief vacation. When we came back to pick up Zeb, we all had lunch with Sean. He had been in Los Angeles since doing a MA in computer animation, moving up rapidly through several Hollywood companies. He now had an executive position at Cinesite, a wholly owned Kodak subsidiary that produced computer animation sequences for movies. Sean was thirty-one and enjoying enormous success in what he loved: cinema. I have always been fascinated by verbal symbols, but for Sean it was visual images. (Strange, I don't even go to movies, and I've never touched a computer.)

Sean was fifteen years into remission from Hodgkin's disease, and we had mostly put it out of mind. But at lunch that day we could see the swelling in his neck, and suddenly I was transported back to that fateful biopsy fifteen years earlier. In a few days Sean entered Cedars Sinai Hospital in Los Angeles for what the doctors said would probably be a thyroidectomy. But halfway through the surgery they came out to the waiting room to tell us that they had halted the operation. They were looking rather into irregularities that would require further biopsies. The results soon came back: Hodgkin's disease. Sean was as stoic as he had been years earlier, but Pamela and I (and Norma) were terrified. The disease was advanced, perhaps in Stage 3.

This time Sean had chemotherapy rather than radiation. The treatments lasted for about six months and were devastating. Somehow he continued working the entire time, taking off only a few hours to rest. The people at the company were magnificent. Often, we were told later, he was more concerned about his fellow employees at Cinesite than about himself. As always, he was cheerful, wanted no pity, and maintained his infectious humor. He came home at Thanksgiving and Christmas but was clearly debilitated. We hardly dared to be hopeful, but by late winter, Sean appeared to be better. We even envisioned his recovery a second time from Hodgkin's disease, but that was not to be.

Sean came home the last time in early April, and as I walked him to the car I joked that he was going to get well and would live forever. He gave me a rueful smile and said, "I don't think so, Dad." I hugged him and said that I loved him. I never saw him alive again. He died in Los Angeles on Friday, April 13, 2001—Good Friday. He was thirty-two.

At a memorial service a few days later, his company hired a large Rodeo Drive restaurant and invited anyone who knew Sean from the several computer animation companies in Hollywood for which he had worked in his ten years in the city. There was a buffet and an open bar. More than two hundred people turned up, few of whom Norma and I knew. Sean seemed to have been famous as a party animal in Los Angeles,

Fig. 51. With Zeb and Sean shortly before the end, December 2000.

even though he was quite serious about his work. Life in the fast lane, I suppose. His friends had gone to his apartment and had found his black leather pants and Hawaiian shirt and had placed them in a life-like pose in a chair in the middle of the restaurant. Beside the chair was a table, on it a large portrait of Sean and a lit candle.

It was a surreal evening—almost a celebration of Sean's life by his many friends in the business, some of whom seemed a bit bizarre to me. Norma and I stood to one side in a receiving line, meeting dozens and dozens of people we had never seen. They stopped by to praise Sean, not just for his professional accomplishments, but more significantly for the impact he had had on many of his colleagues and friends. One young woman flew all the way from Australia to tell us how Sean had saved her life. He had met her at a symposium there and had dropped his own work to hear her out in a time of deep depression; she had taken courage from that. Countless people told us similar stories of Sean's compassion for others—perhaps because of his own condition. In this, Sean was certainly my superior, as he was also in his amazing courage and good cheer in the face of death. How different our children are! And how little we really know them.

I never did understand what Sean did. He would take me through the vast facilities at Cinesite and show me how computers could simulate reality in scenes the company did for movies. But I have never touched a computer, and that whole world of visual imagery is foreign to me. Nor did I understand Sean's frenetic lifestyle in Los Angeles. He thrived on risk, it seems. He went bungee-jumping and sky-diving. He went scuba diving with sharks. He would fly to Los Vegas with a friend who owned a small plane for a weekend of gambling in the casinos (he claimed that he always made money). He loved fast cars. He was attractive to girls and was attracted to them. As I looked back at his behavior, so unlike my characteristically prudent way of doing things, I was inclined to be a bit judgmental. But now I think I understand. When he unexpectedly recovered from cancer at sixteen, he was determined to live life to the fullest, in case he hadn't much time left. In some ways Sean experienced more in his brief life than I have in my nearly ninety years. I can't fault him for wanting to do that. I just wish the adventure had lasted longer.

At his memorial service in Tucson, Saint Philip's in the Hills Episcopal Church was filled with our friends, as well as many of his old school teachers and chums. He had gone from first grade though college in Tucson, and his closest school friends gave eloquent tributes, recalling how Sean had always been a bit of a clown. His friend Josh from Los Angeles gave a heartbreaking tribute, revealing once again how little we had known of Sean's life and circle of friends there. My colleague in biblical studies at the university, Ed Wright, delivered the eulogy. I sat between my wife and former wife, my surviving children beside us, and listened as my own choir, the Lane Justus Chorale, sang from the rear of the church. I looked through the huge picture window behind the altar, an unobstructed view of the pristine Sonoran Desert that I loved, seemingly stretching forever. I thought, "Life goes on." And it did—but nothing was ever the same again.

We had also planned a memorial service for Sean at the W. F. Albright Institute of Archaeological Research in Jerusalem, where he had spent his earliest years. The service, in July, was held in the spacious and serene garden of the institute and was attended by dozens of Israeli and American colleagues, as well as a few faithful Arab friends. I especially valued the presence of Ali Musa Abu Argoub, my old foreman in digs in the West Bank after the 1967 war. He risked arrest in coming from his village of Samua, hiking across the back country and climbing through a hole in the border fence.

His son, named William after me, was about the same age as Sean would have been. We two bent old men embraced, sharing memories that the Israeli crowd could scarcely have understood. Nor did it matter. These were private moments, remembering a time and place gone forever. And Ali, too, is dead now.

We placed a plaque commemorating Sean's birth and death in the garden of the Albright. Norma and I, with the help of our friends, established the Sean W. Dever Memorial Scholarship of $1,000 per year to the graduate student in archaeology and biblical studies with the best oral or written paper.

In August, Pamela and Zeb moved to New York, since a few weeks before Sean's death she had signed a contract as school principal at Congregation B'nai Yisrael in Armonk. She had to honor that commitment, and in any case we had been moving in the direction of my retirement. My life in Tucson, like so many other things, was over. But I stayed all the next school year to honor my own commitments, mostly to my remaining graduate students. Then I had to prepare the house for sale and plan to move the rest of our things to New York.

That year alone I grieved in my own way, as one must. There are no designs for such things. In the first few weeks, almost in a daze, I wrote the complete manuscript of *Who Were the Early Israelites and Where Did They Come From?* Had I not kept busy with work, as usual, I would have lost my mind. Even so, there are long stretches of that awful year of which I have no memory. I simply survived, sustained by the memory of Sean and his unfinished work. I often thought of Nietzsche's observation: "That which does not kill us makes us stronger." In late May I sold the house, packed everything up, and left Tucson. I had been there for twenty-seven years, by far the longest time I had lived anywhere. I still miss the desert and the life we lived there, but I have learned that all good things come to an end.

8
IN LIMBO: MY EIGHTH LIFE

I arrived in Mount Kisco, New York, in June of 2002, driving a big U-Haul truck containing the remainder of our personal belongings that had been left behind in Tucson when Pamela and Zeb had moved to New York a year earlier. She was living in a rented house in Mount Kisco, and we planned to look for something to buy when I arrived. Using the proceeds from the sale of our house in Tucson, plus an advance I had just gotten from a book, we managed to find a pleasant enough Cape Cod house in nearby Bedford Hills.

Before moving in, we all went as usual to Cyprus and Israel for the summer. Pamela was directing her own excavations at Idalion. I was visiting digs in Israel, as well as working some in the office I had kept all those years at HUC in Jerusalem, where my excavated materials and records were housed. I returned earlier than Pamela and Zeb and made some improvements on the house, and in early September we moved in.

Trying to Retire

I made no secret of my misgivings about retiring from a long and active academic career, even though I was almost seventy, or having to move to New York, where I had no job, connections, or friends. I felt as though I were in limbo, and the sense of loss and alienation was made all the more poignant by the still-unresolved grief over Sean's recent death. But work had always been the only therapy that I have known, so resuming regular visits to Israel helped me to think that I was still keeping my hand in. Even though I was now a reluctant armchair archaeologist, I could nevertheless keep up with the ongoing fieldwork of others in Israel and

Jordan, many of them my own students. I would have to get used to being the old man.

There are, fortunately, some advantages to getting older—especially in a field such as archaeology. Mathematicians may peak in their twenties, but archaeologists deal better with their antiquities when they become one. It takes a lifetime of fieldwork when you are younger, research and publication in mid-career, and reflection in your mature years to gain a proper perspective on the past—yours and the discipline's. I was now in that final phase, where one's remaining efforts are best concentrated not on digging or amassing more data but rather on synthesis: interpreting the results of archaeological investigation on a broader scale. So, in addition to working on the completion of a few remaining final report volumes from some thirty seasons in the field, I turned to essays, especially in Festschrift volumes honoring old friends and colleagues (all now retiring, like me). I also published another semipopular book, *Did God Have a Wife? Archaeology and Folk Religion in Ancient Israel* (2005). It appeared to some that I now had more questions than answers, but that's what archaeology does: it raises new questions. Now I also began the manuscript of an early version of this work.

Although retired, I was writing more than ever, a necessity for a workaholic like me, but also a luxury since I now had more time for writing. Becoming a popularizer was a luxury in another sense, since I could afford to risk my hard-earned reputation by taking on controversial subjects or being accused by colleagues of oversimplification. I no longer needed to prove that I was a competent excavator or a serious scholar. At last I could say what I *damned well pleased!* (Smart alecks said that I always had.)

Attempting to communicate the results of biblical and Levantine archaeology to a larger public took on another aspect besides writing. I became a familiar figure on the lecture circuit, even a minor celebrity of sorts. I had long since been invited regularly to do TV programs for the Discovery and Learning channels, as well as for public television, and now that exposure was increased by the semipopular books out there. I was never paid for the appearances, but they sold books and, of course, led to invitations to travel and lecture widely.

My Fifteen Minutes of Fame

I had discovered another benefit of not having to waste time talking to deans who were failed academics or teaching undergraduate students who were never going to be academics. I had a bigger and more appreciative audience now—and despite being a popularizer, I was still a teacher. That was what I had always wanted to be. I often thought, "How lucky I am to be alive, reasonably well, in command of most of my facilities, and able to do useful work, work that I love!" In the academic year of 2003–2004, I made twenty-one trips and gave forty-five lectures. Maybe retirement wasn't going to be so bad after all.

Fig. 52. Lecture tours while in New York, 2002–2008.

With no classes to restrict my schedule, I now had time for more serious lectures as well, especially at international symposia that required travel time. I gave an invited paper on ethnology and ancient music in Rio in 2001. In the summer of 2002 I was invited to give the plenary lecture in Dublin for the eighth Annual Meeting of the British Society for Old

Testament Studies. In March of 2003 I spoke in Rome at an international symposium on historiography and ancient Israel—the nastiest public encounter I have ever had with other scholars. The revisionists were furious with my critiques and were out for blood, especially Philip R. Davies, who launched a personal attack on me that left the audience stunned. (When you have no facts, demonize your opponents.)

In the spring of 2004 I gave the nationwide Charles Elliott Norton lectures for the Archaeological Institute of America (for the second time); in October of that year I spoke at the British Museum on "The Golden Age of Solomon—Fact or Fiction?" In late summer of 2005 I led a ten-week seminar at Oxford, then gave a paper there at a symposium on "Carbon 14 Dating and the Bible" (Solomon again). Some of these papers were published, either state-of the-art summaries or further attempts at dialogue with the revisionists or (more likely) mainstream biblicists.

Scholarly recognition in retirement is not really needed, but it can be especially satisfying. My book *Who Were the Early Israelites?* (2003) won the Irene Levy-Salz Prize in Israel in 2003, as the best popular book in archeology that year. I also received another honorary doctorate in 2005, from Lycoming College in Pennsylvania. My uncle, a country preacher, used to say that an honorary doctorate is like the tail on a hog: it doesn't do anything useful, but it tickles the ham. So it did.

Final Reports

I had hoped in retirement to do two large final scholarly works. The first was to be entitled *The Lives of Ordinary People* (it finally appeared in 2012). This would take up the challenge often thrown at me when I argued that *archaeology*, not the Hebrew Bible, is now our primary source for writing new and better-balanced histories of ancient Israel. Skeptics would say, "But can you write a history of ancient Israel *without* the Bible?" Of course, you can: it all depends upon what kind of history you want and think possible. Mine, restricted to a single epochal century, would be disinterested in secular history, hopefully devoid of any theological agenda. Most of the data would come from archaeology and be focused on the daily life of the masses. The biblical texts would be introduced only subsequently and largely for the light they might shed on the intellectual ideas of the elites, those minorities who wrote and edited the Hebrew Bible. I thought then that this was an idea whose time had come, but my time was running out, and I did not publish the fully mature work until 2017, under the title *Beyond the Texts: An Archaeological Portrait of Ancient Israel and Judah* (SBL Press). This was the first new, mainstream history of ancient Israel to be published in English in more than thirty years., and it was the first to take the archaeological data as primary.

The other work was the final report volume on my excavations of two EB IV sites (ca. 2500–2000 BCE): Jebel Qaʻaqir in the Hebron hills in 1967–1971; and Beʼer Resisim in the Negev in 1978–1980. These were pioneering excavations of a dark age at the time, and they should have been published long ago. But both were salvage projects, added perforce onto my usual obligations. And once I left the materials behind in Israel, it was difficult to work on them. But the volume went to press for the Harvard Semitic Museum in 2011 and appeared in 2014.

Few twentieth-century Near Eastern archaeologists have lived to publish their final field reports—none of my teachers or the founding generation of Israeli archaeologists. It takes as much as twenty-five years after the end of a major excavation to work up and publish all the materials. I had vowed to be out of the field before sixty, and I was, giving me a fighting chance to publish. Do I miss fieldwork? Of course! (And finally, I know how to do it right.) But to excavate without publishing is systematic destruction, and it is immoral. There must be a special corner of hell reserved for archaeologists who do not publish (right next to the one for lawyers and politicians?). I may go to hell anyway, but I hope in that case for other reasons.

Frivolities

Retirement is supposed to provide a bit of play to compensate for the diminished career satisfactions one experiences. But I was never very good at play, as my family will attest. There is in my Irish temperament a certain morbidity, profoundly cherished. Then there's the manic side of my bipolar disorder, long undiagnosed but always the defining trait of my personality—surprisingly, similarly cherished since it works for me.

In my mid-forties in Tucson, I was still undiagnosed but beginning once again to experience what I thought was burnout. I consulted my physician, also a close family friend. He asked what was bothering me. What did I really want to do? The answer was obvious: I wanted to work. I'll never forget the wise advice of my medical friend: "Forget about trying to relax. That could *kill* you! Just get back to work." I did that, and ever since I have known that I am one of the lucky ones among those with a bipolar disorder. I feed off the mania. Fortunately, the highs are long and sustained, and they give me an energy that rarely fails me, one that is best satisfied by plunging into productive work. Happily, the work of scholarship is never finished.

I do have *some* avocations (not really hobbies, I insist, for that would be frivolous), but these activities must be creative. From my adolescent days in Jamaica, I have always done cabinetmaking, and I still do. For many years I have sailed a 4.20-m class boat (a Lido 14), a sport that requires more skill than brawn and suits my tendency to be a loner rather than a team player. And I have always sung in choral groups.

In retirement in New York, I channeled my woodworking and related skills into a sizeable sweat equity in our house. But advancing arthritis and knee replacements ended all that and sailing as well. So I focus now on singing as a diversion. I've sung with several auditioned amateur and semiprofessional choirs, including Amor Artis in New York, directed by the distinguished European conductor Johannes Somary. Most of these groups specialize in liturgical music, usually Renaissance or Baroque. We have performed, for instance, the Verdi Requiem in Carnegie Hall. While I may no longer subscribe to the theological motifs of these compositions, I am deeply moved by them. Indeed, I could not live without such music, which is always in the background as I write.

It is characteristic that these works I love are not popular but terribly serious. I have no interest whatsoever in popular music and scarcely any interest in contemporary music of any sort. I remain, in all things, an unabashed traditionalist. Perhaps that's why archaeology suits me so well. The title of my second Festschrift sums it up well: *Confronting the Past* (2006).

9
CYPRUS: MY NINTH LIFE

Much of my energy in New York had been focused on leaving the place, even though it had served me well as a base for extended operations in my brief postcareer phase as a traveling salesman for archaeology. Pamela has worked in Cyprus nearly every summer for the past thirty-five years, and I visited there frequently even before we were married. We know many people on the island, both foreign excavators and local Greek Cypriots. The children have spent numerous summers there, and in 1996 the whole family lived in the village of Dhali, near Pamela's site of ancient Idalion. So it was natural that we always hoped to be able to retire in Cyprus when the time came.

Israel, where I worked for more than fifty-five years and where we met, was out of the question because it had become too expensive and, frankly, too stressful. But Cyprus is a relative bargain and easily accessible for brief trips to Israel. It is also calm at the moment, since the Turks are making nice in the hopes of getting into the European Union, as the Greeks on their side already were. In Cyprus, Pamela can work on her publication of the Idalion materials, and I can sit under my own fig tree, as the biblical ideal has it. What could be better in old age?

By the summer of 2007, Zeb was nearing the end of his high school years at Fox Lane in Bedford Hills. To be honest, Pamela and I were looking forward to liberation (four children is a lot). In addition, as school principal of a synagogue, Pamela was growing increasingly disillusioned about the superficiality of up-scale Westchester society and a congregation of nouveau riche Jews who weren't really interested in Judaism in its historical and ethical context. "Just make our children feel Jewish." (And in six years as a member of Congregation B'nai Yisrael in Armonk, I had never once been invited to speak for any group, even though the senior rabbi had been my student in Jerusalem in the 1970s.) So we began to form our thoughts more and more on Cyprus and possibly a new beginning there.

In November we went to our timeshare in Tucson for Thanksgiving with some of the family, and we even looked seriously at a lovely condominium overlooking the Sonoran Desert in Tucson, where I had lived for twenty-seven years and all my children had been raised. Tucson was a possible retirement venue, home base in case full-time residency in Cyprus didn't work out.

Back in New York in December, however, Pamela was offered a half-time appointment in archaeology and Judaic studies at Lycoming College, a small liberal arts college in northcentral Pennsylvania. Lycoming students and faculty had come to Gezer back in the 1960s, and in recent years both Pamela and I had formed relationships with the college. She had been director of a field school at Idalion in Cyprus, where student volunteers were coming; I had been a scholar in residence in 2004 and had received an honorary doctorate from Lycoming in 2005. So we both accepted appointments for the fall semester for a projected five years, Pamela as professor of archaeology and Judaic studies and I as distinguished visiting professor of Near Eastern archaeology. Soon we added adjunct professorships at Penn State University, forty-five minutes away, where there were close colleagues in archaeology and biblical studies, with especially close ties to Israel.

Soon thereafter, in January of 2008, we purchased a new home in Montoursville, a reconfigured restored brick grist-mill in the countryside, built in 1842 on a branch of the Susquehanna River. It was in remarkable condition, but it reeked of age and the character that only age can bring. In July we finally sold the New York house, while Pamela was digging in Idalion, and Zeb and I moved all our belongings (where did we *get* all this stuff?) to Williamsport.

The fall semester at Lycoming College went exceptionally well; the people were so much friendlier than fancy-pants New Yorkers, and we *loved* our stately old house. In January we decamped for Cyprus to begin what would be our new life for the foreseeable future: six months in United States, then six months at our old farmhouse in Cyprus. It has already become, for us at least, the best of both worlds. We felt extremely fortunate to be alive, in reasonably good health, and confronting an exciting new life ahead of us.

9. CYPRUS: MY NINTH LIFE

Fig. 53. The 1842 millhouse in Montoursville, Pennsylvania, 2008–.

Moving from Westchester County, New York, in the spring and summer of 2008 marked a major change for our family. Now out of high school, after helping us to move, Zeb went to Israel for a year to participate in a program run by Habonim Dror ("the generation of builders"). This was a Zionist youth social reform movement in Israel whose utopian goal was to reestablish the egalitarian ethos of the early days of the Jewish settlement and the formation of the State of Israel—but this time in an *urban* setting, rather than that of the old kibbutzim, now moribund.

Zeb was eighteen that summer. I had first gone to Israel when I was twenty-three; Pamela had first gone when she was twenty. In time, Zeb would drop out of the University of Arizona, move to Los Angeles to further his Zionist education and experience, and in 2014 make *aliyah*, to "go up to Zion," to become an Israeli citizen. He would master Hebrew, do his military, and begin to move up in the Habonim Dror movement, which by now has some fifty cell groups. He is an idealist—like his parents.

The nest was now empty. Jordana had stayed in Tucson. She finished an MA and another graduate certificate in psychology and began a career in practice and training other counselors. A son and daughter followed, Julian Saletan Hall and Sasha Saletan Hall, our only grandchildren.

Hannah had graduated from the Savannah College of Art and Design on a full fellowship, then returned to Tucson to finish an MA in Near

Eastern Studies in the department at the University that I had founded, with a double major in photo journalism. She has done documentaries in Oman, Morocco, and Cyprus, as well as a Pulitzer Prize–winning documentary on the American political scene. Now she is with *USA Today* in Washington.

Both girls, as well as Zeb, had gone almost all the way through the school system in Tucson. But for all the attachments, Tucson no longer remained home for most of our family.

At Lycoming College after 2008, Pamela's career blossomed. At last, she had a college/university connection that gave her a full professorship, students of her own in an archaeology program that she pioneered, support for the continuing fieldwork at Idalion in Cyprus, and facilities for applying for grants. Best of all, the one-semester teaching assignment in the fall left us free to spend half a year in Cyprus, where she could work on her excavated material.

Our Cyprus American Archaeological Research Institute in Nicosia— the sister institute to the ASOR-affiliated school in Jerusalem that I had directed—greatly facilitated Pamela's work. She became a trustee, and one of my former students, Tom Davis, became a long-term director.

Beginning in 2008 and continuing to the present, we spend half the year in rural Pennsylvania, the other half at our old farm in Cyprus. We continued to develop the original 275-year-old farmhouse into a completely self-contained guest house (and my sometime man cave). The gatehouse, originally the farmer's shop for selling produce, is Pamela's office and lab. Two buildings at the back of the property house Pamela's excavated materials.

On the property we have olive, citrus, almond, chinaberry, and pine trees, as well as bougainvillea, jasmine, rosemary, and other flowering bushes. There are two old grape arbors, but the grapevines no longer flourish. The new house on the middle terrace, some 225 years old, became our residence. We did not modernize it, only made it more livable, filled with antique furniture or reproductions that I made. The mud-brick walls are nearly 2 feet thick, the exposed beams of the tile roof are up to 14 feet high, the floors are mostly old stone slabs or rough gypsum tiles. There are few modern appliances. We heat with a fireplace. We live very much the way Cypriot villagers lived a hundred years ago. As antiquarians by temperament and training, this way of life suits us.

Fig. 54. Our old farmhouse in Alampra, Cyprus, circa 2008.

Since settling in both Cyprus and Pennsylvania in 2008, when I turned seventy-five, I have enjoyed a sort of second retirement. I have maintained some academic affiliations, as distinguished visiting professor of Near Eastern archaeology at Lycoming College and adjunct professor of classical and Mediterranean studies at nearby Penn State University (both honorary appointments). This way I have a library and other facilities, colleagues, and occasional opportunities to teach a bit. I miss my doctoral students, but now I can pick and choose my academic responsibilities. I can say no to deans and department heads, and I have much more time to write.

During these further retirement years, I published a coedited ASOR Centennial volume (already in 2003 with Sy Gitin) and a Festschrift for Sy Gitin (2007). On my own, I published a volume on everyday life in ancient Israel (2012), a large final report volume on my excavations at EB IV sites (2014), and a massive synthetic history of ancient Israel entitled *Beyond the Texts: An Archaeological Portrait of Ancient Israel and Judah* (2017; more below). A short, popular version appeared in 2020, entitled *Has Archaeology Buried the Bible?*—a frankly didactic work stressing how a critical reading of the Hebrew Bible and a revisionist history of ancient Israel need not rob us of the ethical and moral values that undergird the Western cultural tradition (my missionary zeal again).

In addition, a collection of some thirty of my older essays, most in obscure places, some nearly forty years old, is in press. So is this autobiography. As of this writing, my bibliography amounts to more than five hundred publications; they have all been written by hand, printed on yellow pages. Nearly all these manuscripts, over a period of more than fifty years, were typed by Norma, who was unique in understanding my work and to whom I remained indebted until her death in 2019.

None of these publications in my late seventies and eighties would have been possible without the support of a generous benefactor, who, however, prefers to remain anonymous. She called me in 2009 after having discovered several of my recent semipopular books, which she said had saved her life. When I asked her in astonishment what she meant, she explained that I had helped her resolve a life-threatening dilemma: how to reconcile her devotion to the Bible and her critical training in science.

She then asked whether she might contribute in some way to my continuing work, especially in publication. I recall saying "Madame, I'm *retired*." She replied "No you're not! You have more work to do." I protested that I had sold my library, but she said, in effect, "Buy it back." We left it at that, but in the end she prevailed. So at seventy-six I began to rebuild my library and to travel back and forth to Israel to keep up again with fieldwork and to do the research needed to produce what would turn out to be my magnum opus—the cumulative work of a lifetime, *Beyond the Texts* (2017). This was the first attempt of any scholar to write a comprehensive history of ancient Israel based on the revolutionary idea that henceforth any such history would have to be based on the archaeological data—*not* the textual data—as the primary evidence. The 747-page work is dedicated "With profound gratitude to an anonymous benefactor whose generosity is outstripped only by her modesty."

In addition, the 2012 and 2014 volumes were the result of our collaboration, as the volumes of essays mentioned above and my autobiography will also be. But our most ambitious project—I don't know whether I really saved her life, but she certainly saved mine. If I had tried any longer to retire, I would have withered and died. Work is my life, and she has prolonged it so that my late seventies and eighties have been my most productive years, capping a long, adventuresome, and (I hope) productive career.

The renewal of my career also included several visiting professorships: at Beijing Normal University in China (2012), at UCLA (2013), and at La

Sierra University in California (2016). I also did a three-week lecture tour in Australia with Pamela (2012), and together we led several tours of Israel.

In 2008, I gave a lecture in the Jarvis Lectures in Christianity and Culture series at Eastern Carolina State University. In 2012 I gave the Petrie Ovation for the Australian Institute of Archaeology in La Trobe, and in 2014 I gave the Meyers W. Tennenbaum Lecture at Emory University.

In publication, I produced numerous articles and book chapters, including a final state-of the-art piece (2010) and Festschrift essays for Sy Gitin (2007), Eric Meyers (2007), Richard Friedman (2008), Shalom Paul (2008), Rainer Albertz (2008), Ephraim Stern (2009), Larry Stager (2009), Amnon Ben-Tor (2011), Walter Rast and Tom Schaub (2011), Carol Meyers (2015), Ziony Zevit (2017), and Larry Stager again (2018). During these years I published several invited papers from international seminars on Israelite family religion in Germany (2009, published 2014), on the biblical exodus and conquest narratives in San Diego (2013, published 2015), and on state-formation processes in ancient Israel in Jerusalem (2019).

In 2017 I won ASOR's rarely given Richard J. Scheuer Medal for lifetime service to the profession. Most important, my life was prolonged enough to allow me to become one of the oldest scholars in the world in my discipline—old enough to see some of my students near retirement age.

Old age may give one a unique perspective, but the view now focuses on the end, on the most fundamental aspect of our humanity, mortality. Already at sixty-seven I had outlived my parents (now by more than twenty years), all my teachers and mentors, some of my friends and colleagues, and one of my own children. My turn next?

In New York, I began to experience my first serious health issues. I had both knees replaced in 2004, and in Pennsylvania in 2010 I had back surgery. Eventually skin cancer, an occupational hazard of archaeologists, began to take its toll. By now, everything hurts, but I can still write. And in my mature, final years, I have become more philosophical, perhaps a bit less confrontational. I still hold my ground when defending what I think is right, but I recognize that other views may prevail.

Unlike so many others, I have been able to fulfill nearly all my personal and professional ambitions, even to go beyond them. I consider myself to have been extraordinarily fortunate, and I am grateful for the opportunities I have had, particularly in family, in friends, in colleagues, and in those who have appreciated and supported my work. I am grateful even to my adversaries, who have helped to sharpen my focus, to order priorities. I have had two Festschrift volumes: one by my own students (2003) and another entitled, significantly, *Confronting the Past* (2006). Perhaps I believe in Providence after all.

An Old House for Old Folks

In the summer of 2005 Pamela and I had discovered by accident that part of a three-hundred-year-old farm in the nearby village of Alampra (aka Alambra), near Pamela's site of Idalion, was for sale. It had been owned for twenty years by a Swiss archaeologist and had been used now and then as a dig house and storage facility, but the two old houses on the grounds had not really been residences and had long been abandoned. We learned that, despite having sunk a good bit of money into improving the property, the owner, a friend, was anxious to get out from under the obligation. We found him in Athens, made an offer over the telephone, and became the new owners of a *very* old property. It was a dream come true. I have already described how we had begun living part-time in this house in 2008, but let me elaborate on life in the village.

Fig. 55. Pamela in the field at Idalion.

The oldest part of the village of Alampra consists of a few dozen old mud-brick houses, our house among the oldest; a venerable Greek Orthodox church whose bells punctuate the day; two elementary schools; and a farmers' cooperative and grocery. The population is about five hundred, many of them the parents of younger people who have built fancy new houses on the outskirts of the village. The central square of the village was recently put on the National Registry and is slated for renovation. Further, the restoration of our two houses seems to have galvanized neighbors to undertake the rehabilitation of their own houses and other old buildings. The village can never really modernize because it is on a dead-end road, and the village streets are too narrow for much vehicular traffic. That suits our antiquarian tastes: living in a village first occupied in the Middle Cypriot I period, some four thousand years ago.

Life in the tiny village of Alampra is slow, traditional, unexciting—and wonderful. It is like living in a small town in America seventy-five years ago. Everyone knows everyone else, and many people are related by blood. The older folks remain at home and are cared for by their families. There are no policeman in the village, and no one can recall a crime of any significance. The few children have the run of the village, and their parents know that they will be safe anywhere and will be returned home when it is time. People are outdoors a lot, the women shopping in the small co-op and socializing, the older men who are not working playing backgammon and drinking Greek coffee in the local cafe.

The Cypriots love to eat, and the local foods and wines are superb. Some food is organically grown, and everything is eaten only when fresh and in season. There are dozens of excellent local wines, all reasonably priced, some of the best made in small monasteries. People often prefer to cook outside on an open charcoal fire, and from late afternoon on the smells in the air are heady. If you don't like what you have, you can drift next door.

The hospitality of the Greek Cypriots is legendary, especially in the villages. The older houses, and even some newer ones, have a large plastered stone oven in the garden, as our house has. Especially on feast days, these ovens are fired up, stuffed with lamb, pork, and various casserole dishes, then sealed to cook slowly for hours. Then all three generations of the extended family gathers around to feast, the wines flow, and the meal is finished off with a glass or two of 120-proof "sivania," Cyprus's version of "white lightning."

While the village of Alampra is primitive by some criteria, all the facilities and conveniences of modern life are available within a few miles. Nicosia, the modern capital, is only 12 miles away. There we have an American postdoctoral archaeological research institute (CAARI), with a superb library both in Cypriot and in Syro-Palestinian archaeology. The long term director of the Cyprus American Archaeological Research Institute was one of my early PhDs, Thomas Davis.

In summers there are several dozen American, British, and other foreign archaeologists on the island, so we are hardly isolated. In addition,

Fig. 56. Back: Hannah Gaber, Zeb Dever. Front: Julian Hall, Sasha Hall, Jordana Saletan, Pamela, and me.

there is a large expatriate British population, many of them retired from the British airbase there. Finally, Israel is only a thirty-five-minute flight away, Athens only an hour, and Cyprus is connected by boat to most of the other Greek islands—our favorite place to travel. In short, we have the best of both worlds: the traditional life we archaeologists prefer and the modern world when (and if) we need it. Some of my friends are skeptical about all of this. They doubt that someone like me, who has spent all his life in the public eye, can simply retreat and live in relative obscurity. At any rate, how could one leave America? (The answer to this last question is easy.) But that's the point: I am tired of public life, and I am entitled at last to leave it behind and pull my thoughts together in my latter years. I was seventy-five when we settled in Cyprus, and it's time to abandon the lecture circuit. If I can still manage to put a few words together, I can publish now and then. I have easy access to a first-rate library at CAARI, and Israel is close enough for me to keep up with the field as my interests and abilities will still allow and see our son Zeb, now a citizen. Always something of a loner, despite being thrust into public life early on, I am looking forward to some solitude. That will comfort and fulfill me in my ninth and final life.

10
DOES BIBLICAL ARCHAEOLOGY HAVE A FUTURE?

Most of this story has been about the past—the discipline's and mine. But what of the future? Along with others, I have written numerous state-of-the-art summaries over the past forty years, often predicting and highlighting trends (see bibliography). Let me try a final summation, especially since the reader will now be in a better position to see both how far we have come in sixty years and how far we may have yet to go.

What Is Biblical Archaeology?

Let me begin with some definitions. More than forty-five years ago I began (with others) to argue for the separation of what was then popularly called biblical archaeology from biblical studies generally and theological studies in particular. Although novel and controversial at the time, the agenda was to establish our branch of archaeology as an independent, professional, secular discipline with its own aims and methods. The name we young Turks (imagine!) preferred, Syro-Palestinian archaeology, was actually coined by Albright back in the 1920s, but it soon became a battle cry. We won that battle, but did we win the war?

Today it is universally acknowledged that old-fashioned prove-the-Bible archaeology is dead, and except for a few diehard fundamentalists no one mourns its passing. I am often accused of killing biblical archaeology. I'm flattered, but I simply observed its death throes and was among the first to write its obituary.

Yet by the 1990s, I myself was beginning to ask whether a new style of biblical archaeology might be possible and desirable. Today, both American and Israeli archaeologists (not to mention the public and the media) do use the term *Syro-Palestinian archaeology*, albeit inconsistently and casually, mostly as a kind of shorthand for what we all recognize to be the larger parent discipline. Meanwhile, for Israeli archaeologists the term *Palestinian* has become so politicized that many of us have abandoned it for *the archaeology of the southern Levant* or, better, simply *the archaeology of Israel, Jordan, the West Bank*, and so on.

What I want to emphasize here is that, beyond the terminological confusion, there is a widespread consensus today that biblical archaeology is not a discipline itself (certainly not a substitute for the larger discipline). It is rather a complex, fascinating inquiry between two disciplines—archaeology and biblical studies—a dialogue at the intersection of text and artifact. It may be silly or serious, amateur or professional, but it matters, because fundamental issues of history, faith, and self-identity are at stake. Thus biblical archaeology, properly defined, ought to have a future.

The Larger Discipline of Archaeology in Israel, Jordan, and the West Bank

In the following I want to keep in mind that biblical archaeology is a very small part of the larger discipline of archaeology in Israel and Jordan. At least 75 percent of our fieldwork, research, and publication has nothing whatsoever to do with the Bible, though that is nonetheless important. Here I am being deliberately selective, omitting world-class Israeli prehistoric archaeology.

Throughout this survey I have focused almost exclusively on the relevance of Levantine archaeology for the Old Testament/Hebrew Bible and ancient Israel. That simply addresses the reality of the biblical archaeology movement and its focus, as well as the balance of current archaeological work in Israel, where Second Temple archaeology is, surprisingly, of less interest. This focus here also reflects the reality that Old and New Testament studies are separate disciplines, with different scopes and demands in competence, so no one attempts to master both.

Furthermore, an archaeology of early Judaism and Christianity would take us far from Israel and the Levant to the entire Mediterranean basin and from the Hellenistic world to the Byzantine Empire. A recent, massive work illustrates the challenges: *The Eerdman's Encyclopedia of Early*

Christian Art and Archaeology (3 vols., 2018). It is significant that this work concentrates on art, religion as *practiced*, and artifacts rather than just texts. That is what several of us have been doing with the impact of archaeology on ancient Israelite folk or household and family religion. (We would also use art history if we could, that is, if we had more art.) Again, biblical archaeology is a dialogue between several disciplines.

Call it what you will, the health of the parent discipline of archaeology is fundamental to the hoped-for dialogue. Yet archaeology is hardly a monolithic enterprise. For purposes of analysis, let us look first at the Middle East, keeping in mind that here I am focusing largely on American and Israeli work, that is, in the heartland of the biblical world.

Israel

Israel is certainly dominant, and not just because we in the West think of it as the Holy Land (i.e., ours). On the bright side, archaeology in Israel appears to have flourished in the last thirty years. Standards in fieldwork have improved exponentially. The best digs are as good as those anywhere, and the embarrassing projects that some of us remember are no longer tolerated.

There are also more projects in the field than ever, of every size, variety, and focus. Israeli excavations at the time of this survey are too numerous to mention. Many are smaller or salvage projects, as always, but there are large, ongoing excavations (some joint) at Abel-beth-maacah, Kabri, and in the Negev, as well as in Akko, Beth-Shemesh, Azekah, Tell Zafit (Gath), Tel Buma, Khirbet al-Ra'i, Khirbet Qeiyafa, and Tell 'Eton—altogether representing all the Israeli university institutions of archaeology. In addition, longer-running reexcavation projects at Hazor, Megiddo, and Gezer continue in the field. There are also excavations at later period sites (Second Temple period, in Israeli parlance) beyond our purview here, since, for better or for worse, biblical archaeology has been overwhelmingly about the Old Testament/Hebrew Bible and ancient Israel.

It is difficult to see any clear trends in these and other current Israeli excavations. Some are clarifying the Bronze and Iron Age history of Israel's neighbors, the Phoenicians and Philistines. Others focus on Iron Age Israel, but overall there is no obvious concentration on biblical Israel.

One has the impression that current Israeli archaeology no longer has a center in one or two universities, certainly not in the activities of the Israel Antiquities Authority (IAA). It is much more opportunistic and realistically so in light of reduced and uncertain resources. One trend, however, is that science, especially C-14 dating, looms large, more so than more traditional historical concerns and certainly more than any adoption of overall theory, which has always been of relatively little interest, at least until recently. Nearly all recording in the field and in surveys is now digitized, which enables much faster processing of data and publication. Field reports now routinely include several appendices by scholars in various sciences: paleozoology and botany, geology, and neutron analysis. In addition, models are adopted from many ancillary disciplines: anthropology, ethnology, sociology, and economics. The Weitzman Institute at Rehovot, a world-class center for applied science with multimillion grants from the European Union, does its own analyses, including C-14 dating. (That, of course, gives the Israelis enormous advantages over American commuter archaeologists.) Finally, another development: with the retirement or death of several prominent senior archaeologists who have no obvious heirs, the golden age is over.

On the bright side, however, there are five thriving institutes of archaeology, all with graduate programs, in Jerusalem, Tel Aviv, Ramat Gan, Haifa, and Beersheba. The archaeological division of the Israel Museum has its own large interdisciplinary professional staff, excellent laboratories, and modern galleries that rank it among the world's great museums. The old Department of Antiquities has morphed into a much more professional and ambitious Israel Antiquities Authority. Despite the opposition of many, it has raised standards, for instance, in required conservation of sites. A new world-class national storage and research center has been opened by the Authority at Beth-Shemesh. Finally, with the assistance of American funding, the IAA has built an elaborate facility in Jerusalem to replace its old headquarters in the Rockefeller Museum in the Old City.

Younger Israeli archaeologists are much more sophisticated than their venerable teachers in their wide reading of the literature, their use of socioanthropological theory typical of archaeology elsewhere, and their openness to cross-cultural comparisons. One simply did not see these things a generation ago. (In the wings, unheard of as yet by most outsiders, awaits a superb fourth generation of even younger and better

Israeli archaeologists.) Israeli archaeologists, long accused of not publishing, are pouring out a flood of both analytical research papers and final report volumes. There are numerous journals and serials of the IAA and the universities, nearly all in English, which are now the leading publications. The most recent event is the publication of five lavish volumes of the excavations at Lachish by David Ussishkin and others, which I have hailed as a landmark. The Israelis now vastly outpace us in publication, largely because they have the institutional support that we Americans lack. In all this, the Israelis have grown in professionalism, so that theirs is per capita (Israel is a small country) arguably one of the most impressive national archaeological schools in the world, with unparalleled popular support. But there are danger signs.

First, budgets for both the IAA and the universities have been slashed. Recently the IAA put a third of its employees on part-time nonbenefit status and let some of them go permanently. The university institutes have suffered 10 percent cuts annually for several years. My Israeli colleagues tell me privately that, without direct American subsidies to the institutes, as well as the profits from American student volunteer programs in the summer, Israeli archaeology could not survive. Now, with fewer and fewer American universities (and parents) willing to insure students and send them to Israel, income is dwindling further. The fact is that, in today's beleaguered Israel, archaeology is simply not a high priority for the government or all that attractive to foreign institutes. The latter are severely handicapped by the fact that the Israelis now require that all American excavations include an Israeli codirector. There will no longer be any independent American flagship projects such as those at Gezer, Ashkelon, or Ekron in days gone by.

The Israel Antiquities Authority has been compromised by rebellion within its ranks, as well as by budgets cuts. I have already mentioned the scarcity of foreign student volunteers and institutional commitments, which makes it difficult to launch new field projects. Israel continues to tolerate the black market in antiquities and to license dealers, and it does little to stop tomb robbing in the occupied territories. The latest is the scandal of fakes manufactured and traded by Israelis such as Oded Golan, who as I write still has not been convicted and sentenced. Some suggest that the James ossuary and the temple pomegranate are just the tip of the iceberg.

Perhaps the most serious problem of Israeli archaeology is the inability to place younger archaeologists in secure academic positions, rather than what are perceived to be dead-end jobs in the IAA. I can name half a dozen superb young Israeli archaeologists with PhDs who have virtually disappeared in the last decade. Particularly disturbing is the fact that there are so few Israeli women who are well placed, none yet in prominent positions, despite some impressive talent. Where are today's equivalents of Ruth Amiran or Trude Dothan? There are a few women archaeologists in academia, but others are in the Israel Antiquities Authority, in archaeology and science at the Weitzman Institute at Rehovot, at the Israel Museum, and working as independent scholars. University retirement funds have been raided, so they cannot conform to requirements on benefits and thus are hiring virtually no new people in archaeology. Meanwhile, the third generation of Israeli archaeologists—Finkelstein, Mazar, and others—has retired (at sixty-eight, as the law requires), and there are few replacements who can aspire to their singular positions of leadership. Israeli archaeology will be less focused in the future, but that may be beneficial. The era of great men is over.

Fig. 57. Reading pottery with Ruth Amiran.

Finally, I note with some hesitation the polarization of the Israeli archaeological community. Small and somewhat ingrown, this community is becoming characterized by intense rivalries and, worse still, by the cult of personality swirling around Finkelstein. He may have achieved celebrity status abroad, but he is not the centrist he claims to be, and in the minds of many of his colleagues he has given Israeli archaeology a bad name, as though everything is about controversy. It is not. Here there also lurks the danger of politicizing archaeology in the service of radical new movements such as post-Zionism, although to their credit most Israelis thus far have managed to avoid the alignment of archaeology and nationalism. Staying neutral has proven to be a particular challenge since the Orthodox political parties declared open war on archaeology and archaeologists three decades ago. They have not prevailed, but neither have they given up. If they had their way, all archaeology in Israel would be forbidden. The irony is that, in America, fundamentalists love archaeology; in Israel, they hate it.

Jordan

I am less familiar with archaeology in Jordan, although I often visit digs there and know most of the Jordanian archaeologists personally. One thing stands out: the expanding number of field projects, both Jordanian and American, some of them large and long-running (e.g., the fifty-year-old Madeba Plains Project). Forty years ago, Jordan was seen as the hinterland, largely unknown, and was thought to be relatively unimportant. There were few digs, especially American ones; publications were scant, and there was no national school.

All that has changed dramatically. There are now dozens of excavations, many of them Jordanian and even more foreign excavations supported by the Department of Antiquities. The department follows the lines of the old efficient British department but with more modern standards. Proof of its enlightened policies under the direction of its directors is that the department issued an excavation permit to Tom Levy, a Jewish scholar with a long history of involvement in Israel—a first.

Despite Jordan's precarious political situation, plus the fact that several of its archaeologists are Palestinians, I see few signs that archaeology there is being politicized or perverted by nationalism—except where younger archaeologists have been subverted by European minimalism. The Jordanian universities do not yet offer their own doctoral degrees in archaeology, but there are more than a dozen Jordanians with PhDs from abroad, including degrees from some of the world's finest universities. At one time, women were poorly represented, if at all, but today there is a growing group of women in the department and on dig staffs, some with graduate degrees. Every two years the Department of Antiquities organizes an impressive international symposium somewhere abroad under Crown sponsorship, with the papers published in a series of lavish volumes. Prince Hasan of the royal family has been an enthusiastic patron of archaeology in Jordan, and I have met him while visiting digs there. He is also a frequent visitor at our flourishing school there, founded in 1968, the American Center for Oriental Research. Jordan still does not have a modern archaeological museum (only the old British one), but plans for one are underway. In sum, archaeology in Jordan understandably lags somewhat behind its progress in Israel, but it is making extraordinary strides. Today we know probably ten times what we knew forty years ago about the history and archaeology of Jordan. It is no longer the neglected other half of the Holy Land but a fascinating archaeological culture area in its own right (see bibliography).

The West Bank

We used to speak of Palestinian archaeology, but now there are real Palestinians in the field, native Arab archaeologists working with the Palestine Authority, under its own Department of Antiquities, led until recently by Dr. Hamdan Taha. There are departments of archaeology at several Palestinian universities, such as Al-Quds University in Jerusalem, where one faculty member (Dr. Hani Nur al-Din) holds a doctorate from the Sorbonne. At Bir Zeit University, Professor Hamed Salim teaches archaeology, having done his MA with me at the University of Arizona before advancing to his PhD. Several young Palestinian archaeologists are collaborating with foreign excavators, for example, with the Italians at Jericho or the French in the Gaza Strip.

However, formidable obstacles remain. The Palestinian Authority is in such dire straits, so unstable, that archaeology is nearly at the bottom of the list of priorities. There are not even enough resources for basic conservation of sites. And, sad to say, some Palestinian archaeologists are not cosmopolitan enough to rise above politics and nationalist rhetoric. One hope is the W. F. Albright Institute of Archaeological Research, where the director Sy Gitin has created a neutral ground where Palestinian archaeologists are able not only to work in the library but also to socialize with Israelis and Americans. The West Bank has marvelous antiquity sites (including many of biblical importance) and a great deal of pride in its own cultural heritage. Given half a chance, Palestinian archaeology could come into its own. But everything depends upon peace, and the Messiah may come first.

American Archaeology

Coming closer to home, let us look at American archaeology, first in the field abroad and then in this country

Abroad

I have already noted the numerous American projects in Israel and Jordan (none yet in the West Bank, despite the attempts of several of us). In Jordan, the number of digs has grown impressively. More of my students now work in Jordan than in Israel, partly because it is less expensive, apparently safer, and has the appeal of being on the frontier. Nevertheless, at least one American archaeologist who has worked in Jordan for nearly twenty-five years has transferred his projects to Cyprus because his university will no longer send students to Jordan. In Israel, on the other hand, our greatest challenge is to launch new American field projects. The great twenty-year projects at Tel Miqne/Ekron and Ashkelon have ended their fieldwork phase, and no other large projects seem remotely feasible. There is little university interest and virtually no financial support; and there are few tenured young professors with sufficient security and resources to mount a project. To compound the difficulties, the Israel Antiquities Authority will no longer give a license to any American excavator unless he or she has an Israeli codirector, as noted above. The problem is that the Americans provide the money and the people, but the Israeli collaborator, who has all the advantages, tends to get the credit and the publications. To be sure, there are a half dozen or more American projects in the field in

Israel today, but most are small, and they are not sponsored by universities that are training graduate students in the discipline. We desperately need new American field projects in Israel, but at the moment the prospects are not good. A small project such as Ron Tappy's dig of Tel Zayit (possibly biblical Libnah) is significant, relatively speaking, but this is a joint Israeli-American project, like all the others. So was the project at Khirbet Qeiyafa, where my student Michael Hasel was codirector (and did share in publication).

There is some good news, however. For a long time, biblical scholars could claim with some justification that they had no access to the burgeoning archaeological data, since much of it was unpublished. Nor were there any synthetic treatments of the technical data available. Now all that has changed. As I noted above, there are voluminous final reports of excavations in Israel, most of them prompt, all in English. More significantly, there are numerous handbooks, dictionaries, and encyclopedias, all of them providing brief but useful syntheses of the data. For those sources, many with full references to the wider literature, see the "Further Reading" section below.

There is no longer any excuse for biblicists being ignorant of the archaeological data—the data that are now of primary importance for comprehending the reality and the richness of ancient Israel. What is still lacking, however, is a detailed comprehensive overall synthesis. That is what I tried to supply in my 2017 *Beyond the Texts: An Archaeological Portrait of Ancient Israel and Judah* (below).

The great American success story in Israel is the Albright Institute in Jerusalem, until recently under the brilliant guidance of Sy Gitin as director for thirty-four years. It is the only remaining viable foreign archaeological institute in Israel, having survived incredible difficulties both political and financial. (The French, British, and German schools are virtually defunct.) Without the unwavering support of the Albright, few if any American digs would be in the field, and a whole generation of younger American archaeologists might never have gotten their start in Israel.

I am aware that I have not dealt with Syria, but there are virtually no American excavations there, there are bleak prospects for them, and they have nothing to do directly with our topic. In Cyprus, we have a thriving American institute (CAARI), and there are numerous American projects on the island. But again, the archaeology of Cyprus, while important, is beyond our purview here.

At Home

The foundation of American archaeology in the southern Levant as a research and teaching enterprise, not to mention as an intellectual partner in the dialogue of biblical archaeology, is here at home. How are we faring?

The good news is that the discipline has survived at all—survived in spite of the bitter controversy over biblical archaeology that began nearly fifty years ago, growing pains as the discipline came of age, declining support from American academic institutions, and the worsening political situation in the Middle East. ASOR and the Jerusalem school celebrated their centennial in Jerusalem in 2000. Further, during these perilous last thirty years, we have produced at least forty young PhDs. As the mentor of more than half of them, I can attest that they are the best yet: fiercely dedicated to our discipline, willing to risk and to sacrifice beyond reasonable expectations, multitalented, and so well versed in today's archaeological theory and method that I am glad I'm retired.

It is also a very ecumenical group. When I began nearly sixty years ago, biblical archaeology was an exclusive old-boys club: nearly all white males, mostly Protestant clerics. The demographic makeup of the group alone demonstrates the paradigm shift. The vast majority of young people in our field today are simply not practicing what we used to call biblical archaeology. And a discipline, regardless of the terminology, *is* what it *does*.

By the time younger archaeologists get their degrees, many of them have had ten years or more of field experience; a few are already legendary as dirt archaeologists. I'm immensely proud of them and hopeful for their future—our future. Perhaps the best gauge of the overall progress of our field is the Annual Meeting of ASOR. The papers read by young people, compared with those when I began sixty years ago, are light years ahead, and not only because of PowerPoint. Many of the papers are more sophisticated than papers given back then by senior archaeologists. Young people are now stepping into office in ASOR. They are reading papers at national and international meetings, and their burgeoning publications are as good as anything their teachers (and mine) ever did.

On the larger scene, the American public continues to be fascinated by what we archaeologists do, as witness our bombardment by the subject in all the media, especially television. As the success of the magazine *Biblical Archaeology Review* demonstrates, and as I can attest from huge audiences wherever I speak, biblical archaeology in America appears to be alive and well. However, appearances can be deceptive.

The crucial threat to our branch of archaeology is the lack of academic opportunities for young people entering the field. We have plenty of highly qualified candidates, as we have seen, indeed, a surplus. But there are few tenure-track positions at leading universities that can provide adequate resources to support a long-term professional career: library, colleagues in allied fields, a graduate program, funds and commitments for fieldwork. It is true that, miraculously, most recent PhDs are surviving, working at something or another. But many are languishing in dead-end jobs, carrying a teaching load that makes research and publication impossible, unable to continue fieldwork, and postponing personal development and family. Some of our most talented young PhDs have simply dropped out, lost to the field. This is a tragedy, one that I personally feel deeply.

It is true that a few new jobs have been created, notably at Penn State University, the University of North Carolina, Pacific School of Religion, UC San Diego, and UCLA. But after thirty years of leading a distinguished program at the University of Arizona, the program is closed, and the budget line has been redirected to Islamic Thought. Even Harvard let Ernest Wright's position go unfilled for eleven years after his death, and the chair is now empty. Endowed chairs at Duke once held by Carol and Eric Meyers have been converted to biblical studies and reduced to a single full position.

The fact is that, with the shift of priorities from the arts and humanities to science and technology (where the big money is), American universities have lost interest in archaeology, especially in the troubled Middle East. One would like to think that theological seminaries—the home of biblical archaeology in its heyday—might take up the slack, but seminaries such as Drew and McCormick, which sponsored the famous Shechem dig, no longer have any archaeological faculty or do any fieldwork. There is only one full-time professorship in archaeology in a mainstream North

American seminary: at Pittsburgh Theological Seminary—and the chair is not fully endowed. However, there are a number of PhD candidates at evangelical seminaries such as Southwestern Baptist Seminary, and there are also graduate students at Andrews University, an Adventist school. Perhaps the future?

The American public may support us, but this does not translate into what we really need: academic positions. The only hope for our field is to create endowed chairs such as the one at UC San Diego, created recently through the extraordinary generosity of Norma Kershaw. To show you how extraordinary, this is only the second endowed chair in our entire field, the other being at Harvard. Now we need a few endowed positions for *junior* scholars. Without that security, our discipline will remain marginal and imperiled in American academic life.

I once published an article in *Biblical Archaeology Review* entitled "Death of a Discipline?" (1995). Nobody liked it, but the possibility is real. In Europe, the discipline is already moribund because the major universities have abandoned it (as they have their institutes in Jerusalem). The only place in Europe still offering a PhD in our branch of archaeology (and with little emphasis on the biblical connection) is the Institute of Archaeology at the University of London, and it has no stars such as Kenyon on its faculty.

Biblical Archaeology as Dialogue

Having given a state-of-the-art assessment of biblical or Levantine archaeology, let me turn finally to its connection with biblical studies as a partner in dialogue. Over the past forty-five years I have made many attempts to define biblical archaeology, its proper role, and the specific way in which it can and cannot illuminate the Bible. Here I can only repeat a statement of the late 1980s, which is more timely than ever.

Biblical archaeology—or, stated accurately, the archaeology of Syria-Palestine in the biblical period—may indeed survive, although not in the classic 1950s sense. But it is not a surrogate for Syro-Palestinian archaeology or even a discipline at all in the academic sense; it is a subbranch of biblical studies, an interdisciplinary pursuit that seeks to utilize the pertinent results of archaeological research to elucidate the historical and cultural setting of the Bible. In short, biblical archaeology is what it always was, except for its brief bid during the Albright-Wright era to dominate the field of Syro-Palestinian or Levantine archaeology. The crucial issue for biblical archaeology, properly conceived as a dialogue, has always been (and is even more so now) its understanding and use of archaeology, on the one hand, and its understanding of the issues in biblical studies that are fitting subjects for archaeological illumination, on the other—and the proper relationship between the two (Dever 1985, 60, 61).

I want to look now specifically at the American scene, since there can be no question that biblical archaeology is a uniquely American phenomenon, one aspect of a peculiar *religious* atmosphere that does not exist in either Europe or Israel. There is no doubt that archaeology has revolutionized our understanding of the Bible and the biblical world, as Albright had confidently predicted—but not in the way that he and most of the American public expected. I would argue that archaeology is now an indispensable tool in biblical studies, indeed a primary source for writing the history of ancient Israel and early Judaism and Christianity. But the results have been mixed and often disappointing for those who had hoped that archaeology would prove the truth of the Bible. Archaeology has provided a real-life context within which the Bible now appears to many more concrete and tangible and therefore more credible in general. But the historicity of the individual stories of the Bible has often been thrown further into doubt, so that the question of what the supposed events mean seems as elusive than ever.

I cannot go into detail here, but four of my popular books summarize the current status and results of biblical archaeology (2001, 2003, 2005, 2012). Collectively, they present the following conclusions. (1) Relatively few laypeople realize it, but archaeology today demonstrates that the patriarchal stories, while they may have some historical basis in memory and oral tradition, are mostly legendary. (2) The story of the exodus from Egypt has no direct archaeological support and appears to be largely fiction. (3) A pan-military Israelite conquest of Canaan never occurred, much less the annihilation of the native populace. There may have been a small exodus group, but most early Israelites were, in fact, displaced Canaanites. (4) Solomon's golden age is a myth; he did exist (contra the revisionists), but he was the petty chieftain of a few highland tribes, not the ruler of an empire that stretched from the Mediterranean to the

Euphrates. (5) Mosaic monotheism is a relatively late phenomenon, and throughout the settlement period and the monarchy the majority of Israelites were polytheists. (6) For the New Testament era, we have to confess that, however much we can reconstruct the Palestinian world in which Jesus lived, we are as uncertain as ever in our search for the historical Jesus or what he may actually have said. (7) As for early Judaism, I doubt that archaeology has contributed much that is revolutionary. Even the pluralism of the Jewish community revealed by the Dead Sea Scrolls was already known to good scholars. This is summarized in my *Has Archaeology Buried the Bible?* (2020).

All this may appear to make us mainstream archaeologists, both American and Israeli, as much minimalists as the radical European biblicists whom we are vigorously opposing. But there is a critical difference, and therein lies the real threat to the future of biblical archaeology.

Biblical revisionism began in the 1990s, largely in Europe around the Copenhagen and Sheffield schools. The term, which I took from their own writings when I began to oppose them in the mid-1990s, may seem harmless (all good historians revise); however, the most radical of these skeptics are *nihilists*. When they are finished, there is no ancient Israel: the biblical stories are all foundation myths, concocted late in Hellenistic Palestine by Jews desperately seeking an identity. The Hebrew Bible is a monstrous literary hoax. Recently Thomas L. Thompson has extended his deconstruction to the New Testament: there was no historical Jesus; it is all Christianity's self-serving lie. Elsewhere I have demonstrated that the revisionists are really closet postmodernists, since for them there is no truth ("all claims to knowledge are social constructs"), no *history* ("all history writing is fiction"). The latter are all-too-typical postmodern slogans, as typical as the method of deconstructing texts or the claim that all cultural values are relative.

Now, one would think that the revisionists, having discarded the Hebrew Bible as worthless historically (and, of course, theologically), would fall back on archaeology, the only other possible source for history writing. But instead, they ignore or caricature the archaeological data, and they demonize archaeologists like me. Examples are too numerous to cite, but here are a few. (1) In his 1992 book *In Search of Ancient Israel*, Philip R. Davies cites only one archaeological handbook, that of Mazar, and that only in a single footnote discarding it because it deals with the Iron Age and not with Davies's Persian-period literary construct. (2) The group to which Davies belongs—the European Seminar on Methodology in Israel's History—issued a volume on the Assyrian campaigns of Sennacherib in Judah in 701 BCE (Grabbe 2004), for which we have abundant archaeological evidence, including that from twenty-five years of excavations at Lachish. However, there is no chapter by an archaeologist. (3) Thompson held a symposium on the history and archaeology of Jerusalem, the papers from which have been published (2003). The symposium was held in Amman, Jordan; no American or Israeli archaeologists were invited; and the scholars included were all in the revisionist camp, a few of them so virulently anti-Israel that they sound like closet anti-Semites to me. So much for dialogue.

The fact is that the revisionists are not only totally ignorant of modern archaeology, but they are secular fundamentalists: "My mind is made up; don't confuse me with facts!" I have argued that in real intellectual circles, the revisionists' fundamental epistemology, postmodernism, is passe and that, in any case, their influence outside Europe is marginal. However, in 2005 a noted biblical scholar at Yale, John Collins, published a judicious, state-of-the-art analysis of American biblical scholarship in which he argues that revisionism has created a new, skeptical paradigm in biblical studies that will prevail. If so, it will irrevocably undermine our confidence in the historicity of the Bible. Henceforth, the Bible's only claims to appeal to religious beliefs or claims to moral standards will be philosophical—arbitrary matters of personal need or choice. If Collins is right, there is no one out there for us *historians* to talk to. Again, it may be too late for dialogue, at least with mainstream biblical scholars, even in Christian America. I can tell you this much from my own widespread travels and lectures over many years. The average liberal Protestant seminary professors are no longer much interested in the actual history of ancient Israel, only in the Bible as literature. Often the biblical faculty don't bother to attend my lectures. There *is* no real dialogue with archaeology. And despite all that we have learned, no new history of ancient Israel has been written in America in the past thirty years except for a recent evangelical work (Provan, Long, and Longman 2003).

What about other circles? The American public, unlike the European public, still takes the Bible seriously. In some communities there probably is a future for biblical archaeology, even though it would become a purely amateur pursuit, should the professional academic base collapse. It would be either ultimately unsustainable or else wholly dependent upon the archaeological data produced by the Israelis for their own, very different purposes. That is not satisfactory. The production of data is not neutral. How you excavate and publish influences what you find; the answers you get depend largely upon the questions you ask. Israeli-style biblical archaeology is different, and it is not *our* future. Where does that leave us?

It is obvious that the colonial era is over. The archaeology of Israel belongs to Israelis, and rightly so. For many years, in the early history of the field, we Americans pioneered, especially in theory and method, but the Israelis have long since been in the lead. We need them, but they no longer need us (except to supply money and student volunteers, as noted above).

Israelis now define what our branch of archaeology is: not *biblical* or *Syro-Palestinian* archaeology or, even as many of us now acknowledge, *Southern Levantine* archaeology but simply the *archaeology of Israel*. To be sure, Israelis do speak in English of biblical archaeology. But the Hebrew form simply denotes the archaeology of the biblical *period*, that is, the Iron Age, circa 1200–600 BCE, the other time periods being prehistory and the later era, the Second Temple period. Furthermore, the Bible for Israelis means the *Hebrew Bible*, read not as American Jews and Christians read it but, in effect, as the constitution of the State (Israel has no secular constitution.)

The upshot of all the above is that, for us Americans, archaeology in Israel must now be constructed not as an independent discipline but as a dialogue, a conversation between *two* disciplines: archaeology and biblical studies, both Old and New Testaments. The Israelis will increasingly control the production of the essential material culture data, which we in turn will have to employ for *our* distinctive interests. Further, new and relevant understanding of ancient Israel and its relevant contributions to American culture will depend on a productive dialogue between the two sources for history writing: texts and artifacts. Yet there is little evidence of dialogue at all. No new mainstream history of ancient Israel has been written in more than thirty years (see further below).

Archaeologists have not been so skeptical, but they, too, have worked in isolation, usually ill-trained in biblical studies and, moreover, unaccustomed to thinking of themselves as historians. The failure to engage in dialogue has resulted in a stalemate—precisely at the time when

Albright's archaeological revolution really *could* become a reality in our understanding of the life and times of ancient Israel, as well as its enduring cultural and religious values.

It was to meet this challenge that I was emboldened to attempt a major synthesis in my mid-eighties, *Beyond the Texts: An Archaeological Portrait of Ancient Israel and Judah* (SBL Press, 2017). This is the first history of ancient Israel to attempt a dialogue between the biblical text and the archaeological data, but using the latter as the primary data. It is not *the* history of ancient Israel but an effort to inspire more new and different histories, balancing both of our sources.

While I congratulate these Christian groups (and have trained some of their excavators), a monopoly by any group is unhealthy, and if conservative Christian groups come to dominate, suspicions about a biblical bias may arise again. Where are *mainstream* liberal Protestant seminaries? The only archaeological project is Pittsburgh Theological Seminary's recent excavation at Tel Zayit (1991–).

One would think that Jewish institutions would have taken up the theme of archaeology and the Bible, especially since Jewish scholars began entering the field a generation ago. But in Judaism, tradition (as in the Talmud and the Mishnah) is more fundamental than biblical history. (Classic biblical archaeology was almost exclusively a Christian, Protestant enterprise.) In any case, most American Jews think that supporting Israeli archaeology is sufficient. The Hebrew Union College–Jewish Institute of Religion, my own first employer, still maintains an archaeological program at the Jerusalem school, but it has no faculty members in archaeology at the New York, Cincinnati, or Los Angeles campuses, and it has virtually closed the Jerusalem archaeological facility, leaving only the rabbinical program.

I have been speaking of inadequate funding. In the last few years, two major endowments for our field have been established: one at Brown University by Artemis Joukowsky, and the other in New York through a bequest of the late Leon Levy. But neither has yet clarified its aims, and I confess that I am not terribly sanguine about the actual benefits—particularly if endowed chairs are not envisioned. The only fully endowed position in our branch of archaeology is the Dorot chair at Harvard, and as of this writing it has been vacant for several years. Meanwhile, the doctoral programs at Duke and Arizona have been closed. For the first time in many years, American PhD candidates are going to Israel to pursue graduate programs. This loss of our autonomy does not bode well.

Clearly the question about the future of biblical archaeology has no simple answer. I can only suggest that we do face a crisis as serious as any that we have ever confronted. I am convinced that our best hope lies in steering a cautious mid-course between radical skepticism, on the one hand, which rejects the Bible altogether (and archaeology as well), and fundamentalism, which reads the Bible in a literal, simple-minded fashion that most of us can no longer accept.

The middle ground is the position that I have staked out in my recent popular books, but I get criticism from all sides. If the extremists prevail, as they already do in Europe and most of the Middle East, there is little hope for either our kind of biblical archaeology or the enlightened Western cultural tradition that gave rise to the inquiry. After my sixty years observing all these challenges and changes, am I optimistic? The answer is yes and no. My story is almost over. It all depends now on the next generation.

EPILOGUE

Psychologists tell us that we all essentially live out our lives according to a script—as though we are players on a stage (as Shakespeare also put it). The script is unwritten, of course, and it is often subconscious. The script may originate partly from our DNA and partly from the way we are socialized, but the script is always decisive. It governs our most private thoughts and characteristic actions as individuals, on and off the stage. The script largely determines whether we emerge stage front and center or remain a bit player in the wings. And through many acts and scene changes, the plot unfolds and propels us inevitably toward the final curtain. To be sure, some things may depend on how well, how authentically, we act out our part. It is not all fate. And if our script is perverse, then the play will end in tragedy. But the play is the thing in the end.

Like most of us, I was unaware of my script throughout much of my life. Indeed, I thought myself as an autonomous individual, acting on my own free will and proud that *my* motives and achievements were deliberate and clear—and yes, maybe superior. I was different.

As I have grown older, a bit wiser (I hope), and more philosophical in looking back at a long and adventuresome life, I have begun to realize that there does appears to have been a script. But what *was* it? And how has it affected who I became and what I accomplished in all these years?

Socrates famously declared that "the unexamined life is not worth living." After much reflection and soul-searching, I have reviewed my life, and I see that there was a script of sorts and one with a central theme in the plot (like a *Leitmotif* in a novel). It had to do with what I would call a mission: to find the truth as best I could (maybe *the* Truth), to align myself with it and thereby achieve satisfaction (not to "have fun"), and, most of all, to do my duty to communicate whatever knowledge I had accumulated to others.

Early on, I seized first on theology (in seminary) and then on archaeology as the key to acquiring knowledge, not only about the past, but about the future. And for sixty years, most of my life has been about carrying out the mission, *my* mission.

I come by this sense of moral obligation, of duty, naturally, raised in the household of an evangelical pastor. That influence can, of course, make me judgmental and often a bit self-righteous. But it also has kept me on course.

As I look back, there was a remarkable consistency in the theme of all that I have attempted in career, in personal life, and in family life. I wanted to be a professional and to make biblical archaeology a more professional discipline. But I never wanted for myself simply a profession, much less a job; I had a *vocation* (even if not a divine calling).

I always thought about the moral lessons to be gained from studying the past. I was obligated to publish what I learned, in hundreds of both scholarly and popular publications, in more that three hundred public lectures, and in many television documentaries. I also trained more than two dozen PhDs; above all, I was a *teacher*, using whatever skills I had, even a big voice. My wife Pamela is a fellow academic. My children are all in public service, teachers in various ways. Their scripts are very much like my own (Providence?).

I feel fortunate to have had this vocation, and I would gladly do it again, only probably better. Yet I try to be realistic. I have done my best, but it may not be enough, and it probably will make little difference in the end. So the play comes to an end, part comedy, part tragedy. And the stage is turned over to other actors—some, I hope, my students. They are the future.

FURTHER READING

1. On the History of Biblical Archaeology in General

Davis, Thomas W. 2004. *Shifting Sands: The Rise and Fall of Biblical Archaeology.* New York: Oxford University Press.
Dever, William G. 1974. *Archaeology and Biblical Studies: Retrospects and Prospects.* Evanston, IL: Seabury-Western Theological Seminary.
———. 1985. "Syro-Palestinian and Biblical Archaeology." Pages 31–74 in *The Hebrew Bible and Its Modern Interpreters.* Edited by Douglas A. Knight and Gene M. Tucker. Philadelphia: Fortress.
———. 1992. "Archaeology, Syro-Palestinian and Biblical." *ABD* 1:354–67.
———. 1995. "The Death of a Discipline?" *BAR* 21.5:50–55, 70.
———. 2000. "Biblical and Syro-Palestinian Archaeology: A State-of-the-Art Assessment at the Turn of the Millennium." *CurBS* 8:91–116.
———. 2003. "Syro-Palestinian and Biblical Archaeology: Into the Next Millenium." Pages 513–27 in *Symbiosis, Symbolism, and the Power of the Past: Canaan, Ancient Israel, and Their Neighbors from the Late Bronze Age through Roman Palaestina.* Edited by William G. Dever and Seymour Gitin. Winona Late, IN: Eisenbrauns.
———. 2003. "Whatchamacallit: Why It's So Hard to Name our Field. *BAR* 29.4:67–71.
———. 2017. "A Critique of Biblical History and Interpretation." Pages 141–57 in *The Old Testament in Archaeology and History.* Edited by Jennie Ebeling, J. Edward Wright, Mark Elliott, and Paul V. M. Flesher. Waco, TX: Baylor University Press.
Hallote, Rachel. 2006. *Bible, Map, and Spade: The American Palestine Exploration Society, Frederick Jones Bliss, and the Forgotten Story of Early American Biblical Archaeology.* Piscataway, NJ: Gorgias.
Hoffmeier, James Karl, and A. R. Millard, eds. 2004. *The Future of Biblical Archaeology: Reassessing Methodologies and Assumptions.* Grand Rapids: Eerdmans.

Levy, Thomas Evan, ed. 2010. *Historical Biblical Archaeology and the Future: The New Pragmatism*. London: Equinox.

Moorey, P. R. 1991. *A Century of Biblical Archaeology*. Cambridge: Lutterworth.

Silberman, Neil Asher. 1982. *Digging for God and Country: Archaeology and the Secret Struggle For the Holy Land 1799-1917*. New York: Doubleday.

2. The American Schools of Oriental Research and the American School

Clark, Douglas R., and Victor Matthews, eds. 2003. *One Hundred Years of American Archaeology in the Middle East*. Boston: American Schools of Oriental Research.

Dever, William G. 1973. "Two Approaches to Archaeological Method: The Architectural and the Stratigraphic." *ErIsr* 11:1-8.

King, Philip J. 1983. *American Archaeology in the Mideast: A History of the American Schools of Oriental Research*. Winona Lake, IN: Eisenbrauns.

———. 1988. "American Archaeologists." Pages 15-35 in *Benchmarks in Time and Culture: An Introduction to Palestinian Archaeology*. Edited by Joel F. Drinkard, Gerald M. Mattingly, and J. Maxwell Miller. ABS 1. Atlanta: Scholars Press.

Seger, Joe D. 2001. *An ASOR Mosaic: A Centennial History of the American Schools of Oriental Research*. Boston: American Schools of Oriental Research.

Wright, G. Ernest. 1952. *God Who Acts: Biblical Theology as Recital*. London: SCM.

———. 1969. "Archaeological Method in Palestine: An American Interpretation." *ErIsr* 9:120-33.

———. 1970. "The Phenomenon of American Archaeology in the Near East." Pages 3-40 in *Near Eastern Archaeology in the Twentieth Century: Essays in Honor of Nelson Glueck*. Edited by James A. Sanders. New York: Doubleday.

3. The Israeli School

Dever, William G. 1980. "Archaeological Method in Israel: A Continuing Revolution." *BA* 43:41–48.
———. 1989. "Archaeology in Israel Today: A Summation and Critique." Pages 143–52 in *Recent Excavations in Israel: Studies in Iron Age Archaeology*. Edited by Seymour Gitin and William G. Dever. Winona Lake, IN: Eisenbrauns for the American Schools of Oriental Research.
Bar-Yosef, Ofer, and Amihai Mazar. 1982. "Israeli Archaeology." *World Archaeology* 13:310–25.
Kletter, Raz. 2006. *Just Past? The Making of Israeli Archaeology*. London: Equinox.
Mazar, Amihai. 1988. "Israeli Archaeologists." Pages 109–28 in *Benchmarks in Time and Culture: An Introduction to Palestinian Archaeology*. Edited by Joel F. Drinkard, Gerald M. Mattingly, and J. Maxwell Miller. ABS 1. Atlanta: Scholars Press.
Stern, Ephraim. 1987. "The Bible and Israeli Archaeology." Pages 31–40 in *Archaeology and Biblical Interpretation: Essays in Memory of D. Glen Rose*. Edited by Leo G. Perdue, Lawrence E. Toombs, and Gary L. Johnson. Atlanta: John Knox.

4. The Jordanian School

Bienert, Hans-Dieter, Bernd Müller-Neuhof, Ute Wagner-Lux, and Ingrid Liedgens, eds. 2000. *At the Crossroads: Essays on the Archaeology, History and Current Affairs of the Middle East*. Amman: German Protestant Institute of Archaeology in Amman.

5. The British School

Davies, Graham I. 1988. "British Archaeologists." Pages 37–62 in *Benchmarks in Time and Culture: An Introduction to Palestinian Archaeology*. Edited by Joel F. Drinkard, Gerald M. Mattingly, and J. Maxwell Miller. ABS 1. Atlanta: Scholars Press.

6. The French School

Benoit, Pierre. 1988. "French Archaeologists." Pages 63–86 in *Benchmarks in Time and Culture: An Introduction to Palestinian Archaeology*. Edited by Joel F. Drinkard, Gerald M. Mattingly, and J. Maxwell Miller. ABS 1. Atlanta: Scholars Press.

7. The German School

Weippert, Manfred, and Helga Weippert. 1988. "German Archaeologists." Pages 87–108 in *Benchmarks in Time and Culture: An Introduction to Palestinian Archaeology*. Edited by Joel F. Drinkard, Gerald M. Mattingly, and J. Maxwell Miller. ABS 1. Atlanta: Scholars Press.

8. Archaeological Encyclopedias and Handbooks

Encyclopedias and Dictionaries

Freedman, David Noel, ed. 1992. *Anchor Bible Dictionary*. 6 vols. New York: Doubleday.
Master, Daniel M., ed. 2015. *The Oxford Encyclopedia of the Bible and Archaeology*. New York: Oxford University Press.
Meyers, Eric M. 1996. *The Oxford Encyclopedia of Archaeology in the Near East*. 5 vols. New York: Oxford University Press.
Stern, Ephraim, ed. 1993–2008. *New Encyclopedia of Archaeological Excavations in the Holy Land*. 5 vols. Jerusalem: Israel Exploration Society.
Sasson, Jack M., ed. 1995. *Civilizations of the Ancient Near East*. 2 vols. New York: Charles Scribner's Sons.
Steiner, Margreet L., and Ann E. Killebrew, eds. 2014. *The Oxford Handbook of the Archaeology of the Levant, c. 8000–332 B.C.E.* New York: Oxford University Press.

Handbooks

Ben-Tor, Amnon, ed. 1992. *The Archaeology of Ancient Israel*. New Haven: Yale University Press.
Ebeling, Jennie, J. Edward Wright, Mark Elliott, and Paul V. M. Flesher, eds. 2017. *The Old Testament in Archaeology and History*. Waco, TX: Baylor University Press.
Fritz, Volkmar. 1994. *An Introduction to Biblical Archaeology*. Sheffield: JSOT Press.
Levy, Thomas Evan, ed. 1995. *The Archaeology of Society in the Holy Land*. London: Leicester University Press.
Lewis, Ariel. 2005. *The Archaeology of Ancient Judah and Palestine*. Los Angeles: Getty Museum.
Mazar, Amihai. 1990. *Archaeology of the Land of the Bible, 10,000–586 B.C.E.* New York: Doubleday.
Richard, Suzanne, ed. 2003. *Near Eastern Archaeology: A Reader*. Winona Lake, IN: Eisenbrauns.
Weippert, Helga. 1988. *Palästina in vorhellenisischer Zeit*. Tübingen: Beck.

9. Atlases

Bahat, Dan. 1994. *The Atlas of Biblical Jerusalem*. Jerusalem: Carta.
Har'el, Menashe, 2005. *Understanding the Geography of the Bible: An Introductory Atlas*. Jerusalem: Carta.
Rainey, Anson F., and R. Steven Notley, eds. 2006. *The Sacred Bridge: Carta's Atlas of the Biblical World*. Jerusalem: Carta.

10. Archaeology and Biblical Interpretation, Especially Revisionism

The literature is too extensive to cite any but a few recent works, although with full bibliography. See also several works cited above, especially under section 1.

Barr, James. 2000. *History and Ideology in the Old Testament: Biblical Studies at the End of a Millennium*. Oxford: Oxford University Press.

Collins, John J. 2005. *The Bible after Babel: Historical Criticism in a Postmodern Age.* Grand Rapids: Eerdmans.
Dever, William G. 2001. *What Did the Biblical Writers Know and When Did They Know It? What Archaeology Can Tell Us about the Reality of Ancient Israel.* Grand Rapids: Eerdmans.
———. 2020. *Has Archaeology Buried the Bible?* Grand Rapids: Eerdmans.

11. Individual Archaeologists: Critiques and Festschrift Volumes with Bibliographies

William F. Albright

Freedman, David N., ed. 1975. *The Published Works of William Foxwell Albright: A Comprehensive Bibliography.* Cambridge: American Schools of Oriental Research.
Long, Burke O. 1997. *Planting and Reaping Albright: Politics, Ideology, and Interpreting the Bible.* University Park: Penn State University Press.
Feinman, Peter Douglas. 2004. *William Foxwell Albright and the Origins of Biblical Archaeology.* Berrien Springs, MI: Andrews University Press.

Nelson Glueck

Brown, Jonathan M., and Laurence Kutler. 2005. *Nelson Glueck: Biblical Archaeologist and President of Hebrew College-Jewish Institute of Religion.* Cincinnati: Hebrew Union College Press.
Sanders, James A., ed. 1970. *Near Eastern Archaeology in the Twentieth Century: Essays in Honor of Nelson Glueck.* Garden City, NY: Doubleday.

George Ernest Wright

Cross, Frank Moore, Werner E. Lemke, and Patrick D. Miller, eds. 1976. *Magnalia Dei, the Mighty Acts of God: Essays on the Bible in Memory of G. Ernest Wright.* New York: Doubleday.
Dever, William G. 1980. "Biblical Theology and Biblical Archaeology: An Appreciation of G. Ernest Wright." *HTR* 73:1–15.

King, Philip J. 1987. "The Influence of G. Ernest Wright on the Archaeology of Palestine." Pages 15–29 in *Archaeology and Biblical Interpretation*. Edited by Leo G. Perdue, Lawrence E. Toombs, and Gary Lance Johnson. Atlanta: John Knox.

Yigael Yadin

Dever, William G. 1989. "Yigael Yadin: Prototypical Biblical Archaeologist." *ErIsr* 20:44*–51*.
Silberman, Neil A. 1993. *A Prophet from amongst You: The Life of Yigael Yadin; Soldier, Scholar, and Mythmaker of Modern Israel*. New York: Addison-Wesley.

Kathleen M Kenyon

Davis, Miriam C. 2008. *Dame Kathleen Kenyon: Digging up the Holy Land*. Walnut Creek, CA: Left Coast Press.
Dever, William G. 2004. "Kathleen Kenyon (1906–1978)." Pages 525–33 in *Breaking Ground: Pioneer Women Archaeologists*. Edited by Getzel M. Cohen and Martha Sharp Joukowsky. Ann Arbor: University of Michigan Press.
Moorey, Roger, and Peter Parr, eds. 1978. *Archaeology in the Levant: Essays in Honour of Kathleen M. Kenyon*. London: Aris & Phillips.

William G. Dever

Nakhai, Beth Alpert, ed. 2003. *The Near East in the Southwest: Essays in Honor of William G. Dever*. Winona Lake, IN: Eisenbrauns.
Gitin, Seymour, J. Edward. Wright, and J. P. Dessel, eds. 2006. *Confronting the Past: Archaeological and Historical Essays on Ancient Israel in Honor of William G. Dever*. Winona Lake, IN: Eisenbrauns.

12. New Histories of Ancient Israel

Dever, William G. 2017. *Beyond the Texts: An Archaeological Portrait of Ancient Israel and Judah*. Atlanta: SBL Press.

13. Popular Histories of Ancient Israel

Dever, William G. 2001. *Who Were the Early Israelites? Archaeology and Israelite Origins.* Grand Rapids: Eerdmans.

———. 2012. *The Lives of Ordinary People in Ancient Israel: Where Archaeology and the Bible Intersect.* Grand Rapids: Eerdmans.

WORKS CITED

Aharoni, Yohanan. 1973. "Remarks on the 'Israeli' Method of Excavation" [Hebrew]. *ErIsr* 11:48–53.
Bahat, Dan. 1994. *The Atlas of Biblical Jerusalem.* Jerusalem: Carta.
Bar-Yosef, Ofer, and Amihai Mazar. 1982. "Israeli Archaeology." *World Archaeology* 13:310–25.
Ben-Tor, Amnon, ed. 1992. *The Archaeology of Ancient Israel.* New Haven: Yale University Press.
Broshi, Magen. 1987. "Religion, Ideology and Politics and Their Impact on Palestinian Archaeology." *IMJ* 6:17–32.
Carta. 1996. *Carta's Historical Atlas of Israel: A Survey of the Past and Review of the Present.* Jerusalem: Carta.
Coe, Michael. 2006. *Final Report: An Archaeologist Excavates His Past.* Thames & Hudson.
Collins, John J. 2005. *The Bible after Babel: Historical Criticism in a Postmodern Age.* Grand Rapids: Eerdmans.
Crawford, Sidnie White, Amnon Ben-Tor, J. P. Dessel, William G. Dever, Amihai Mazar, and J. Aviram, eds. 2007. *"Up to the Gates of Ekron": Essays on the Archaeology and History of the Eastern Mediterranean in Honor of Seymour Gitin.* Jerusalem: Israel Exploration Society.
Cross, Frank Moore, Werner E. Lemke, and Patrick D Miller, ed. 1976. *Magnalia Dei, the Mighty Acts of God: Essays on the Bible and Archaeology in Memory of G. Ernest Wright.* New York: Doubleday.
Davies, Philip R. 1992. *In Search of Ancient Israel.* Sheffield: Sheffield Academic.
Dever, William G. 1966. "The EBIV–MBI Period in Syria-Palestine, ca. 2150–1850 B.C.E." PhD diss. Harvard University.
———. 1967a. "Archaeology and the Six Day War." *BA* 3:73, 102–8.
———. 1967b. "Excavations at Gezer." *BA* 30:47–62.
———. 1969–1970. "Iron Age Epigraphic Material from the Area of Khirbet el-Kôm." *HUCA* 40:139–204.

———.1970a. "The Middle Bronze I Period in Syria and Palestine." Pages 132–63 in *Near Eastern Archaeology in the Twentieth Century: Essays in Honor of Nelson Glueck*. Edited by James A. Sanders. New York: Doubleday.

———. 1970b. "Vestigial Features in MB I: An Illustration of Some Principles of Ceramic Typology." *BASOR* 200:19–30.

———. 1971. "The Peoples of Palestine in the Middle Bronze I Period." *HTR* 64:197–226.

———. 1973a. "'Biblical Archaeology'—or 'The Archaeology of Syria-Palestine'?" *Christian News from Israel* 22:21–22.

———. 1973b. "Two Approaches to Archaeological Method: The Architectural and the Stratigraphic." *ErIsr* 11:1–8.

———. 1974a. *Archaeology and Biblical Studies: Retrospects and Prospects*. Evanston, IL: Seabury-Western Theological Seminary.

———. 1974b. "The MB IIC Stratification in the Northwest Gate Area At Shechem." *BASOR* 216:31–52.

———. 1975. "A Middle Bronze I Cemetery at Khirbet el Kirmil." *ErIsr* 12:18*–33*.

———. 1976. "The Beginning of the Middle Bronze Age in Syria-Palestine." Pages 1–38 in *Magnalia Dei, the Mighty Acts of God: Essays on the Bible in Memory of G. Ernest Wright*. Edited by Frank Moore Cross, Werner E. Lemke, and Patrick D. Miller. New York: Doubleday.

———. 1978. "Palestine in the Second Millennium B.C.E.: The Archaeological Picture." Pages 70–120 in *Israelite and Judean History*. Edited by John H. Hayes and J. Maxwell Miller. Philadelphia: Westminster.

———. 1980. "Biblical Theology and Biblical Archaeology: An Appreciation of G. Ernest Wright." *HTR* 73:1–15.

———. 1981. "The Impact of the 'New Archaeology' on Syro-Palestinian Archaeology." *BASOR* 242:15–29.

———. 1982. "Recent Archaeological Confirmation of the Cult of Asherah in Ancient Israel." *Hebrew Studies* 23:37–43.

———. 1983. "Material Remains and the Cult in Ancient Israel: An Essay in Archeological Systematics." Pages 571–87 in *The Word of the Lord Shall Go Forth: Essays in Honor of David Noel Freedman*. Edited by Carol L. Meyers and M. O'Connor. Winona Lake, IN: Eisenbrauns.

———. 1984. "The Late Bronze, Iron Age, and Hellenistic Defences at Gezer." Pages 19–34 in *Essays in Honour of Yigael Yadin*. Edited by Géza Vermes and Jacob Neusner. Totawah, NJ: Allanheld, Osmun.

———. 1985a. "Relations between Syria-Palestine and Egypt in the Hyksos Period." Pages 69–87 in *Palestine in the Bronze and Iron Ages: Papers in Honour of Olga Tufnell*. Edited by Jonathan N. Tubb. London: University College of London Institute of Archaeology.

———. 1985b. "Syro-Palestinian and Biblical Archaeology." Pages 31–74 in *The Hebrew Bible and Its Modern Interpreters*. Edited by Douglas A. Knight and Gene M. Tucker. Philadelphia: Fortress.

———. 1987. "The Contribution of Archaeology to the Study of Canaanite and Early Israelite Religion." Pages 209–48 *Ancient Israelite Religion: Essays in Honor of Frank Moore Cross*. Edited by Patrick D. Miller, Paul D. Hanson, and S. Dean McBride. Philadelphia: Fortress.

———. 1988. "Impact of the 'New Archaeology.'" Pages 337–52 in *Benchmarks in Time and Culture: An Introduction to Palestinian Archaeology*. Edited by Joel F. Drinkard, Gerald M. Mattingly, and J. Maxwell Miller. ABS 1. Atlanta: Scholars Press.

———. 1989a. "Archaeology in Israel Today: A Summation and Critique." Pages 143–52 in *Recent Excavations in Israel: Studies in Iron Age Archaeology*. Edited by Seymour Gitin and William G. Dever. Winona Lake, IN: Eisenbrauns for the American Schools of Oriental Research.

———. 1989b. *Recent Archaeological Discoveries and Biblical Research*. Seattle: University of Washington Press.

———. 1993. "Biblical Archaeology—Death and Rebirth?" Pages 335–44 in *Biblical Archaeology Today, 1990: Proceedings of the Second International Congress on Biblical Archaeology, Jerusalem, June–July 1990*. Edited by Avraham Biran. Jerusalem: Israel Exploration Society.

———. 1995. "The Death of a Discipline?" *BAR* 21.5:50–55, 70.

———. 1998. *Gezer: At the Crossroads of Ancient Israel* [Hebrew]. Tel Aviv: Hakibbutz Hameuchad.

———. 2001. *What Did the Biblical Writers Know and When Did They Know It? What Archaeology Can Tell Us about the Reality of Ancient Israel*. Grand Rapids: Eerdmans.

———. 2003. *Who Were the Early Israelites and Where Did They Come From?* Grand Rapids: Eerdmans.

———. 2005. *Did God Have a Wife? Archaeology and Folk Religion in Ancient Israel*. Grand Rapids: Eerdmans.

———. 2007a. "Archaeology and the Fall of the Northern Kingdom: What Really Happened?" Pages 78–92 in *"Up to the Gates of Ekron": Essays on the Archaeology and History of the Eastern Mediterranean in Honor of Seymour Gitin*. Edited by Sidnie White Crawford, Amnon Ben-Tor,

J. P. Dessel, William G. Dever, Amihai Mazar, and J. Aviram. Jerusalem: Israel Exploration Society.

———. 2007b. "Ethnicity and the Archaeological Record: The Case of Early Israel." Pages 49–66 in *The Archaeology of Difference: Gender, Ethnicity, Class and the "Other" in Antiquity; Studies in Honor of Eric M. Meyers*. Edited by Douglas R. Edwards and C. Thomas McCollough. Boston: American Schools of Oriental Research.

———. 2008a. "Ahab and Archaeology: A Commentary on 1 Kings 16–22." Pages 475–84 in *Birkat Shalom: Studies in the Bible, Ancient Near Eastern Literature, and Postbiblical Judaism Presented to Shalom M. Paul on the Occasion of His Seventieth Birthday*. Edited by Chaim Cohen. Winona Lake, IN: Eisenbrauns.

———. 2008b. "Can Archaeology Serve as a Tool in Textual Criticism of the Hebrew Bible?" Pages 225–37 in *Sacred History, Sacred Literature: Essays on Ancient Israel, the Bible, and Religion in Honor of R. E. Friedman on His Sixtieth Birthday*. Edited by Shawna Dolansky. Winona Lake, IN: Eisenbrauns.

———. 2008c. "Folk Religion in Ancient Israel: The Disconnect between Text and Artifact." Pages 425–39 in *Beruhrungspunkte: Studien zur Sozial- und Religionsgeschichte Israels und seiner Umwelt; Festschrift für Rainer Albertz zu seinem 65. Geburtstag*. Edited by Ingo Kottsieper. Münster: Ugarit-Verlag.

———. 2009a. "Archaeology and the Fall of Judah." *ErIsr* 29:29*–35*.

———. 2009b. "Merneptah's 'Israel,' the Bible's, and Ours." Pages 9–96 in *Exploring the Longue Duree: Essays in Honor of Lawrence E. Stager*. Edited by J. David Schloen. Winona Lake, IN: Eisenbrauns.

———. 2011. "Earliest Israel: God's Warriors, Revolting Peasants or Nomadic Hordes?" *ErIsr* 30:4*–12*.

———. 2011. "Religion and Cult in the Early Bronze Age IV Period in Palestine." Pages 89–100 in *Life in Early Bronze Age Communities: Papers in Honor of Walter Rast and R. Thomas Schaub*. Edited by Meredith S. Chesson. Winona Lake, IN: Eisenbrauns.

———. 2012. *The Lives of Ordinary People in Ancient Israel: Where Archaeology and the Bible Intersect*. Grand Rapids: Eerdmans.

———. 2015. "The Exodus and the Bible: What Was Known; What Was Remembered; What Was Forgotten?" Pages 399–408 in *Israel's Exodus in Transdisciplinary Perspective—Text, Archaeology, Culture, and Geoscience*. Edited by Thomas E. Levy, Thomas Schneider, and William H. C. Propp. Cham: Springer.

———. 2014a. *Excavations at the Early Bronze IV Sites of Jebel Qa'aqir and Be'er Resisim*. Winona Lake, IN: Eisenbrauns.

———. 2014b. "The Judean 'Pillar-Base Figurines': Mothers or 'Mother-Goddesses'?" Pages 129–41 in *Family and Household Religion: Toward a Synthesis of Old Testament Studies, Archaeology, Epigraphy, and Cultural Studies*. Edited by Rainer Albertz, Beth Alpert Nakhai, Saul M. Olyan, and Rüdiger Schmitt. Winona Lake, IN: Eisenbrauns.

———. 2015. "Israelite Women as 'Ritual Experts': Orthodoxy or Orthopraxis?" Pages 187–203 in *Celebrate Her for the Fruit of Her Hands: Essays in Honor of Carol L. Meyers*. Edited by Susan Ackerman, Charles E. Carter, and Beth Alpert Nakhai. Winona Lake, IN: Eisenbrauns.

———. 2017a. *Beyond the Texts: An Archaeological Portrait of Ancient Israel and Judah*. Atlanta: SBL Press.

———. 2017b. "History from Things: On Writing New Histories of Ancient Israel." Pages 3–20 in *Le-ma'an Ziony: Essays in Honor of Ziony Zevit*. Edited by Frederick E. Greenspahn and Gary Rendsburg. Eugene, OR: Cascade.

———. 2018. "Shoshenq and Solomon: Chronological Considerations." *ErIsr* 33:50*–58*.

———. 2020. *Has Archaeology Buried the Bible?* Grand Rapids: Eerdmans.

Dever, William G., and H. Darrell Lance. 1978. *A Manual of Field Excavations: Handbook for Field Archaeologists*. Cincinnati: Hebrew Union College.

Dever, William G., H. Darrell Lance, and Reuben G. Bullard. 1986. *Gezer IV: The 1969–71 Seasons in Field VI; The "Acropolis."* Jerusalem: Nelson Glueck School of Biblical Archaeology.

Dever, William G., H. Darrell Lance, Reuben G. Bullard, Dan P. Cole, and Joe D. Seger. 1974. *Gezer II: Report of the 1967–70 Seasons in Fields I and II*. Jerusalem: Hebrew Union College Biblical and Archaeological School.

Dever, William G., H. Darrell Lance, G. Ernest Wright, and Aaron Shaffer. 1970. *Gezer I: Preliminary Report of the 1964–66 Seasons*. Jerusalem: Hebrew Union College Biblical and Archaeological School.

Dever, William G., and Seymour Gitin, eds. 2003. *Symbiosis, Symbolism, and the Power of the Past: Canaan, Ancient Israel, and Their Neighbors from the Late Bronze Age through Roman Palaestina*. Winona Late, IN: Eisenbrauns.

Gitin, Seymour, J. Edward Wright, and J. P. Dessel, eds. 2006. *Confronting the Past: Archaeological and Historical Essays on Ancient Israel in Honor of William G. Dever. Winona Lake, IN: Eisenbrauns.

Grabbe, Lester L. 2004. *"Like a Bird in a Cage": The Invasion of Sennacherib in 701 BCE*. London: Clark.

Finney, Paul Corby, ed. 2017. *The Eerdmans Encyclopedia of Early Christian Art and Archaeology*. 3 vols. Grand Rapids: Eerdmans.

Kletter, Raz. 2006. *Just Past? The Making of Israeli Archaeology*. London: Equinox.

Levy, Thomas Evan, ed. 1995. *The Archaeology of Society in the Holy Land*. London: Leicester University Press.

Mazar, Amihai. 1988. "Israeli Archaeologists." Pages 109–28 in *Benchmarks in Time and Culture: An Introduction to Palestinian Archaeology*. Edited by Joel F. Drinkard, Gerald M. Mattingly, and J. Maxwell Miller. ABS 1. Atlanta: Scholars Press.

———.1990. *Archaeology of the Land of the Bible, 10,000–586 B.C.E.* New York: Doubleday.

Nakhai, Beth Alpert, ed. 2003. *The Near East in the Southwest: Essays in Honor of William G. Dever*. Boston: American Schools of Oriental Research.

Provan, Iain W., V. Philips Long, and Tremper Longman. 2003. *A Biblical History of Israel*. Louisville: Westminster John Knox.

Silberman, Neil A. 1993. *A Prophet from amongst You: The Life of Yigael Yadin; Soldier, Scholar, and Mythmaker of Modern Israel*. New York: Addison-Wesley.

Stern, Ephraim. 1987. "The Bible and Israeli Archaeology." Pages 31–40 in *Archaeology and Biblical Interpretation: Essays in Memory of D. Glen Rose*. Edited by Leo G. Perdue, Lawrence E. Toombs, and Gary L. Johnson. Atlanta: John Knox.

———, ed. 1993–2008. *New Encyclopedia of Archaeological Excavations in the Holy Land*. 5 vols. Jerusalem: Israel Exploration Society.

Thompson, Thomas L. 1999. *Mythic Past: Biblical Archaeology and the Myth of Israel*. London: Basic Books.

———, ed. 2003. *Jerusalem in Ancient History and Tradition*. London: T&T Clark International.

Whitelam, Keith. 1995. *The Invention of Ancient Israel: The Silencing of Palestinian History*. New York: Routledge.

Woolly, Leonard, and T. E. Lawrence. 1915. *The Wilderness of Zin*. London: Cape.

Wright, G. Ernest. 1937. "The Pottery of Palestine from the Earliest Times to the Eighteenth Century B.C." PhD diss. John Hopkins University.
———. 1937. "The Troglodytes of Gezer." *PEQ* 69:67–78.
———. 1944. *The Challenge of Israel's Faith*. Chicago: University of Chicago Press.
———. 1950. *The Old Testament against Its Environment*. London: SCM.
———. 1952. *God Who Acts: Biblical Theology as Recital*. London: SCM.
———. 1957. *Biblical Archaeology*. Philadelphia: Westminster.
———. 1965. *Shechem: The Biography of a Biblical City*. New York: McGraw-Hill.
———. 1971. "What Archaeology Can and Cannot Do." *BA* 34:69–76.
———. 1975. "The New Archaeology." *BA* 38:104–15.
Wright, G. Ernest, and Floyd V. Filson. 1945. *The Westminster Historical Atlas to the Bible*. Philadelphia: Westminster.
Yadin, Yigael. 1963. *The Art of Warfare in Biblical Lands*. 2 vols. New York: McGraw-Hill.

GENERAL INDEX

Abel-beth-maacah 191
Abu Issa 126
Achziv 40, 149
ACOR. *See* American Center for Oriental Research
Aharoni, Yohanan 38–41, 89, 106, 108–9, 115–16, 118, 137, 139, 149–50, 161
Ai 89, 109, 138
Aijalon Valley 38
'Ajrud, Kuntillet 108
Akko 131, 162, 191
Albertz, Rainer 185
Albright Institute. *See* W. F. Albright Institute of Archaeological Research
Albright, Ruth Norton 101, 103–4
Albright, William Foxwell 38, 40, 42, 49–50, 59, 61, 65, 77, 99, 101–5, 110, 112–16, 119–20, 122–27, 129, 131–35, 142–43, 147, 152, 158, 189, 198, 202, 206
American Center for Oriental Research 125, 196
American Philosophical Society 78
American School of Oriental Research. *See* W. F. Albright Institute of Archaeological Research
American Schools of Oriental Research 40, 75, 87–88, 109, 111–12, 118, 125–27, 129, 132, 134, 139–40, 142–43, 148, 152, 155, 157, 165–66, 182–83, 185, 199
Amiran, David 78, 115
Amiran, Ruth 38, 39, 78, 106, 115, 194
Amman 59, 86, 88, 89, 109, 204
Anafa 138
Andrews University 201
Aphek 137–38
Arad 64, 106, 108, 118, 122, 131, 150
Arav, Rami 162
Argoub, Ali Musa Abu 92, 96, 171
Artzy, Michal 105, 149, 162
Asherah 94, 102, 154
Ashkelon 125, 152, 162, 193, 197
Ashod 106, 131
ASOR. *See* American Schools of Oriental Research
Atlit 108
Avdat 107
Avigad, Nahman 39, 68, 78, 89, 106, 108, 136, 149–50, 161
Avi-Yonah, Michael 39, 79
Avi-Yonah, Yael 79
Ayalon, David 115
Azekah 191
Bâb edh-Dhrâ 126
Babylon 59
Baghdad 59
Bahat, Dan 149, 163
Baidun, Mahmoud 91
Baidun, Musa 91
Balatah 51, 99
Band, Arnold 130, 141
Banks, John 47–48, 54
Bar-Adon, Pesach 39, 106
Barag, Dan 39, 115
Barakat, Victor 91
Bar-Ilan University 149, 162
Barkay, Gaby 105
Bar Kokhba 106, 116
Bar-Yosef, Ofer 153

-227-

Batash, Tel 137–38, 150
Beck, Pirhiya 105, 108–9, 115
Beek, Gus van 138
Be'er Resisim 137–38, 144, 177
Be'erotayim 144
Beersheba 64, 102, 106, 108, 118, 122, 131, 137, 142, 145, 150
Beit Mirsim, Tell 61, 104, 126, 134
Beit-Arieh, Itzhaq 105, 108, 115, 137
Ben-Gurion, David 144
Ben-Gurion University of the Negev 137, 149–50, 162
Bennett, Crystal 124, 135
Benoit, Pierre 123
Ben-Tor, Amnon 38–39, 115, 136, 138, 162–64, 185
Ben-Yehuda, Eliezer 102
Bernstein, Leonard 87–88
Bethsaida 162
Beth-Shean 150, 162
Beth Shearim 40
Beth-Shemesh 162, 191, 192
Bilgray, Albert 130
Biran, Avraham 39, 76, 78, 84, 106, 115, 150, 158
Bliss, Frederick 67
Boston University 55
Boysie 12–13
Braun, Eliot 105
Briend, Jacques 138
British Mandate 40, 77
British Museum 136, 156, 176
British School of Archaeology 119
British Society for Old Testament Studies 175
Broshi, Magen 117, 153
Buber, Martin 37
Bull, Odd 83
Bull, Robert 52–53, 127, 138
Buma, Tel 191
Bunimovitz, Shlomo 108, 149, 162
Butler School of Religion 32–34, 42, 45
Byfield, Brother 17–18
CAARI. *See* Cyprus American Archaeological Research Institute

Caesarea 127, 137–38, 162
Caesarea Maritina 164
Callaway, Joseph 53, 109, 119, 138, 153–54
Campbell, Ted 53
Carthage 125
Casey, William Van Etten 88
Christian Normal Institute 3
Christian Theological Seminary. *See* Butler School of Religion
Churches of Christ 21, 24
City of David 136, 151
Coe, Michael xi
Cohen, Haim 87
Cohen, Rudolph 105, 137–38, 144–45
Collins, John 204
Cross, Frank Moore, Jr. 32, 47, 49, 56, 68–69, 77, 80, 84, 99, 102, 119, 154
Cyprus xiii, 67, 73, 75, 125, 148, 154, 156, 165–66, 173, 179–80, 182–83, 187–88, 197–99
Cyprus American Archaeological Research Institute 154, 166, 182, 187–88, 198
Daliyeh, Wadi ed- 109
Damascus 59, 88, 148
Dan 131, 149–50
Davies, Philip R. 176, 203–4
Davis, Thomas 154, 182, 187
Dayan, Moshe 85, 115
Deir al-Balah 136
Department of Antiquities, Israel 76, 84, 92, 105, 109, 192
Department of Antiquities, Jordan 195–96
Department of Antiquities, Palestine Authority 196
Dessel, J. P. xiii, 152, 162
Dever, Claudine Watts xii, 1–7, 9–13, 15, 19–20, 55, 69, 111, 130, 142,
Dever, Evan Jacob Gaber. *See* Dever, Zeb
Dever, Lee 1, 2, 4–6, 9–10, 12, 17–22, 27–29, 33, 36–37, 42, 46, 55, 65, 111–12
Dever, Lonnie Earl xii, 2

GENERAL INDEX   229

Dever, Myrna Sue 4–6, 9, 11–12, 16–17, 19, 111, 130, 140
Dever, Norma Spangler xiii, 26–27, 29–30, 33, 42–43, 46–48, 55–56, 58–59, 61, 63–65, 67, 72, 75, 77, 79, 81–83, 85, 87–88, 97, 99–101, 110–12, 114–15, 120, 122, 125, 127–30, 133, 140, 142–43, 145, 147, 155–59, 168–71, 184, 201
Dever, Sean William xiii, 99, 100–101, 110–11, 114, 122, 128–30, 135, 140, 142, 145, 147, 155–59, 165, 168–73
Dever, Sudie Murphy 1
Dever, Zeb xiii, 3, 160, 165–66, 168–69, 171, 173, 179–82, 188
Din, Hani Nur al- 196
Disciples of Christ 9, 24, 46
Dor 136, 150, 162
Dothan, Moshe 38–39, 106, 115, 161
Dothan, Trude 38–39, 115, 136, 152, 162, 194
Drew Theological Seminary 51
Dunayevsky, Immanuel 39
Ebenezer. *See* ʿIzbet Ṣarṭah
École Biblique 41, 85, 103, 123, 135
Eglon. *See* Ḥesi, Tell el-
ʿEin-Gedi 106
Eitan, Avi 105
Ekron. *See* Miqne, Tel
Elliot, Luke 10, 14, 19
Elliot, Mrs. 20
Elusa 162
En Gev 162
Epstein, Claire 39
Esdar, Tel 108
ʿEton, Tell 191
Ezion-geber 114
Falconer, Steve 154
Farʿah, Tell el- 41, 53
Farʿah (North), Tell el- 107
Feinstein, Rosaline 97
Filson, Floyd 134
Finkelstein, Israel 108, 137, 148–50, 162, 164, 194–95

Freedman, David Noel 99, 102, 106, 119, 154, 158
Friedman, Richard 185
Ful, Tell el- 109
Gaber, Hannah Susan xiii, 156–57, 159, 181
Gaber, Jordana Lee. *See* Saletan, Jordana Lee Gaber
Gaber, Martin 159
Gaber, Pamela xiii, 67, 120–21, 156–60, 165–66, 168, 171, 173, 179–82, 185–86, 188, 210
Gamla 137, 162
Garber, Paula. *See* Gaber, Pamela
Garfinkel, Yosef 162
Gath. *See* Ṣafi, Tell eṣ-
Gerar. *See* Haror, Tel
Gerizim, Mount 162
Gezer 38–39, 50–52, 58–67, 69, 72–77, 79, 81–82, 90, 96, 98–99, 101, 106–8, 110–11, 113–14, 116–22, 124–28, 130, 134–41, 143, 145, 147, 149, 154, 156–57, 160, 164–65, 180, 191, 193
Gibeon. *See* Jib, Tell el-
Gilboa, Ayelet 149, 162
Gilmore, Garth 164
Giloh 137–38
Ginsberg, H. L. 37
Girlie 11–12, 17–18
Gitin, Seymour (Sy) xiii, 99, 110, 126, 147, 152, 162, 164, 183, 185, 197–98
Glueck, Charles 100, 101
Glueck, Helen 101
Glueck, Nelson xii, 56–57, 59, 64–66, 71, 74–79, 82, 85–91, 96–100, 102, 107, 110–15, 117, 119, 121–22, 125
Golan, Oded 193
Gophna, Ram 105, 108, 115
Greenberg, Rafi 108
Greenfield, Jonas 131, 158
Gutman, Shmaryahu 137
Gwinn, Henry 3
Haifa University 149, 162–63
Ḥalif, Tel 138, 162
Hall, Julian Saletan 181, 188

Hall, Sasha Saletan 181
Hamdan Taha 196
Hammond, Philip 92
Hanfman, George 156
Haror, Tel 150
Harvard Divinity School/University 31–32, 40, 45–48, 50–51, 53–56, 58, 62–63, 65–66, 68, 71–72, 77, 80, 99, 119–20, 125, 132–34, 143, 152–53, 156, 200–201, 206
Hasel, Michael 154, 198
Hassan. *See* Talal, Hassan bin, Prince
Hatra 59
Hazor 38–41, 105–7, 116, 162, 191
Hebrew Union College-Jewish Institute of Religion 56–59, 61–65, 69, 72, 77, 79–80, 84–86, 88, 91–92, 96–99, 101, 110–12, 114–15, 121–23, 126–27, 136, 147, 149, 158, 173, 206
Hebrew University of Jerusalem 40, 105, 116, 128, 139, 147, 149–50, 152, 155, 161
Hebron 92
Hennessey, Basil 86
Herbert, Sharon 107, 138
Herodion 162
Herzog, Ze'ev 105, 137, 150
Ḥesi, Tell el- 127, 138, 152, 164
Holladay, Jack 50, 62
Holy Cross College 88
Horn, Siegfried 53, 57
HUC. *See* Hebrew Union College-Jewish Institute of Religion
Humbert, Jean-Baptiste 138
Hussein, King 84
IAA. *See* Israel Antiquities Authority
Idalion 67, 125, 156, 165, 173, 179, 180, 182, 186
Institute of Archaeology in Tel Aviv 137
'Ira, Tel 108, 137, 138
Iskander, Khirbet 126
Israel Antiquities Authority 139, 162, 192–94, 197
Israel Museum 78, 95, 153–54, 192, 194
Issa, Abu 99

'Izbet Ṣarṭah 137–38
Jabber 99, 126
Jacobsen, Thorkild 68, 69
Jalamie 107
Jebel Qa'aqir 94–95, 98–99, 107, 145, 177
Jemmeh, Tell 138
Jerash 59
Jericho 41, 50–51, 75, 84, 86, 89, 119, 135, 162, 196
Jerusalem xii, 36–37, 40–42, 50, 53, 56–62, 64, 71–72, 75–79, 81–91, 99–103, 105–16, 118–19, 122–23, 127–33, 135–38, 140, 142–43, 147–52, 158, 161–64, 171, 173, 180, 182, 185, 192, 196, 199, 201, 204, 206
Jezreel 162
Jib, Tell el- 41, 53, 58, 89, 107
Jibrin, Omar 85–86
Joesler, Josiah 146
Joukowsky, Artemis 206
Kabri 162, 191
Kaplan, Jacob 39–40
Katsh, Abraham 35–37
Keisan, Tell 135, 138
Kempinski, Aharon 105, 108, 137, 162
Kenyon, Kathleen 39, 41, 51, 61, 74–75, 109, 115–16, 119, 124, 135–36, 138, 201
Kerak 59
Kershaw, Norma 111
Ketco, S. 163
Kheleifeh, Tell el- 114
King, Philip 125, 129
Kirmil, Khirbet el-s 128
Kiryat-Sefer. *See* Beit Mirsim, Tell
Kitan 138
Kletter, Raz 40
Kloner, Amos 105
Knauf, Ernst Axel 161
Kochavi, Moshe 105–9, 115, 137
Kurnub 107
Kyle, Melvin Grove 104
Lachish 108, 137, 149–50, 193, 204
LaGrange, Marie-Joseph 124

Lahav. *See* Ḥalif, Tel
Lambdin, Thomas 49
Lance, Darrell 50, 57–61, 63, 65–66, 90, 117, 125, 127, 139, 145, 164
Landgraf, John 92, 99
Lapp, Paul 51, 53, 86–87, 109
Lawrence, T. E. 144
Lederman, Zvi 162
Levine, Lou 137
Levy, Leon 152, 206
Levy, Moshe 79
Levy, Tom 75, 142, 164, 195
Lexington Theological Seminary 3–4
Libnah. *See* Zayit, Tell
Licht, Jacob 36
Linder, Elisha 108
Lycoming College 176, 180, 182–83
Macalister, R. A. Stewart 59–60, 98
Magness-Gardiner, Bonnie 154
Maier, Aren 162
Malamat, Avraham 36, 78, 115, 131
Malamat, Naʾama 115
Malḥata, Tel 108
Mansoor, Menahem 154
Maresha 162
Masada 73, 106, 116, 150
Masos, Tel 108, 137
Mazar, Amihai 137, 149–50, 153, 162–64, 194, 203
Mazar, Benjamin 40–41, 78, 102, 115, 136–37, 149, 161
Mazar, Eilat 149–50
McCormick
McCormick Theological Seminary 45, 51, 134, 200
McNamara, John R. 157
Megiddo 162, 191
Meiron 127
Meshel, Zeʾev 105, 108
Metzer, Ehud 137
Mevorakh 136, 138
Meyers, Carol 127, 137–38, 152, 162, 185, 200
Meyers, Eric 127, 130, 137–38, 141, 152, 162, 185, 200

Michal, Tel 137–38, 150
Milligan College 24–27, 31, 33
Miqne, Tel 152, 162, 193, 197
Miroschedji, Pierre de 162
Mishmar, Nahal 106
Mizrahi, Yonathan 109
Mosul 59
Murphy, Sudie. *See* Dever, Sudie Murphy
Nablus 51, 85, 99, 134
Nabratein 152
Nagileh, Tell en- 106
Nakarai, Toyozo Watanabi 32, 35–36, 38
Nakhai, Beth Alpert 152
Nami, Tel 162
National Endowment for the Humanities 143, 144, 155–56
Nazareth 162
Negbi, Ora 105, 115
Negev, Avraham 105, 107, 115
NEH. *See* National Endowment for the Humanities
Nelson Glueck School of Biblical Archaeology 106
Nessana 162
Netzer, Ehud 162
Nigro, Alphonso 162
Nimrod 59
Nineveh 59
Novack, Michael 58
Old City 37, 40, 53, 58, 76, 82, 84–86, 90, 97, 99, 108, 149, 151, 192
Omar 85–86, 129, 132–33, 140
Oren, Eliezer 105, 137, 150
Oriental Institute 125
Palmyra 59
Penn State University 180, 183, 200
Perrot, Jean 39
Petra 59
Petrie, Flinders 52, 138
Pittsburgh Theological Seminary 206
Pope, Marvin 77, 80
Prato, Jonathan 78
Prausnitz, Moshe 40
Prignaud, Jean 135, 138
Pritchard, James B. 41, 53, 58, 107, 143

Qashish, Tel	136
Qasile, Tel	40, 137–38
Qeiyafa, Khirbet	191, 198
Qiri, Tel	136
Qôm, Khirbet el-	92–93, 95, 98, 100, 119, 126
Qumran	106
Raban, Avner	105, 108, 163
Rabin, Chaim	36
Ra'i, Khirbet al-	191
Rainey, Anson	115
Ras, Tell er-	127
Rast, Walter	126, 185
Reḥov, Tel	162
Reich, Ronny	105, 162
Richard J. Scheuer Medal	185
Richard, Suzanne	126
Rockefeller Museum	40, 53, 84, 192
Rose, Glen	138, 153
Rosen-Ayalon, Miriam	115
Rosenblatt, Paul	130
Rosen, Steve	137
Rosen, Theodore A.	99
Ross, James F.	72, 77
Rothenberg, Benno	108
Rowley, H. H.	32
Rubenstein, C.	163
Rujm el-Hiri	109
Ṣafi, Tell eṣ-	162, 191
Saletan, Jordana Lee Gaber	xiii, 156, 159, 181
Salim, Hamed	196
Samaria	53, 89, 119, 135, 136
Samiyeh	92, 95
Samiyeh, Khirbet es-	91, 95
Sauer, Jim	125–26
Schaeffer, John	130
Schaub, Tom	126, 185
Scoggin, Elmo	145
Seger, Joe	50, 62, 101, 110, 123, 137–38, 162, 164
Sepphoris	127, 152, 162
Sera', Tel	137–38
Sha'ar ha-Golan	162
Sharon, Ariel	148
Sharon, Ilan	162
Sharon Plain	106
Shazar, Zalman	102
Shechem	41, 50–54, 57–58, 61–62, 66–67, 71–72, 74, 89, 99, 107, 109, 120, 126–28, 134, 138, 200
Shema, Khirbet	127, 138
Shiloh	137
Shiloh, Yigal	38–39, 115, 136, 151–52, 161, 164
Shiqmona	106
Shukron, Eli	162
Silberman, Neil Asher	117
Sonia Nadler Institute of Archaeology 108	
Southern Baptist Theological Seminary 31–32	
Southwestern Baptist Seminary	201
Spangler, Norma. See Dever, Norma Spangler	
Spicehandler, Ezra	83, 88, 101
Spicehandler, Shirley	101
Sta B	12
Stager, Larry	125, 185
Stager, Lawrence	152, 162
Steinberg, Paul	65
Stekelis, Moshe	39
Stern, Ephraim	xiii, 38–39, 115, 136, 140, 150, 162–64, 185
Strange, James	127, 137, 152, 162
Sukenik, Eliezer	40–41
Ta'anach	109
Tadmor, Hayim	78, 115
Tadmor, Miriam	38–39, 78, 115
Talal, Hassan bin, Prince	196
Tannur, Khirbet et-	114
Tappy, Ron	162, 198
Tawfeek, Mustapha	51
Tel Aviv University	108–9, 118, 137, 139, 149, 162
Temple Mount	85, 136, 149
Thompson, Thomas L.	161, 203–4
Timnah. See Tel Batash	
Tirzah. See Far'ah, Tell el-	
Toombs, Lawrence	53, 127, 138

Tsafrir, Yoram 105, 149
Tufnell, Olga 119, 154
University of Arizona 97, 130, 141, 154, 160, 167, 181, 196, 200
Ur 59
Ussishkin, David 38–39, 108, 115, 137, 148–50, 162, 164, 193
'Uza, Ḥorvat 108
Vaux, Roland de 41, 53, 85–86, 115–16, 119, 123–24
Vilnay, Ze'ev 37–39
Vincent, Louis-Hugues 124
Virginia Theological Seminary 77
W. F. Albright Institute of Archaeological Research 38, 42, 50–51, 58, 76, 78, 85–88, 99, 102, 109–10, 112–14, 122–23, 126, 128–29, 131–34, 138, 142, 147, 152, 158, 171, 197–98
Wawiyat, Tell el- 152
Weinberg, Gladys Davidson 97, 107
Weinberg, Saul
Weinberg, Saul S. 96–97, 107, 138
Weiss, Ze'ev 162
Wheeler, Mortimer 136
Whitelam, Keith 161
Wilson, Evan 83
Wisthof, Bonnie 152
Woolley, C. Leonard 144
Worrell, John 127, 138
Wright, Carolyn 63
Wright, Ed 171
Wright, Emily 63
Wright, G. Ernest xii–xiii, 41, 45, 47, 49–54, 56–69, 74–75, 77, 79, 86, 99–102, 104, 106, 112–16, 119–20, 123, 126–27, 129, 132–34, 143, 146, 154, 161, 200, 202
Wright, G. R. H. (Mick) 52
Yadin, Carmella 118
Yadin, Yigael 38–41, 73, 78, 89, 101, 106, 108, 115–19, 136, 150–52, 154, 161
Yale University 77, 80
Yarmut, Tel 162
Yeivin, Shmuel 40
Yeruham 108, 137

Yoqneam 136
Zayit, Tell 162, 198, 206
Zeror, Tel 106
Zevit, Ziony 185
Ziklag. *See* Sera', Tel
Zippori, Tel 162

www.ingramcontent.com/pod-product-compliance
Lightning Source LLC
Chambersburg PA
CBHW030824230426
43667CB00008B/1371